Yamaha Trail Bike Owners Workshop Manual

by Mansur Darlington

Models covered:

246 cc: DT series introduced USA only. 1968-1973
DT 250 series introduced UK 1975, USA 1974
Including monoshock models

351 cc: RT series introduced USA only. 1971-1973
DT 360A introduced USA only. 1974

397 cc: DT 400 series introduced UK 1976, USA 1975
Including monoshock models

ISBN 0 85696 519 7

© Haynes Publishing Group 1976, 1978, 1979, 1980

All rights reserved. No part of this book may be reproduced or transmitted in any form or by any means, electronic or mechanical, including photocopying, recording or by any information storage or retrieval system, without permission in writing from the copyright holder.

Printed in England (263—2F3)

**HAYNES PUBLISHING GROUP
SPARKFORD YEOVIL SOMERSET ENGLAND**
distributed in the USA by
**HAYNES PUBLICATIONS INC
861 LAWRENCE DRIVE
NEWBURY PARK
CALIFORNIA 91320
USA**

Acknowledgements

Our grateful thanks are due to R. S. Damerell and Son Ltd, St. Austell, Cornwall, who provided the DT250B machine featured in this manual, together with much useful information. We would also like to thank Mitsui Machinery Sales UK Ltd who provided the cover photograph. Brian Horsfall gave considerable assistance with the overhaul and devised ingenious methods for overcoming the lack of service tools. Les Brazier arranged and took the photographs that accompany the text. Jeff Clew edited the text. Finally we would also like to acknowledge the help of the Avon Rubber Company, who kindly supplied advice about tyre fitting and NGK Spark Plugs (UK) Limited for the provision of spark plug photographs.

About this manual

The author of this manual has the conviction that the only way in which a significant and easy to follow text can be written is first to do the work himself, under conditions similar to those found in the average household.

Unless specially-mentioned and therefore considered essential, Yamaha service tools have not been used. There is invariably some alternative means of loosening or slackening some vital component, when service tools are not available and risk of damage has to be avoided at all costs.

Each of the six Chapters is divided into numbered sections. Within the sections are numbered paragraphs. Cross-reference throughout this manual is quite straight forward and logical. When reference is made 'See Section 6.10' - it means section 6, paragraph 10 in the same chapter. If another chapter were meant, the text would read 'See Chapter 2, Section 6.10'.

All photographs are captioned with a section/paragraph number to which they refer and are always relevant to the chapter text adjacent.

Figure numbers (usually line illustrations) appear in numerical order, within a given chapter. Fig. 1.1. therefore refers to the first figure in Chapter one. Left-hand and right-hand descriptions of the machines and their components refer to the left and right of a given machine, when the rider is seated normally.

Whilst every care is taken to ensure that the information in this manual is correct no liability can be accepted by the author or publishers for loss, damage or injury, caused by any errors in or omissions from the information given.

Modifications to the Yamaha trail bikes

Since the inception of the Yamaha trail bikes in 1971 no major modifications were made until the 1975 season when the 360 cc machine was phased out to be replaced by the 400 cc model. At the same time the 250 cc model was extensively modified. Any minor modifications made up until 1974 are discussed in the text as are the major modifications made for the 1975 season. For clarity all machines produced before 1975 will be referred to generally in the text as **Early Models** and machines built after 1974 as **Late Models.**

Contents

Chapter	Section	Page
Introductory pages	Acknowledgements	2
	About this manual	2
	Introduction to the Yamaha enduro trail bikes	5
	Ordering spare parts	5
	Routine maintenance	6
Chapter 1/Engine, clutch & gearbox	Specifications	8
	Engine/gearbox removal	11
	Dismantling	13
	Examination and renovation	25
	Reassembly	28
	Fault diagnosis	51
Chapter 2/Fuel system & lubrication	Specifications	53
	Carburettor	54
	Exhaust system	58
	Fault diagnosis	62
Chapter 3/Ignition system	Specifications	63
	Contact breakers	64
	Ignition timing	69
	Spark plug	69
	Fault diagnosis	70
Chapter 4/Frame & forks	Front forks	71
	Frame	79
	Swinging arm	79
	Rear suspension units	84
	Fault diagnosis	86
Chapter 5/Wheels, brakes & tyres	Specifications	87
	Wheels	88
	Brakes	88
	Tyres	96
	Fault diagnosis	97
Chapter 6/Electrical system	Specifications	98
	Magneto	99
	Battery	99
	Headlamp	99
	Fault diagnosis	106
	Wiring diagrams	107
Chapter 7/The Yamaha 250 and 400 D and E monoshock models	Specifications	100-113
	Oil pump	114-115
	Rear suspension shock absorber	116
	Rear sub-frame	119
	Other modifications	119
Metric conversion tables		124-125
Index		126-127

1975 Yamaha 246 cc DT250 model

Introduction to the Yamaha enduro trail bikes

Although the history of Yamaha can be traced back to the year 1887, when a then very small company commenced manufacture of reed organs, it was not until 1954 that the company became interested in motorcycles. As can be imagined, the problems of marketing a motorcycle against a background of musical instruments manufacture were considerable. Some local racing successes and the use of hitherto unknown bright colour schemes helped achieved the desired results and in July 1955 the Yamaha Motor Company was established as a separate entity, employing a work force of less than 100 and turning out some 300 machines a month.

Competition successes continued and with the advent of tasteful styling that followed Italian trends, Yamaha became established as one of the world's leading motorcycle manufacturers. Part of this success story is the impressive list of Yamaha 'firsts' - a whole string of innovations that include electric starting, pressed steel frame, torque induction and 6 and 8 port engines. There is also the 'Autolube' system of lubrication, in which the engine-driven oil pump is linked to the twist grip throttle, so that lubrication requirements are always in step with engine demands.

The Yamaha DT and RT series machines complement the smaller range of trail bikes, these being the LT/AT/CT models, which were designed to fulfill the same two main roles, that of providing reliable and economical transport as medium performance road machines and that of off-the-road machines for trail and scrambles work as a leisure pursuit. In addition the DT and RT series are readily converted to competition standard machines for rough-riding with the use of Yamaha supplied tuning parts. All machines are equipped as standard for road use, with those cycle parts necessary for the machine to comply with the law of the country or state of original delivery.

Ordering spare parts

When ordering spare parts for any Yamaha it is advisable to deal direct with an official Yamaha agent who should be able to supply most of the parts ex-stock. Parts cannot be obtained from the manufacturer or his Concessionaire direct; all orders must be routed via an approved agent, even if the parts required are not held in stock. He is in a better position to specify exactly the parts required and to identify the relevant spare part numbers so that there is less chance of the wrong part being supplied by the manufacturer due to a vague or incomplete description.

When ordering spares, always quote the frame and engine numbers in full, together with any prefixes or suffixes in the form of letters. The frame number is found stamped on the right-hand side of the steering head, in line with the forks. The engine number is stamped on the left-hand side of the upper crankcase, immediately below the carburettor.

Use only parts of genuine Yamaha manufacture. A few pattern parts are available, sometimes at cheaper prices but there is no guarantee that they will give such good service as the originals they replace. Retain any worn or broken parts until the replacements have been obtained; they are sometimes needed as a pattern to help identify the correct replacement when design changes have been made during a production run.

Some of the more expendable parts such as spark plugs, bulbs, tyres, oils and greases etc can be obtained from accessory shops and motor factors, who have convenient opening hours, charge lower prices and can often be found not far from home. It is also possible to obtain parts on a mail order basis from a number of specialists who advertise regularly in the motorcycle magazines.

The frame number

The engine number

Routine maintenance

Periodic routine maintenance is a continuous process that commences immediately the machine is used. It must be carried out at specified mileage recordings, or on a calendar basis if the machine is not used frequently, whichever is the sooner. Maintenance should be regarded as an insurance policy, to help keep the machine in the peak of condition and to ensure long, trouble-free service.

There is a maxim used in some quarters of the motorcycling fraternity. 'If it works, leave well alone.' Wise as this saying may be in some respects, don't take it too literally and succumb to the temptation of assuming that your motorcycle is 100 per cent fit merely because it has not broken down. The key to reliability is routine maintenance and constant checking.

It is worthwhile practice as a safety precaution, before each ride, to walk quickly around the machine and check for any loose parts; wheels, chains, cables, brake mechanisms and retaining bolts.

The various maintenance tasks are described under their respective mileage and calender headings. Accompanying diagrams are provided, where necessary. It should be remembered that the interval between the various maintenance tasks serves only as a guide. As the machine gets older or is used under particularly adverse conditions, it would be advisable to reduce the period between each check. Some of the tasks are described in detail, where they are not mentioned fully as a routine maintenance item in the text. If a specific item is mentioned but not described in detail, it will be covered fully in the appropriate Chapter. No special tools are required for the normal routine maintenance tasks. The tools are required for the normal routine maintenance tasks. The tools supplied with every new machine will prove adequate, or if they are not available, the tools found in the average household.

However, it is essential before commencing even a minor engine overhaul to make certain that you have an impact or 'punch' screwdriver in your tool kit. The pan-head screws holding the crankcases and side covers on are screwed up very tightly, and if the engine has not been dismantled since leaving the factory they will be immovable with an ordinary screwdriver. If any bearings or shafts are to be removed from the engine, a pair of special circlip pliers are an invaluable, if not absolutely essential, addition to the tool kit.

Weekly, or every 200 miles

Check the adjustment of the front and rear brakes.
Check the oil level in the gearbox and top up if necessary.
Check the oil level in the oil tank and top up if necessary.
Oil all exposed control cables and joints.
Check the tyre pressures.
Check the electrolyte level of the battery and top up with distilled water, if necessary. DO NOT OVERFILL.
Check final drive chain adjustment.

Three-monthly, or every 2000 miles

Complete all the checks listed in the weekly/200 mile service, and then the following items:
Apply a grease gun to all the greasing points.
Remove, inspect and clean both spark plugs. If necessary, regap the points.
Clean the contact breaker points and reset the gaps.
Verify the accuracy of the ignition timing by the alternator timing marks.
Decarbonise the cylinder heads and the exhaust ports.
Remove and clean the silencer baffles.
Remove, clean and lubricate the final drive chain.
Check or renew the air cleaner element.
Check the setting of the Autolube oil pump and re-adjust if necessary. This is the dealer's responsibility whilst the machine is still under guarantee. Unauthorised tampering may invalidate the guarantee.
Check the clutch action and adjust if necessary.
Remove all control and meter cables and lubricate.
Lightly lubricate twist grip.
Check carburettor action and adjust if necessary.
Remove and flush fuel tap filter.

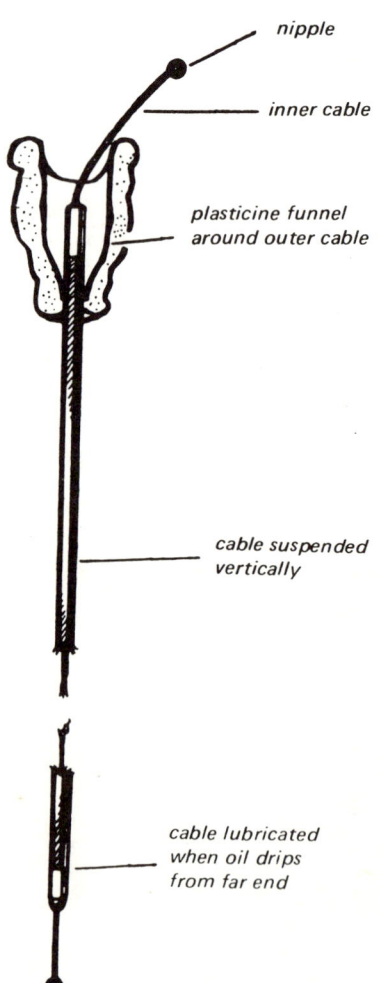

Control cable oiling

Routine maintenance

Six monthly, or every 4000 miles

Complete all the checks listed in the weekly and three monthly services and then the following items:
Dismantle and clean the carburettor.
Repack the wheel hub bearings.
Drain front forks and refill to the correct level.
Re-pack steering head bearings.
Recharge contact breaker cam lubrication wick.
Lightly lubricate tachometer and speedometer housings.

Oil changes

Although a two-stroke engine runs on the total loss principle and does not have an oil content which is recirculated and retained in the crankcase, there is need to change the gearbox oil at regular intervals. The recommended period between oil changes is every 1000 miles or six weeks, whichever is the sooner. If the machine is used for a succession of short journeys, or when temperatures are low, it is advisable to halve this period, to offset the effects of condensation.

Statutory requirements

Although no specific mention has been made of the tyres, lighting equipment, horn or speedometer, statutory requirements relate to the depth of tyre tread permissible before replacement must be made and to the correct functioning of the lighting equipment, horn and speedometer. Whilst the prudent rider will check each of these points during the course of the routine maintenance tasks, as well as the general security of all nuts and bolts etc, it should be remembered that failure to observe the regulations may result in prosecution. Apart from the legal implications, it is best to err on the side of safety.

Recommended lubricants

Component	Grade	Castrol Grade
Engine	SAE 30 two-stroke	Castrol TT Two-Stroke Oil
Gearbox and forks	SAE 10W/30 engine oil	Castrolite Castrol Fork Oil
Final drive chain	Multi-grade oil or graphited grease	Castrol GTX or Castrol Graphited Grease or Castrol Chain Lubricant
All greasing points	Multi-purpose high melting point lithium grease	Castrol LM Grease
Chain		Castrol Chain Lubricant

Chapter 1 Engine, clutch and gearbox

Contents

General description ... 1	assembly (early models) ... 31
Operations with engine in frame ... 2	Engine/gearbox reassembly: replacing the kickstart assembly (early models) ... 32
Operations with engine removed ... 3	Engine/gearbox reassembly: replacing the kickstart assembly (late models) ... 33
Method of engine/gearbox removal ... 4	
Removing the engine/gearbox unit ... 5	Engine/gearbox reassembly: replacing the primary drive pinion ... 34
Dismantling the engine/gearbox: general ... 6	
Dismantling the engine/gearbox unit: removing the cylinder head, barrel and piston ... 7	Engine/gearbox reassembly: replacing the clutch assembly (early models) ... 35
Dismantling the engine/gearbox unit: removing the magneto assembly ... 8	Engine/gearbox reassembly: replacing the clutch assembly (late models) ... 36
Dismantling the engine/gearbox unit: removal of the clutch and primary drive gear ... 9	Engine/gearbox reassembly: replacing the magneto assembly ... 37
Dismantling the engine/gearbox unit: removing the kickstart assembly ... 10	Engine/gearbox reassembly: replacing the final drive sprocket ... 38
Dismantling the engine/gearbox unit: removing the gearchange mechanism ... 11	Engine/gearbox reassembly: replacing the tachometer and oil pump drive shafts ... 39
Dismantling the engine/gearbox unit: removing the primary drive gear ... 12	Engine/gearbox reassembly: replacing the primary drive cover ... 40
Dismantling the engine/gearbox unit: separating the crankcases ... 13	Engine/gearbox reassembly: replacing the piston and piston rings ... 41
Dismantling the engine/gearbox unit: removing the gear assembly and crankshaft assembly ... 14	Engine/gearbox reassembly: replacing the cylinder barrel ... 42
	Engine/gearbox reassembly: replacing the cylinder head ... 43
Dismantling the engine/gearbox unit: removing tachometer and oil pump drive pinion ... 15	Engine/gearbox reassembly: replacing the decompressor units ... 44
Examination and renovation: general ... 16	Refitting the engine/gearbox unit into the frame ... 45
Crankshaft assembly: examination and renovation ... 17	Engine/gearbox reassembly: reconnecting the oil pipes and carburettor ... 46
Small end bearing: examination and renovation ... 18	
Piston and rings: examination and renovation ... 19	Engine/gearbox reassembly: reconnecting bleeding and setting the oil pump ... 47
Cylinder barrel: examination and renovation ... 20	
Cylinder head: examination and renovation ... 21	Engine/gearbox reassembly: replacing the left-hand crankcase cover (early models) ... 48
Oil seals: examination and renovation ... 22	
Gearbox components: examination and renovation ... 23	Engine/gearbox reaassembly: replacing the left-hand crankcase cover (late models) ... 49
Clutch assembly: examination and renovation ... 24	
Crankcase covers: examination and renovation ... 25	Engine/gearbox reassembly: replacing the exhaust system ... 50
Engine/gearbox reassembly: general ... 26	Engine/gearbox reassembly: completion and final adjustments ... 51
Engine/gearbox reassembly: replacing the crankshaft ... 27	
Engine/gearbox reassembly: replacing the gearbox assembly ... 28	Starting and running the rebuilt engine ... 52
Engine/gearbox reassembly: jointing the crankcase ... 29	Fault diagnosis: engine ... 53
Engine/gearbox reassembly: replacing the gearchange assembly (late models) ... 30	Fault diagnosis: gearbox ... 54
Engine/gearbox reassembly: replacing the gearchange	Fault diagnosis: clutch ... 55

Specifications

	DT1 (all suffix)	DT2 and DT3
Model	DT1-F	DT1-F
Engine Type	Single cylinder, two-stroke	
Porting	5 port	7 port
Capacity	15.01 cu in (246 cc)	
Bore	2.756 inch (70 mm)	
Stroke	2.520 inch (64 mm)	

Chapter 1: Engine, clutch and gearbox

Comp. ratio	6.4 : 1	6.8 : 1
B.h.p.	23 @ 7,000 rpm	24 @ 7,000 rpm
Lubrication	Separate pump using 'Autolube' system	

Piston
Cylinder bore clearance	0.0016" - 0.0018" (0.040 - 0.045 mm)
Wear limit	0.0019" (0.050 mm)
Rebore sizes available	0.010" and 0.020" (0.25 mm and 0.50 mm)

Piston rings
No. per piston	Two
End gap	0.007" - 0.015" (0.20 mm - 0.40 mm)
	0.011" - 0.019" (0.30 mm - 0.50 mm)

Gearbox
Type	5 speed constant mesh
Ratios	
1st gear	24.644 : 1
2nd gear	17.408 : 1
3rd gear	12.689 : 1
4th gear	9.728 : 1
5th gear	7.458 : 1

Clutch
Type	Wet, multi-plate
No. of plates	
Plain	7
Inserted	6
Clutch springs	6
Free length	1.433 in (36.4 mm)
Wear limit	1.390 in (35.4 mm)
Inserted plate thickness	0.118 in (3.0 mm)
Wear limit	0.106 in (2.7 mm)

Model	RT1 (all suffix)	RT2 and RT3
Engine	RT1	RT1
Type	Single cylinder, two-stroke	
Porting	5 port	7 port
Capacity	21.42 cu. in (351 cc)	
Bore	3.150 in (80 mm)	
Stroke	2.756 in (70 mm)	
Comp. ratio	6.3 : 1	6.3 : 1
b.h.p.	30 @ 6,000 rpm	32 @ 6,000 rpm
Lubrication	Separate pump using 'Autolube' system	

Piston
Cylinder bore clearance	0.0018" - 0.0020" (0.045 mm - 0.05 mm)
Wear limit	0.0019" (0.05 mm)
Rebore sizes available	0.010" - 0.020" (0.25 mm - 0.50 mm)

Piston rings
No. per piston	Two
End gap	0.011" - 0.019" (0.30 mm - 0.50 mm)

Gearbox
Type	5 speed constant mesh
Ratios	
1st gear	20.387 : 1
2nd gear	14.401 : 1
3rd gear	10.490 : 1
4th gear	8.048 : 1
5th gear	6.170 : 1

Clutch
Type	Wet, multi-plate
No. of plates	
Plain	7
Inserted	6
Clutch springs	6
Free length	1.433" (36.4 mm)
Wear limit	1.390" (35.4 mm)
Inserted plate thickness	0.118" (3.0 mm)
Wear limit	0.106" (2.7 mm)

Chapter 1: Engine, clutch and gearbox

Model	DT 400B
Engine	
Type	Single cylinder, two-stroke
Porting	7 port
Capacity	24.22 cu. in (397 cc)
Bore	3.35 in (85 mm)
Stroke	2.76 in (70 mm)
Comp. ratio	6.4 : 1
b.h.p.	27 @ 5,000 rpm
Lubrication	Separate pump using 'Autolube' system
Piston	
Cylinder wall clearance	0.0018'' - 0.0020'' (0.045 mm - 0.05 mm)
Wear limit	0.0019'' (0.05 mm)
Rebore sizes available	0.010'' - 0.020'' (0.25 mm - 0.50 mm)
Piston rings	
No. per piston	Two
End gap	0.011'' - 0.019'' (0.30 mm - 0.50 mm)
Gearbox	
Type	5 speed constant mesh
Ratios	
1st gear	19.3 : 1
2nd gear	13.6 : 1
3rd gear	9.9 : 1
4th gear	7.6 : 1
5th gear	5.8 : 1
Clutch	
Type	Wet, multi-plate
No. of plates	
Plain	6
Inserted	7
Clutch springs	6
Free length	1.433'' (36.4 mm)
Wear limit	1.390'' (35.4 mm)
Inserted plate thickness	0.118'' (3.0 mm)
Wear limit	0.106'' (2.7 mm)

1 General description

The engines fitted to the Yamaha Enduro trail motorcycles range from the 100 cc fitted to the LT series to the recently introduced DT 400 cc model.

This manual covers those machines with 250 cc, 360 cc and 400 cc engines.

The engines are single cylinder units using 5 port or 7 port induction systems depending on the particular model. Reed valves are fitted to the fuel inlet passages on the 7 port models to reduce the possibility of blow-back and to maintain an even flow of combustible gases precisely when they are required. This feature coupled with the seventh scavenging port produces an economical and powerful unit. All engine castings are of aluminium alloy, including the cylinder barrel, cylinder head and piston. The pistons have two rings of the pegged type, usual to two-strokes.

The built-up crankshaft has full flywheels and runs on two journal ball bearings housed in the crankcases, one each side of the flywheels. The crankcase separates vertically down the centre line of the motorcycle, and effectively houses the crank assembly and gearbox as one unit. Therefore when the engine is dismantled and the crankcase separated the gearbox has to be dismantled too. The inverse also applies.

Starting and lighting are supplied by a flywheel magneto mounted on the left-hand side of the engine, and driven directly off the end of the crankshaft. The 400 model introduced in 1975 is equipped with a CDI (capacity discharge ignition) system which replaces the traditional contact breaker assembly and improves the accuracy of the ignition timing.

Lubrication is effected by the Yamaha 'Autolube' system, which takes the form of a gear driven oil pump drawing oil from a separate oil tank and distributing it to the various working parts of the engine. The pump is interconnected to the throttle, so that optimum lubrication is achieved at all times, corresponding to the requirements of both engine speed and throttle opening. This system completely obviates the need for petroil and the problems that arise when pre-mixing petrol and oil.

2 Operations with engine in frame

It is not necessary to remove the engine unit from the frame unless the crankshaft assembly and/or the gearbox internals require attention. Most operations can be accomplished with the engine in place, such as:

1 *Removal and replacement of the cylinder head.*
2 *Removal and replacement of the cylinder barrel and piston.*
3 *Removal and replacement of the generator.*
4 *Removal and replacement of the clutch.*
5 *Removal and replacement of the contact breaker assembly.*

When several operations need to be undertaken simultaneously it will probably be advantageous to remove the complete engine unit from the frame, an operation that should take approximately two hours, working at a leisurely place. This will give the advantage of better access and more working space.

Chapter 1: Engine, clutch and gearbox

3 Operations with engine removed

1 Removal and replacement of the crankshaft assembly.
2 Removal and replacement of the gear cluster, selectors and gearbox main bearings.

4 Method of engine/gearbox removal

As mentioned previously, the engine and gearbox are built in unit and it is necessary to remove the unit complete, in order to gain access to components. Separation is accomplished after the engine unit has been removed from the frame and refitting can not take place until the crankcase has been reassembled. When the crankcase is separated, the gearbox internals will be exposed.

5 Removing the engine/gearbox unit

1 As the Yamaha trail bikes are not supplied with centre stands it is necessary to securely block the motorcycle in an upright position before commencing removal of the engine. Blocks may be placed below the sump guard without hindering removal of the engine bolts. However, on late machines, the sump guard should be removed and the clutch cable disconnected from the clutch operation arm before the blocks are put in place.
2 Turn the fuel tap to the 'stop' position. Remove the petrol feed pipe which is a push fit on the union and is retained by a spring clip. The ears of the clip should be pressed together to release the tension on the fuel line. The petrol tank is retained by two rubber buffers at the front, which fit into slots on either side of the frame cross tube, and by a rubber strap over a hook, or a single bolt and washer at the rear of the tank. Lift the dual-seat by undoing the over-centre clip that can be found on the left-hand side of the seat, and hinge the seat up to the right. The seat stopper can be pulled out of its slider slot in order to allow the seat to fall back as far as it will go and facilitate tank removal. Alternatively the spring clips holding the seat hinge pins can be removed and the pins pulled from position. This will free the seat for complete removal. The tank can now be eased backwards and lifted clear.
3 As a safety precaution to minimise the risk of shorting out any part of the electrical system, it is wise to remove the battery from the motorcycle. The earth lead is retained to the frame by a cross-head screw, and the live wire by a torpedo connector. With the wire disconnected and the battery strap (where fitted) unclipped, the battery may be lifted out of its cradle.
4 Remove the two bolts which retain the exhaust pipe flange on the cylinder barrel and unscrew the silencer holding bolt(s). On most machines a single bolt, passing through the frame under the seat holds the exhaust system in place. Where two or three-piece systems are used each section is supported by a
5 Remove the throttle slide by unscrewing the knurled ring which retains the carburettor cap and withdrawing. Tape the slide and the cable to the frame cross tube to prevent it getting damaged during engine removal and replacement. Disconnect the spark plug cap and tape it and the HT cable to the frame.
6 Remove the tachometer drive cable from the crankcase unscrewing the knurled union ring in an anticlockwise direction. The cable will pull straight out of the drive housing.
7 Remove the oil pump inspection cover which is held by two or three screws. Disconnect the control cable linking the oil pump with the throttle. A barrel-shaped nipple on the end of the inner cable engages with the oil pump pulley and can be slipped out of position by twisting while the pulley is turned. When the cable is free, remove the adjuster which threads into the outer crankcase cover. The cable can then be withdrawn complete from the engine.
8 Disconnect the main electrical harness from the magneto by pulling the individual connectors apart and release the wires from the clips on the frame.

5.2a Fuel tank held at rear by nut or strap and ...

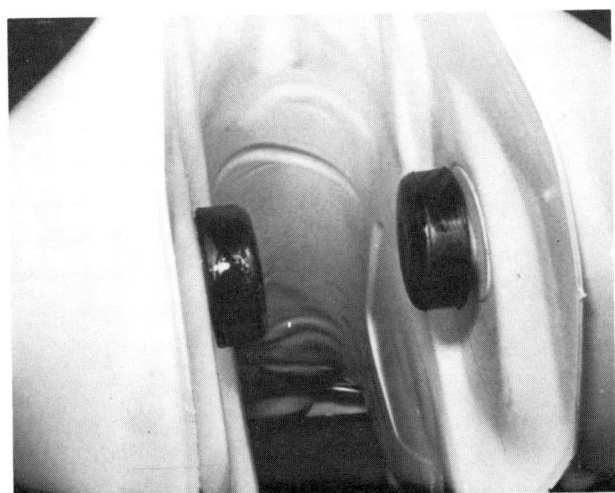

5.2b ...by rubber buffers at front end

5.4a Exhaust pipe held by two nuts on flange and ...

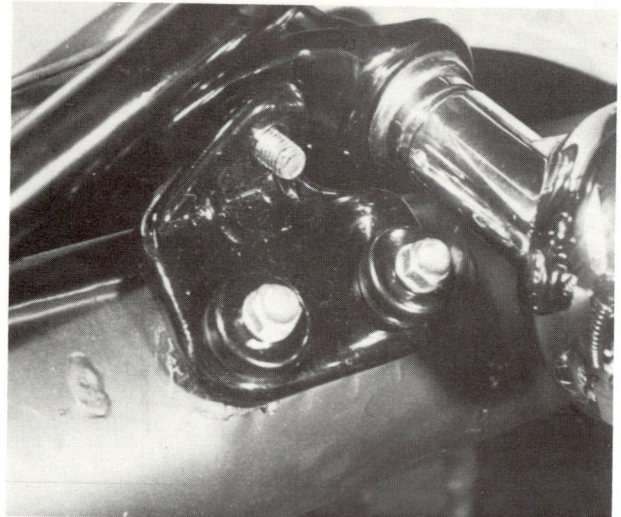

5.4b ... by bracket on silencer body

5.5 Remove throttle slide, retained by screw cap

5.6 Tachometer cable unscrews at casing

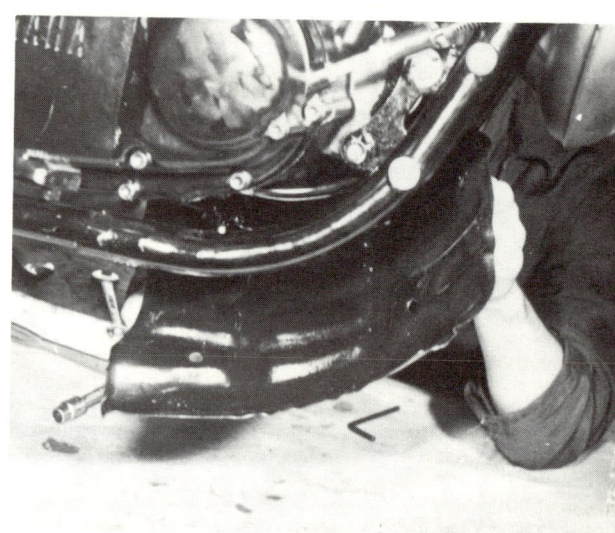

5.12a Remove sump guard to give access to ...

5.12b ... the clutch operating arm and cable (late model)

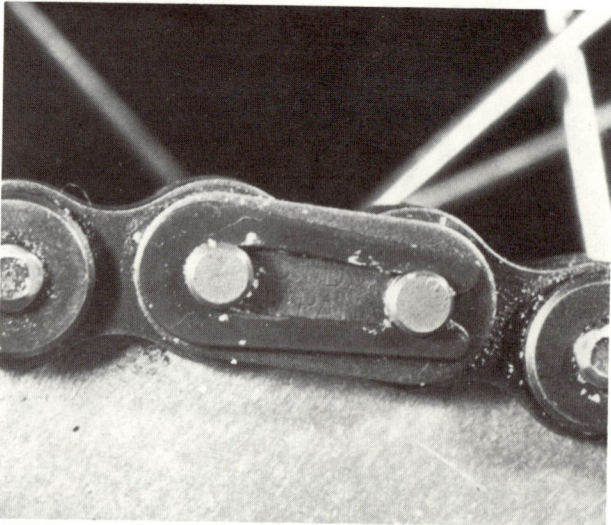

5.15 Detach final drive chain at sprocket

Chapter 1: Engine, clutch and gearbox

9 The gearchange pedal is retained on its shaft by a pinch bolt as is the kickstart lever. The pinch bolts on both kickstart and gearchange lever must be removed before the levers are pulled off their splines.

10 Unscrew the four cross-head screws which retain the magneto cover plate onto the left-hand crankcase and remove the casing.

11 On early models, unscrew the four cross-head screws which retain the outside left-hand casing and gently pull the case away. The casing cannot be completely removed until the clutch cable has been disconnected. First disconnect the clutch cable from the left-hand handlebar lever.

12 With the slack inner cable now available the barrel-nipple at the other cable end can be removed from the clutch actuating arm which is positioned behind the casing. The clutch cable may now be pulled free from the casing top and the casing will be free for removal.

13 Detach the air cleaner hose from the carburettor by undoing the screw clip that is around the hose and carburettor mouth. The hose can then be pulled from the mouth.

14 It is recommended that the carburettor be removed at this stage as it is easily damaged during engine removal. Early models with 7 port cylinder barrels have the carburettor attached to the reed valve housing which in turn is attached to the barrel. To remove the whole assembly, undo the two Allen screws which hold the carburettor flange to the reed valve housing and remove the carburettor. On late 7 port models the carburettor is mounted on a flexible rubber stub which is bolted to the reed valve housing. The carburettor can be removed after the screw clip is loosened. Those machines with 5 port cylinder barrels have the carburettor retained directly onto the inlet manifold stub, either by two Allen screws or two studs, passing through the carburettor flange and heat sink block.

15 Before the final drive chain is removed, it can be usefully employed to lock the final drive sprocket whilst the sprocket centre nut is being loosened. This operation can be troublesome when the engine has been removed from the frame as it is difficult to prevent the drive sprocket rotating. Knock the centre nut tab washer back away from the nut face using a blunt cold chisel or screwdriver. Weight applied over the rear wheel will stop the drive sprocket rotation as the centre nut is undone. Remove the master link from the drive chain and pull the chain out, over the rear sprocket's rotation as the centre nut is undone. Remove the master link to avoid its misplacement when the chain is out of use.

16 The engine mounting bolts can now be removed. On the early models four full length bolts are utilised, two at the front and two at the rear. With the nuts and washers loosened and removed the bolts can be knocked out from the left. Late machines have two full length bolts at the rear of the engine. The two front engine bolts run from left to right, and pass through the crankcase lugs into a threaded plate which is either bolted or welded to the frame. With all engine mounting bolts removed the engine is ready for removal. Although the engine unit can be removed single-handed, it is wise to have a second person at hand to steady the engine as it comes out. This applies particularly with the 400 cc unit.

6 Dismantling the engine and gearbox: general

1 Before commencing work on the engine unit, the external surfaces should be cleaned thoroughly. A motorcycle engine has very little protection from road grit and other foreign matter, which will find its way into the dismantled engine if this simple precaution is not taken. One of the proprietary cleaning compounds such as Gunk or Jizer can be used to good effect, particularly if the compound is permitted to work into the film of oil and grease before it is washed away. Special care is necessary when washing down to prevent water from entering the now exposed parts of the engine unit.

2 Never use undue force to remove any stubborn part unless specific mentioned is made of this requirement. There is

5.16a Engine mounted at the front on detachable plates

5.16b Lift engine out with great care

7.1 Remove cylinder head and gasket

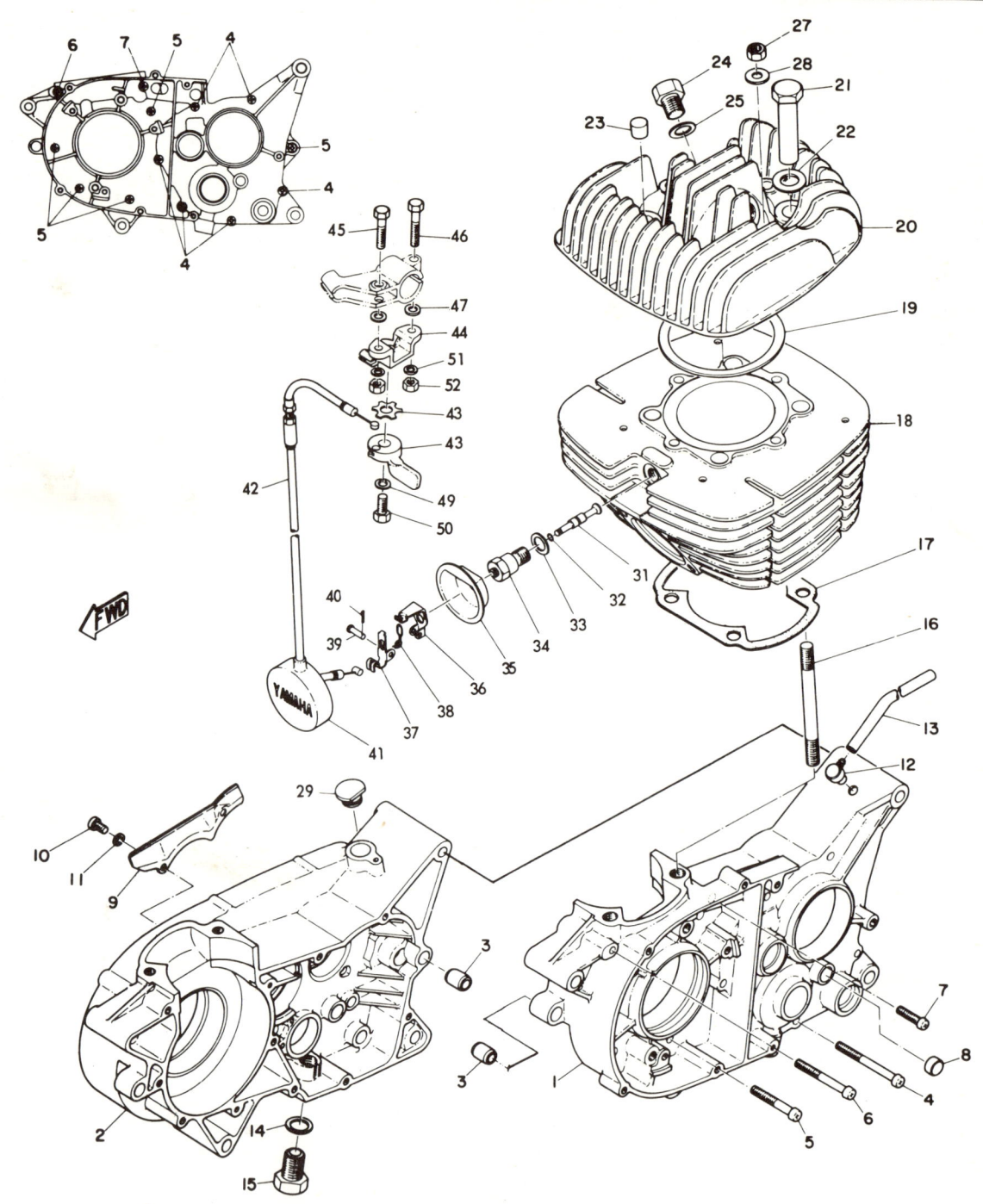

Fig. 1.1 Crankcase assembly

1 Left-hand crankcase
2 Right-hand crankcase
3 Dowel pin - 2 off
4 Pan head screw - 6 off
5 Pan head screw - 5 off
6 Pan head screw - 1 off
7 Pan head screw - 1 off
8 Blind plug
9 Cover - 1 off
10 Pan head screw - 2 off
11 Spring washer - 2 off
12 Breather body
13 Breather pipe
14 Drain plug washer
15 Drain plug
16 Cylinder holding stud - 4 off
17 Cylinder base gasket
18 Cylinder barrel
19 Cylinder head gasket
20 Cylinder head
21 Cylinder head sleeve nut - 4 off
22 Plain washer - 4 off
23 Rubber buffer - 4 off
24 Cylinder head plug
25 Cylinder head plug washer
26 Cylinder head holding stud - 4 off
27 Cylinder head holding nut - 4 off
28 Plain washer - 4 off
29 Tacho drive blind plug
30 Spark plug
31 Decompression valve stem
32 'O' ring
33 Washer
34 Decompression valve body
35 Inner cover
36 Operating arm anchor
37 Operating arm
38 Return spring
39 Clevis pin
40 Split pin
41 Outer cover
42 Cable
43 Compressor lever
44 Lever stock
45 Bolt
46 Bolt
47 Distance washer - 2 off
48 Star washer
49 Plain washer
50 Bolt
51 Spring washer - 2 off
52 Nut - 2 off

Chapter 1: Engine, clutch and gearbox

invariably good reason why a part is difficult to remove, often because the dismantling operation has been tackled in the wrong sequence. Dismantling will be made easier if a simple engine stand is constructed to correspond with the engine mounting points. This arrangement will permit the complete engine unit to be clamped rigidly to the workbench, leaving both hands free.

7 Dismantling the engine/gearbox unit: removing the cylinder head, barrel and piston

1 Four or six nuts retain the cylinder head depending on the model. Loosen the nuts in a diagonal sequence and remove them along with their washers. The cylinder head can now be lifted off together with the head gasket.
2 Remove the oil delivery pipe from the inlet manifold by unscrewing the bolt that passes through the banjo union. On some late models the oil feed pipe runs directly to a union on the carburettor, where it is a push fit retained by a spring clip. In all cases the oil pipe issues from a joint between the right-hand engine cases and should not be pulled through.

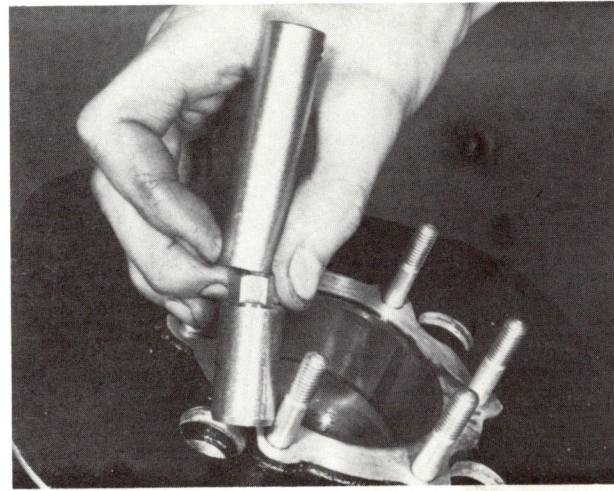
7.2a Cylinder barrel held by four sleeve bolts

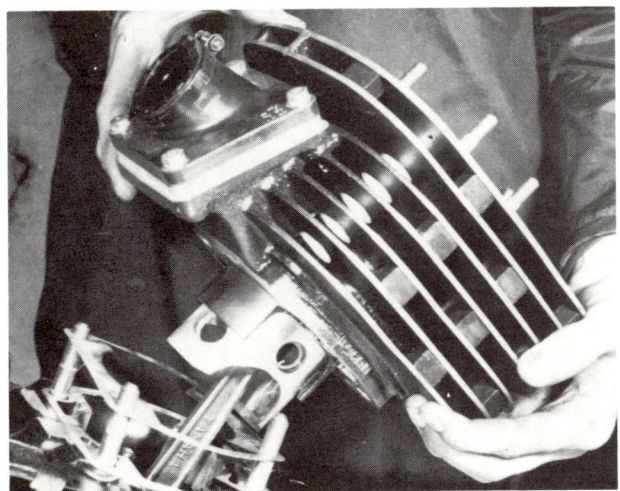
7.2b Remove barrel and old gasket

7.4a Remove circlip with pliers and ...

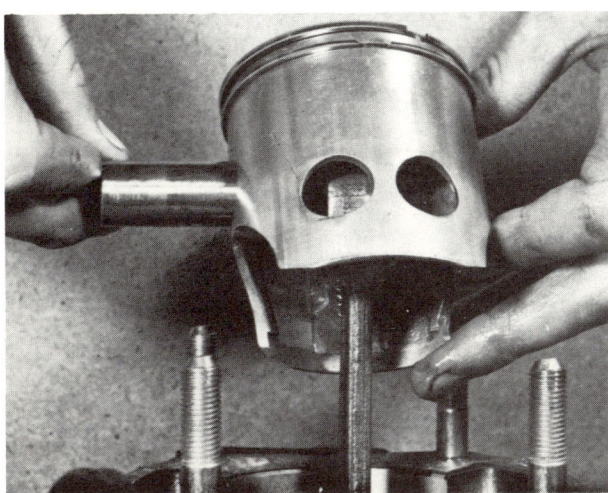
7.4b ... push out the gudgeon pin to ...

7.4c ... remove the piston and small end bearing

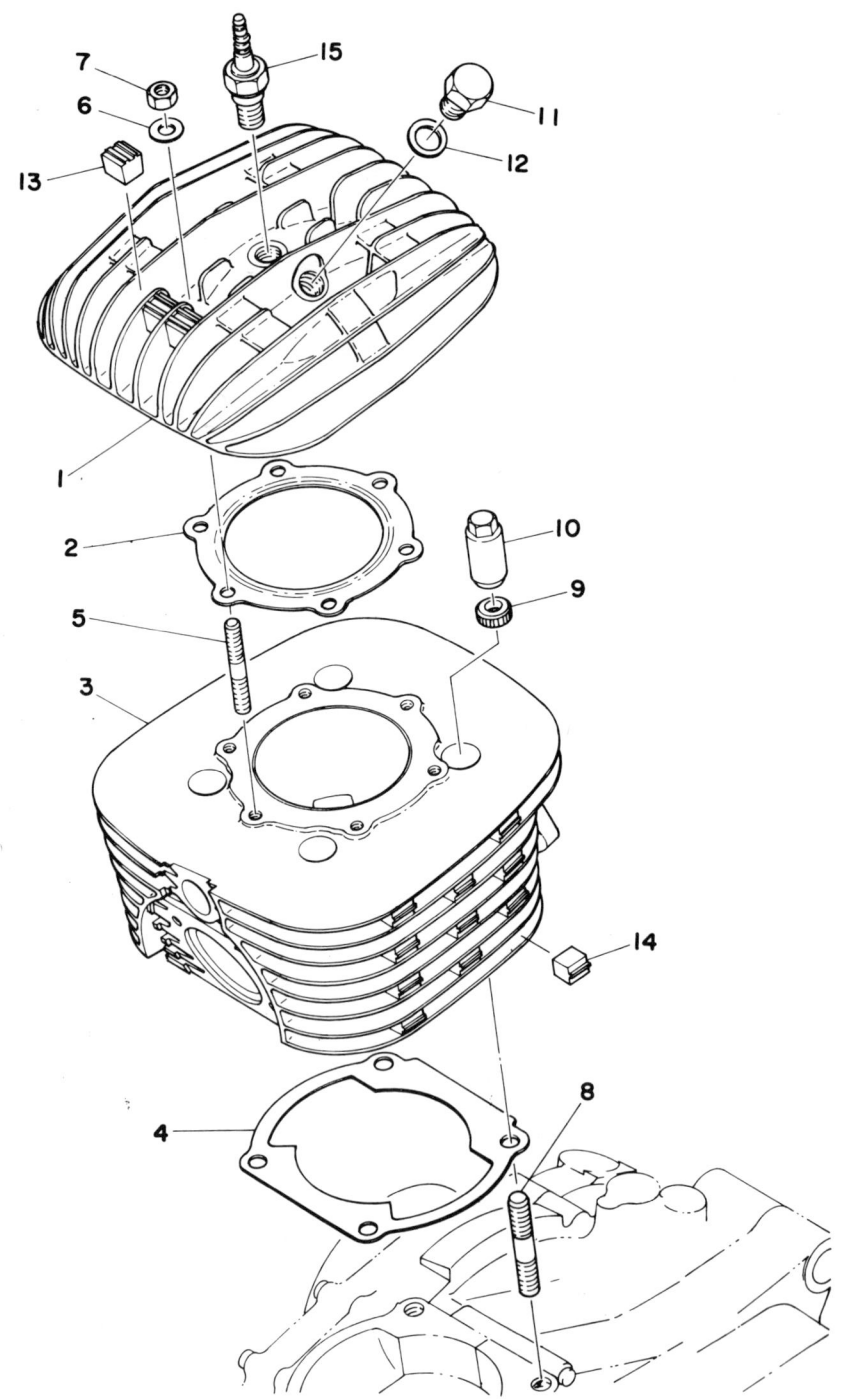

Fig. 1.2 Cylinder head and cylinder (Late models)

1 Cylinder head
2 Cylinder head gasket
3 Cylinder
4 Cylinder base gasket
5 Holding down stud - 6 off
6 Plain washer - 6 off
7 Nut - 6 off
8 Barrel holding stud - 4 off
9 Special washer - 4 off
10 Holding down screw nut - 4 off
11 Cylinder head plug
12 Cylinder head washer
13 Vibration buffer - 3 off
14 Vibration buffer - 24 off
15 Spark plug

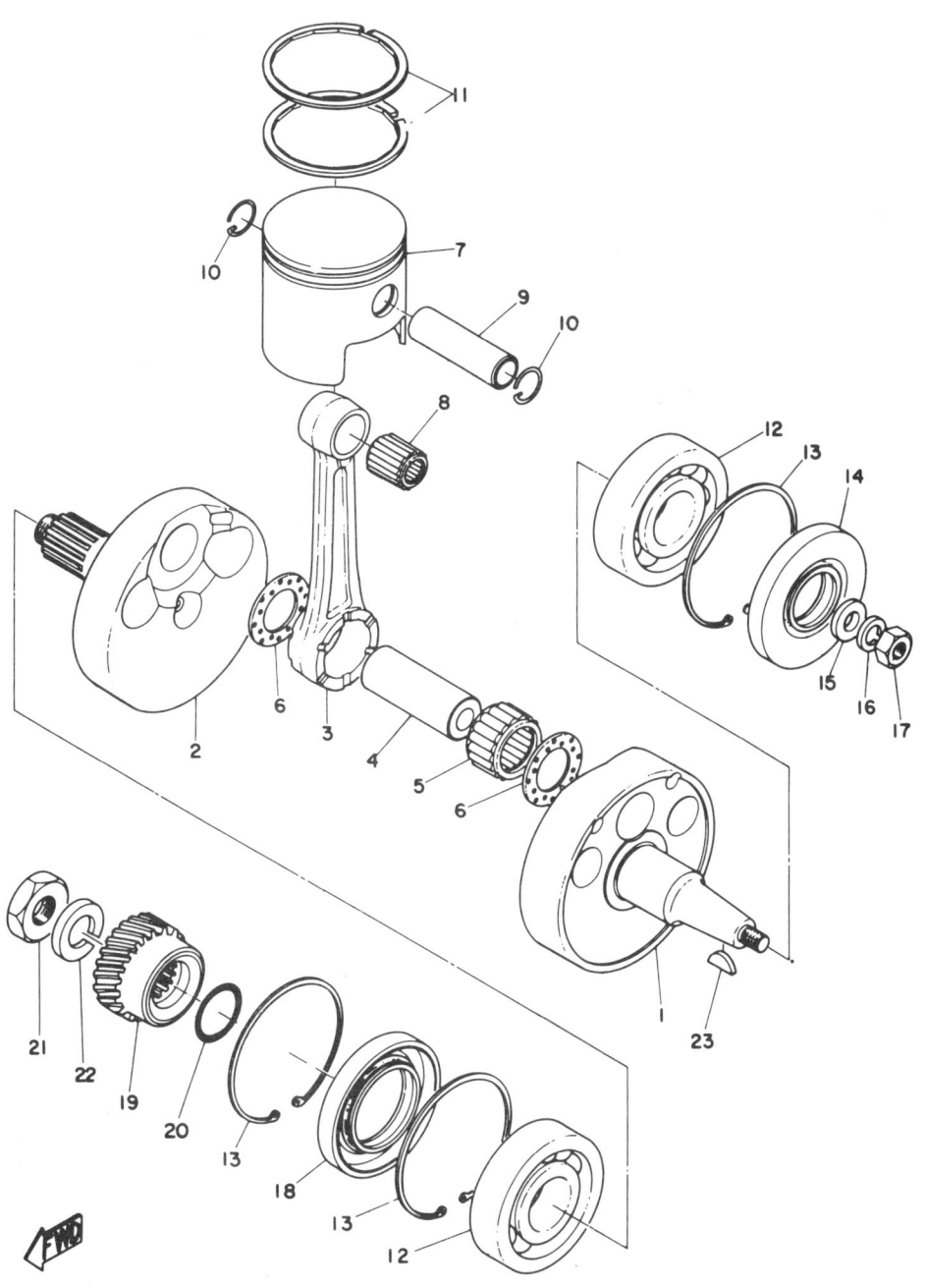

Fig. 1.3 Crankshaft assembly and piston (Early models)

1 Left-hand crankshaft
2 Right-hand crankshaft
3 Connecting rod
4 Crank pin
5 Big-end bearing
6 Thrust washer - 2 off
7 Piston
8 Small-end bearing
9 Gudgeon pin
10 Gudgeon pin circlip - 2 off
11 Piston ring set
12 Main bearing - 2 off
13 Bearing retainer circlip - 3 off
14 Oil seal
15 Plain washer
16 Spring washer
17 Nut
18 Oil seal
19 Primary drive pinion
20 'O' ring
21 Nut
22 Spring washer
23 Woodruff key

8.1a After removing nut and washer(s) ...

8.1b ... pull the magneto flywheel from position ...

8.2 ... to allow removal of stator plate

3 On late models the cylinder barrel is retained by four or six studs and sleeve nuts, which are quite separate from the cylinder retaining bolts. These nuts can be removed using the narrow socket spanner which is supplied in the tool kit.

Withdraw the cylinder barrel from the crankcase by pulling up along the holding down studs and at the same time pushing down on the piston crown with both thumbs. It is a wise precaution to place a rag in the mouth of the crankcase and all around the connecting rod to prevent damage to the crankcase mouth and the connecting rod sides in the event of the two components slapping together when the piston is being removed. The rag so placed will also exclude any broken pieces of piston ring from falling into the crankcase.

4 Before removing the piston, clean the piston crown to ascertain whether it has been marked with a small arrow on the forward edge. All pistons should be marked thus to ensure their correct replacement. Remove the circlips from both sides of the piston and press out the gudgeon pin. If the gudgeon pin is a tight fit in the piston bosses the piston can be slightly warmed to facilitate removal. This may be done by the application of a rag over which boiling water has been poured. If it is necessary to tap out the gudgeon pin, make certain that the connecting rod is securely blocked against side thrust, thereby alleviating the possibility of damage to the big-end bearing or connecting rod itself. Discard the old circlips. **Never re-use old ones.** The piston is now free for removal as is the small end needle roller bearing which is a sliding fit in the connecting rod small end eye.

8 Dismantling the engine/gearbox unit: removing the magneto assembly

1 Remove the magneto centre nut, spring washer and belville washer. It is recommended that a special service tool is used to remove the magneto flywheel; however removal can be accomplished using other means if the requisite tool is not available. It will be necessary to have a second person at hand. It may be found that the flywheel will tap off its keyed taper merely by holding it firmly in two hands, whilst the assistant taps the tapered shaft with a rawhide mallet. If this method fails, the two legs of a flywheel or sprocket puller may be utilised to hold the flywheel while the centre shaft is tapped. The feet of the extractor legs should be placed facing outwards in any opposite two of the four eccentric holes in the flywheel face. Care should be taken not to damage any part of the contact breaker assembly or lighting coils that are housed within the flywheel. One sharp tap on the shaft end is preferable to a number of more gentle taps. With the flywheel removed, prise out the Woodruff key and put to one side in a safe place.

2 Remove the two or three screws which hold the contact breaker assembly face plate and life the assembly off. The main leads connected to the contact breaker assembly run through a rubber grommet in the crankcase edge. this should be slid from its housing and the complete assembly removed. It is helpful to make a scribe line across the contact breaker base plate and the surrounding casing, so that the assembly is eventually replaced in the same position. This should obviate the need for retiming the ignition. On early models which have the clutch operating mechanism in the left-hand crankcase cover, remove the clutch operating rod by pulling it straight out of the mainshaft. Note carefully that between this length of rod and the remainder, which must be removed from the other side of the engine during clutch dismantling, there is a small ball bearing which takes the thrust of the two rods. This should be shaken out by inverting the engine.

9 Dismantling the engine/gearbox unit: removal of the clutch and primary drive gear

1 Place the engine so that the right-hand casing is facing upwards. The oil pump should be unscrewed and pulled off its

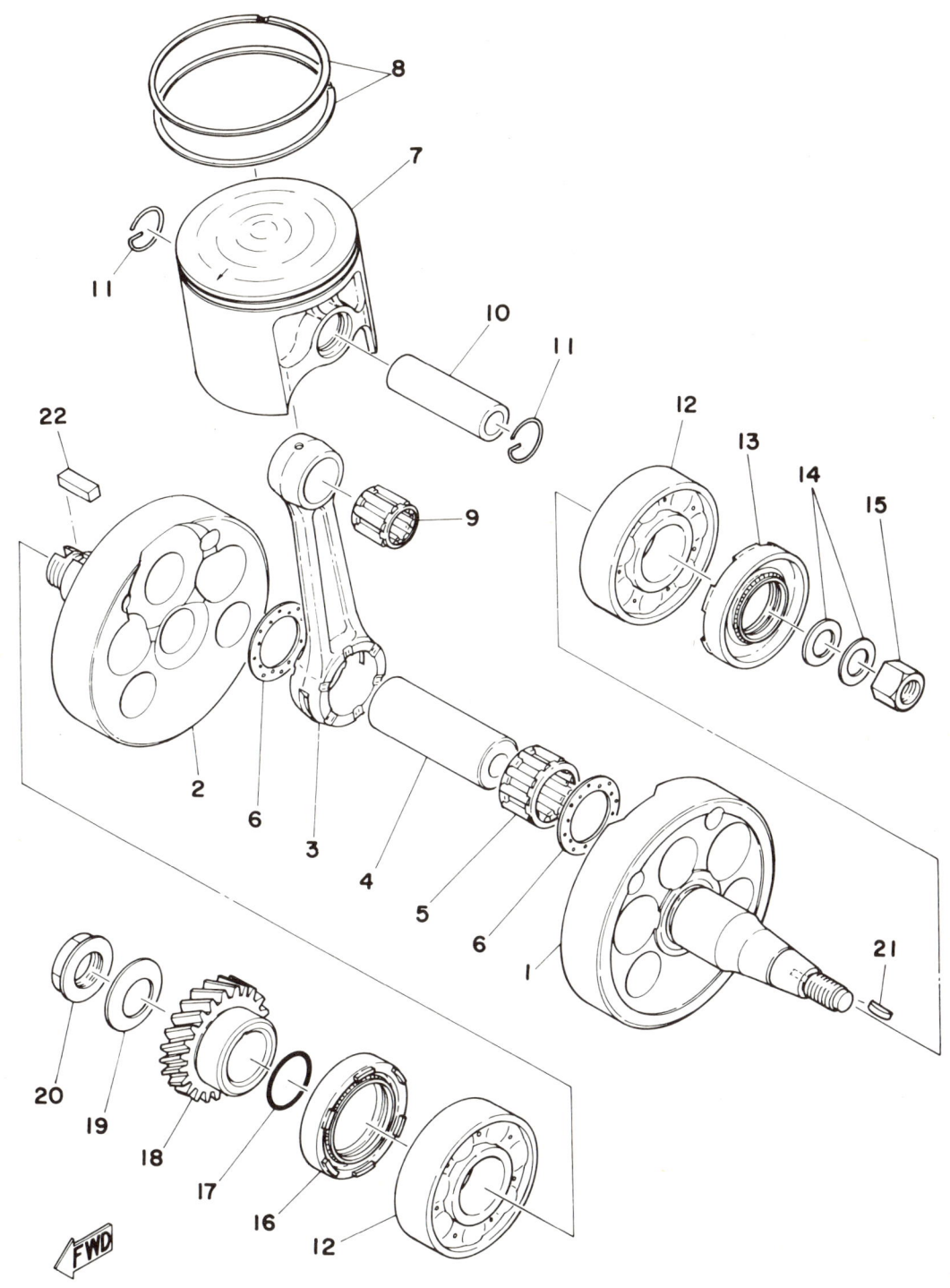

Fig. 1.4 Crankshaft assembly and piston (Late models)

1 Left-hand crankshaft
2 Right-hand crankshaft
3 Connecting rod
4 Crank pin
5 Big-end bearing
6 Thrust washer - 2 off
7 Piston
8 Piston ring set
9 Small-end bearing
10 Gudgeon pin
11 Gudgeon pin circlip - 2 off
12 Main bearing - 2 off
13 Left-hand crankshaft oil seal
14 Plain washer - 2 off
15 Nut
16 Right-hand crankshaft oil seal
17 'O' ring
18 Primary drive pinion
19 Belville washer
20 Nut
21 Woodruff key
22 Straight cut key

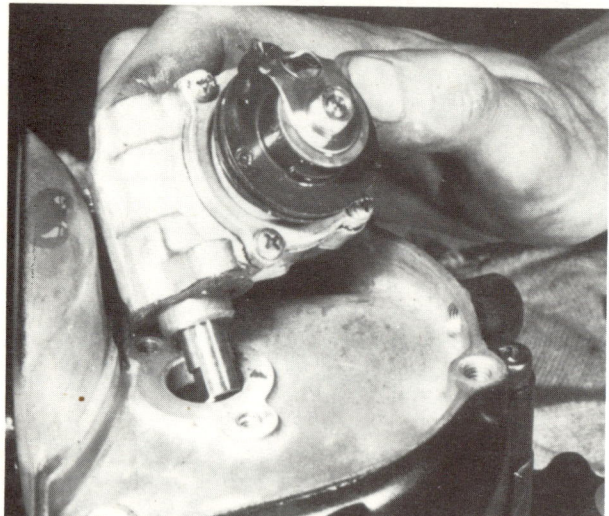
9.1 Pump body held by two screws

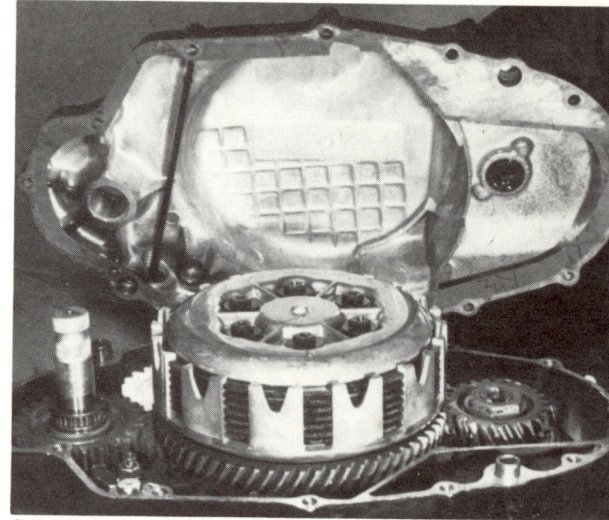
9.2a Remove casing to give access to clutch

9.2b Remove screws complete with springs to ...

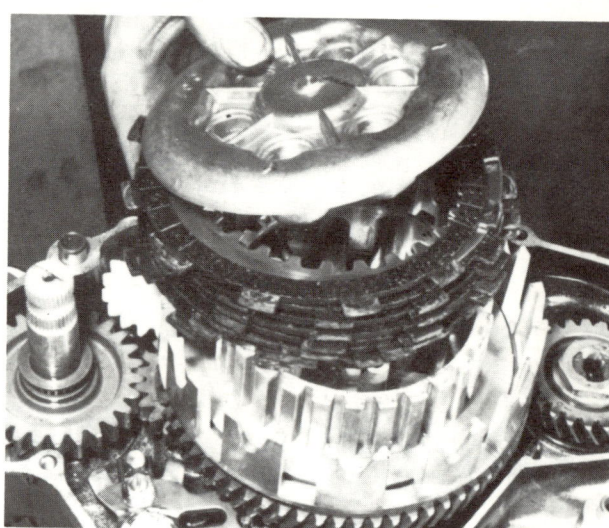
9.2c ... allow plates to be removed

9.3a Remove pushrod and loosen centre nut

9.3b Pull the clutch centre from position followed by ...

Chapter 1: Engine, clutch and gearbox

driveshaft, this particularly on some early models where the pump obscures one forward primary drive cover screw. The two pump retaining screws lie directly below the main pump body; having removed the screws the pump can be pulled out.

2 Loosen the cheese-head screws which retain the primary drive cover and withdraw. The casing is located by two tight fitting dowels and may therefore need gentle tapping with a rawhide mallet to aid removal. Having removed the casing make certain that the dowels are a tight fit in their apertures as they will otherwise fall out and may be misplaced while the engine is dismantled. Remove the casting gasket. Remove the Nylon tachometer drive gear, spacer collar and steel shim. Unscrew the six clutch springs and remove the pressure plate and clutch plates. Note the sequence of plain plates, inserted plates and rubber expander rings (where fitted).

3 Remove the mushroom-head clutch actuating rod by pulling it straight out. On late models the remaining ball bearing and clutch rod will have to be shaken out of position as they cannot be pushed out from the right.

4 In order to loosen the clutch retaining nut, it will be necessary first to lock the crankshaft so that it will not rotate and then to lock together the centre clutch boss and outside clutch drum. To lock the crankshaft, a short rod of approximately the same diameter as the gudgeon pin should be passed through the small end eye. Two blocks of soft wood can now be placed across the crankcase mouth and as the crankshaft is rotated the rod will bear down on the two blocks. If a special service tool is not available to lock the clutch, then a simple makeshift tool should be fabricated. A piece of ¼ inch or similar flat iron of approximately 8" x 1" dimensions when bent into a Z form will lock the clutch. Take great care that the segmented outer clutch drum is not unduly strained during this operation as the individual segments are easily bent or fractured. Bend back the clutch centre nut tab washer and then loosen and remove the centre nut and washer. The clutch centre can now be drawn off its shaft followed by the large thrust washer that is positioned behind.

5 Lift off the clutch outer drum, followed by the kickstart driven pinion (where it is fitted separate from the drum) and the clutch spacer collar and thrust washer(s).

10 Dismantling the engine/gearbox unit: removing the kickstart assembly

Early models

1 The kickstart assembly can be removed as a unit after the return spring has been disengaged from the peg in the casing, thereby releasing the tension. The shaft will have to be rotated slightly so that the ratchet wheel clears the pawl guide. Note the position of the steel shim that lies between the kickstart gear retaining circlip and the crankcase boss.

Late models

1 Remove the circlip and shim which retains the kickstart gear on the shaft and pull the gear from position.

2 Bend up the tab washers that lock the two ratchet wheel guide retaining bolts, loosen and remove the bolts followed by the guide and stopper plates. During this operation the tension in the kickstart spring will be released and the shaft will snap round approximately 1 turn. Mind your fingers!

The kickstart shaft can now be pulled from position. Note that the kickstart spring is located in a sleeve between the two crankcase halves and cannot be removed until the cases are separated.

11 Dismantling the engine/gearbox unit: removing the gear-change mechanism

1 Remove the retaining circlip and kickstart idler gear.

9.3c ... the thrust washer(s) and drum

9.5 Remove spacer and thrust washer(s)

10.1a Remove circlip and slide kickstart gear off shaft ...

10.1b ... pull shaft from position in casing (late models)

11.2a Tachometer nylon gear will slide from shaft ...

11.2b ... but idler gear is held by circlip

11.3a Gear change selector mechanism (late model)

11.3b Pull main change arm out as a unit

11.4 Remove circlip and pull secondary arm off pivot

Chapter 1: Engine, clutch and gearbox

2 The gearchange shaft runs through the crankcase from right to left. On late models the shaft is retained on the left by a circlip and washer which should be removed together with the dust excluder.
3 Pull out the shaft from the right by gripping the main change lever at its central pivot, making sure that the return spring comes away from its stopper peg. On early models the secondary change lever must be guided so that it does not foul the change drum pegs.
4 Remove the circlip which holds the secondary change lever and pull the assembly off the pivot peg. On the early models the change drum guide must be removed; it is held by two cross-head screws and spring washers.
5 Unscrew the neutral stopper bolt from bottom of the left-hand gearbox casing and remove the detent spring and plunger.

12 Dismantling the engine/gearbox unit: removing the primary drive gear

1 Lock the crankshaft using the two blocks of soft wood and short bar. Loosen and remove the retaining nut and belville washer which hold the primary drive pinion.
2 The pinion is located on the mainshaft by parallel splines or a large Woodruff key and should therefore remove with ease. If there is any difficulty in removing the pinion and a puller is not at hand, two screwdrivers can be used to ease it along the shaft. When utilising this method make certain that the screwdrivers do not bear upon any part of the crankcase. Two very thin blocks of wood should be used to protect the crankcase edges. Having removed the pinion, pull off the pinion spacer that passes through the oil seal.

13 Dismantling the engine/gearbox unit: separating the crankcases

1 Remove the cross-head screws which hold the crankcase halves together. Early models have 13 (thirteen) screws and late models only 12 (twelve) screws all of which are in the left-hand casing. The screws should be slackened in a diagonal sequence to avoid distorting the cases.
2 Separate the crankcase by gently tapping the right-hand crankshaft end and the gearbox mainshaft end in turn. NEVER insert screwdrivers or other levers between the crankcase halves to hasten separation. This will almost certainly cause irreparable damage to the mating surfaces. If there is any difficulty encountered while separating it is probable that the two shafts are tying against each other in their bearings, therefore it is important to give each shaft equal attention with the rawhide mallet. On late models note the distance piece between the two rubber mounting bushes on the engine mounting bolt top crankcase lug. This bush will fall clear and may be lost.

14 Dismantling the engine/gearbox unit: removing the gear assembly and crankshaft assembly

1 On separating the crankcases both the crankshaft assembly and the gearbox assemblies should have remained in-situ in the left-hand crankcase. Both units must now be removed.
2 Remove the crankshaft assembly by using a rawhide mallet on the mainshaft end. On some engines crankshaft endfloat shims may be found on one or both mainshafts. The position of these should be carefully noted. As when removing the crankshaft from the right-hand case, the main bearing should remain in its housing in the crankcase. However, if the bearings come off with the shaft, make certain before the crankshaft is replaced that the bearings have been repositioned in their housings.
3 Gearboxes at first sight often look more complicated than they actually are, but by the time the gears have been dismantled and cleaned they have usually taken on a less daunting aspect.

13.2 Crankshaft and gearbox should stay in left-hand case

14.4a Pull out selectors and rods followed by ...

14.4b ... the change cam and ...

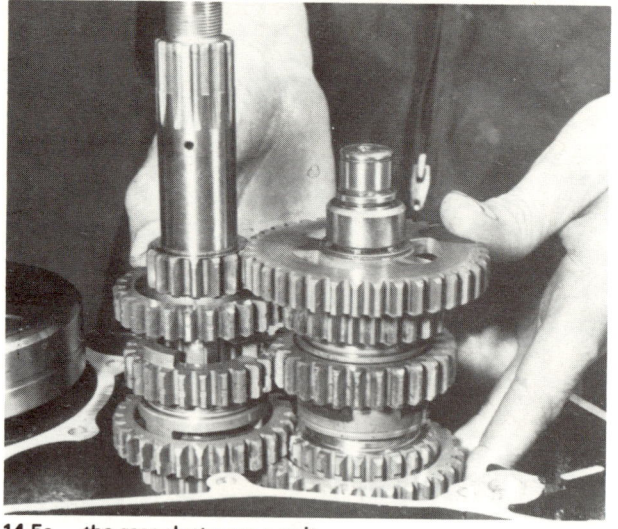
14.5a ... the gear clusters as a unit

14.5b Assemble the gears and selectors for inspection

15.2a Tachometer driven shaft and housing are free ...

15.2b ... after claw retainer is removed.

17.1a Note shim on drive side of crankshaft (late models) and ...

17.1b 'O' ring on timing side shaft.

Chapter 1: Engine, clutch and gearbox

Before removing the gears, shafts and gearchange drum, it is wise to take some time to familiarise yourself with the assembly as a whole.

4 Remove the drive shaft selector rod complete with the two selector forks, followed by the layshaft selector assembly. This can be a difficult operation as the selector forks may foul the pinions; care should therefore be taken. With the selector assemblies removed, the gear change drum can be pulled from position.

5 Note and remove the two shims, one of which will be found on each shaft end. On some machines the shims are retained together with the pinions by circlips, in this case the shims may be left in place. Pull the two shafts from position complete with their gear pinions. The shafts must be removed together. Note any endfloat shims on the drive side end of the shafts; take note also of the split spacer which lies on the drive shaft between the second gear driven pinion and the gearbox wall.

15 Dismantling the engine/gearbox unit: removing tachometer and oil pump drive pinions

Early models

1 It is unnecessary to remove either the tachometer drive pinion and shaft or the oil pump pinion and shaft unless the teeth are badly worn or damaged or the bushes badly worn. Inspection can be easily carried out with the components in place in the primary drive cover.

Tachometer drive

2 Loosen and remove the pan-head screw which holds the clawed plate retaining the tachometer drive shaft top housing. The housing can be pulled out followed by the drive shaft and gear.

Oil pump pinion

3 In order to remove the pump worn shaft it is necessary to remove the drive pinion and pin. Wrap a rag around the nylon pinion and firmly grasp it while the retaining nut is slackened. Do not use a screwdriver or other lever to lock the pinion as it can easily damage the pinion teeth. Remove the pinion and the slide fitting drive pin. The worm shaft can be drawn from the right, once the circlip has been removed.

Late models

Remarks on the tachometer drive apply equally to later models, dismantling being carried out in the same manner. No oil pump pinion is fitted to the later models as the pump is driven by a dog machined in the face of the drive side mainshaft.

16 Examination and renovation: general

1 Before examining the component parts of the dismantled engine/gear unit for wear, it is essential that they should be cleaned thoroughly. Use a paraffin/petrol mix to remove all traces of oil and sludge which may have accumulated within the engine.

2 Examine the crankcase castings for cracks or other signs of damage. If a crack is discovered, it will require professional attention, or in an extreme case, renewal of the casting.

3 Examine carefully each part to determine the extent of wear. If in doubt, check with the tolerance figures whenever they are quoted in the text. The following Sections will indicate what type of wear can be expected and in many cases, the acceptable limits.

4 Use clean, lint-free rags for cleaning and drying the various components, otherwise there is risk of small particles obstructing the internal oilways.

17.3a Bearing retaining plates must be removed ...

17.3b ... together with seal retainer before ...

17.3c ... bearings are knocked from casings

17 Crankshaft assembly: examination and renovation

1 The crankshaft assembly comprises two one-piece full flywheels and crank main pins. These are joined by a press fit central crankpin upon which the big-end bearing and connecting rod run. The whole is run in two journal ball bearings, one on each main pin.

2 The main bearings should be washed free of all old oil deposits, as they cannot be properly tested before this is done. If any play is evident or if the bearings do not run freely and smoothly they must be renewed. Warning of main bearing failure is usually given by a characteristic rumble that can be readily heard when the engine is running. Some vibration will also be felt, which will be transmitted via the footrests and frame in general.

3 The main bearings can easily be renewed in the average garage as they are only a push fit on the crankpins and in their housings. If the bearings remained on the crankpins when the crankshaft was removed, they should be gently prised off their pins, and, as with new bearings, replaced in the crankcase housings. Main bearings should be removed from the crankcases using a brass drift and mallet, tapping them from the outside of the case. Both main bearing oil seals should be removed before the bearings are tapped out; this will necessitate the removal of the oil seal retaining plate from the right-hand casing. Bearings should be replaced with the face stamped with the maker's name facing outwards, or away from the housing shoulder. The marked face of the bearing has been specially hardened to withstand tapping during replacement. Oil seals should be replaced in the same manner.

4 The big-end bearing should be inspected for play by pulling and pushing the connecting rod in a vertical direction. There should be no perceptible play. A certain amount of sideways play is permissible, but no more than 0.019 in (0.4 - 0.5 mm). If there is any excessive play, either laterally or up and down the bearing must be renewed. Because of the method of fixing the central crankpin and of the high accuracy required in re-aligning the flywheels after bearing replacement, this operation is usually beyond the means of the average owner. It is recommended that the crankshaft assembly be returned to a Yamaha specialist for the work to be executed.

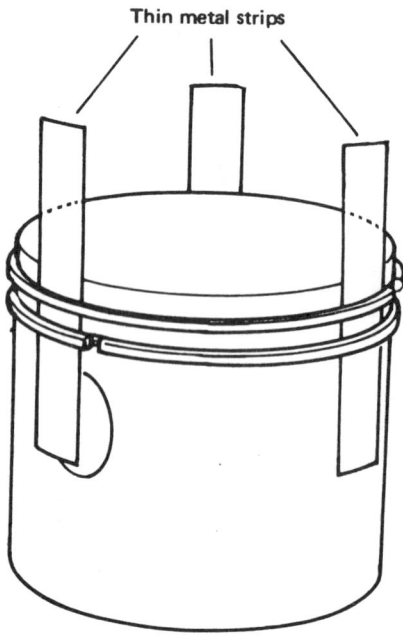

Fig. 1.5 Freeing gummed rings

18 Small end bearing: examination and renovation

1 The small end bearing is a caged needle roller assembly and will seldom give trouble unless lubrication failure has occurred. The gudgeon pin should be a good sliding fit in the bearing without any up and down play. If play develops, a noticeable rattle will be heard when the engine is running, indicative of the need for renewal of the bearing.

2 No problem is encountered when replacing the caged needle roller bearing as it is a light push fit in the small end eye. New small end bearings are normally supplied whenever the crankshaft assembly is renewed or service exchanged.

19 Piston and rings: examination and renovation

1 Attention to the piston and rings can be overlooked if a rebore is necessary as a new piston and rings will be fitted under these circumstances.

2 If a rebore is not considered necessary, the piston should be examined closely. Reject the piston if it is badly scored or discoloured as the result of the exhaust gases by-passing the rings. Check the gudgeon pin bosses to ensure that they are not enlarged or that the grooves retaining each circlip are not damaged.

3 Remove all carbon deposits from the piston crown and use metal polish to finish off, so that a high polish is obtained. Carbon will adhere much less readily to a polished surface. Examination of the piston crown will show whether the engine has been rebored previously, since the amount of rebore is always stamped on the piston crown. Two oversizes are available: + 0.010 in (+ 0.25 mm) and + 0.020 in (+ 0.50 mm).

4 The grooves in which the piston rings locate can become enlarged in use. The clearance between the edge of each piston ring and the groove in which it seats should not exceed 0.002 inch.

5 Remove the piston rings by pushing the ends apart with the thumbs whilst gently easing the ring from its groove. Great care is necessary throughout this operation because the rings are brittle and will break easily if overstressed. If the rings are gummed in their grooves, three strips of tin can be used to ease them free, as shown in the accompanying illustration.

6 Piston ring wear can be checked by inserting the rings one at a time in the cylinder bore from the top and pushing them down about 1½ inches with the base of the piston so that they rest square in the bore. Make sure that the end gap is away from any of the ports. If the piston ring end gap is within the correct range then the rings are suitable for further service.

Piston ring end gaps:
DT models 250 cc, 0.2 mm - 0.4 mm (0.008 in - 0.015 n)
RT models 350 cc, 0.3 mm - 0.5 mm (0.012 in - 0.020 in)

7 Examine the working surface of each piston ring. If discoloured areas are evident, the ring should be renewed because these areas indicate the blow-by of gas. Check that there is not a build-up of carbon on the back of the ring or in the piston ring groove, which may cause an increase in the radial pressure. A portion of broken ring affords the best means of cleaning out the piston ring grooves.

8 Check that the piston ring pegs are firmly embedded in each piston ring groove. It is imperative that these retainers should not work loose, otherwise the rings will be free to rotate and there is danger of the ends being trapped in the ports.

9 It cannot be over-emphasised that the condition of the piston and piston rings is of prime importance because they control the opening and closing of the ports by providing an effective moving seal. A two-stroke engine has only three working parts, of which the piston is one. It follows that the efficiency of the engine is very dependent on the condition of piston and the parts with which it is closely associated.

Chapter 1: Engine, clutch and gearbox

20 Cylinder barrel: examination and renovation

1 There will probably be a lip at the uppermost end of the cylinder barrel which marks the limit of travel of the top of the piston ring. The depth of the lip will give some indication of the amount of bore wear that has taken place even though the amount of wear is not evenly distributed.

2 Insert the piston (without rings) in the cylinder so that it is about ¾ inch from the top of the bore. Measure the distance between the piston skirt and the cylinder wall with a feeler gauge. Repeat measurement at two further positions down the bore. The recommended clearance is from 0.0016 - 0.0018 inch (0.40 - 0.45 mm). If the clearance exceed 0.0019 inch (0.50 mm) the cylinder is in need of a rebore.

3 Give the cylinder barrel a close visual inspection. A powerful torch or hand lamp can assist in showing up irregularities. If the surface of the bore is either scored or grooved, indicative of an earlier seizure, or a displaced circlip and/or gudgeon pin, reboring is essential. Compression loss has a marked effect on performance.

4 Check that the outside of each cylinder barrel is clean and free from road dirt. Use a wire brush on the cooling fins if they are obstructed in any way but take care not to score or damage the light alloy. If the air flow to the cooling fins is obstructed, the engine may overheat badly. Although caustic soda is often recommended for cleaning some of the oiler components of a two-stroke engine, NEVER use on parts made of light alloy. Caustic soda attacks aluminium alloy with great vigour and produces an explosive gas.

5 Clean all carbon deposits from the exhaust ports, using a blunt ended scraper. It is important that all the ports should have a clean, smooth appearance because this will have the dual benefit of improving gas flow and making it less easy for carbon to adhere in the future. Finish off with metal polish, to heighten the polishing effect.

6 Do not under any circumstances enlarge or alter the shape of the ports under the mistaken belief that improved performance will result. The size and position of the ports predetermines the characteristics of the engine and unwarranted tampering can produce very adverse effects.

21 Cylinder head: examination and renovation

1 It is unlikely that the cylinder head will require any special attention apart from removing the carbon deposit from the combustion chamber. Finish off with metal polish; the polished surface will help improve gas flow and reduce the tendency of future carbon deposits to adhere so readily.

2 Check that the cooling fins are clean and unobstructed, so that they receive the full air flow. If a wire brush is used, take care not to scratch or damage the fins.

3 Check the condition of the thread within the spark plug hole. The thread is easily damaged if the spark plug is over-tightened. If necessary, a damaged thread can be reclaimed by fitting a Helicoil thread insert. Most Yamaha agents have facilities for this type of repair, which is not expensive.

4 If there has been evidence of oil seepage from the cylinder head joint when the machine was in use, check whether the cylinder head is distorted by laying it on a sheet of plate glass. Severe distortion will necessitate renewal of the cylinder head, but if the distortion is only slight, the head can be reclaimed by wrapping a sheet of emery cloth around the glass and using it as the surface on which to rub down the head with a rotary motion until it is once again flat. The usual cause of distortion is failure to tighten down the cylinder head bolts evenly in a diagonal sequence.

22 Oil seals: examination and renovation

The crankshaft oil seals form one of the most critical parts in any two-stroke engine because they perform the dual function of preventing oil leaking along the crankshaft and preventing air from leaking into the crankcase.

2 Oil seal failure is difficult to define precisely, although in most cases the machine will become difficult to start, particularly when warm. The engine will also tend to run unevenly and there will be a marked fall-off in power especially in the higher gears. This is caused by the intake of air into the crankcase which dilutes the incoming mixture, giving an exceptionally weak mixture for ignition.

3 Because of the comparitively low cost, it is worthwhile replacing the crankshaft oil seals and the gearbox oil seals whenever the engine is stripped down. If an oil seal is found to be faulty after reassembly, replacement will necessitate the complete dismantling of the engine once again.

4 Make certain that the oil seals are replaced in the same position as they were before removal. In general the spring loaded face of the oil seal lies in the direction that the oil or gas may leak from. Most oil seals are only gas or oil tight in one direction therefore it is of the utmost importance that they are fitted correctly. The seal lips should be greased lightly to aid shaft replacement and avoid damage to the seal. The seals must not be replaced at an angle to their shaft as this will encourage leakage.

23 Gearbox components: examination and renovation

1 Examine each of the gear pinions to ensure that there are no chipped or broken teeth and that the dogs on the end of the pinions are not rounded. Gear pinions with any of these defects should be removed from their shafts and replaced by new gears.

2 The gearbox bearings must be free from play and show no signs of roughness or jamming when rotated. Once again it is necessary to make sure any old oil is removed from the bearings before they are inspected. The gearbox incorporates both journal ball bearings and a caged needle roller bearing. The ball bearings can be tapped from the casing once their retainer plates or circlips have been removed. If any difficulty is encountered, the cases can be heated to 200°F. This will produce expansion in the cases necessary to free the outer races. Heating the cases can either be accomplished with a blow-lamp or in an oven. When using a blow-lamp take care not to hold the flame in one spot for more than a few moments at a time. Remember also that later cases are finished in a matt black paint, and that a blow-lamp will easily destroy this finish.

The drive side end of the mainshaft runs on a caged needle roller bearing. On early models this can be knocked from position from the inside after the pushrod oil seal and circlip have been removed. On late models the bearing lies in a blind recess in the gearbox wall. Removal of the bearing is virtually impossible without the use of the correct expanding withdrawing tool. It is recommended that the casing be taken to a Yamaha specialist who will be able to remove the bearing without damage to the casing.

3 It is advisable to renew the gearbox oil seals irrespective of their condition. Should a re-used oil seal fail at a later date, a considerable amount of dismantling is necessary to gain access and renew it.

4 Check the gear selector rods for straightness by rolling them on a sheet of plate glass. A bent rod will cause difficulty in selecting gears and will make the gearchange action particularly heavy. The remaining circlips on the fork shafts must be removed in order to test them. Replace the circlips once the test is complete.

5 The selector forks should be examined closely, to ensure that they are not bent or badly worn. Wear is unlikely to occur unless the gearbox has been run for a period with a particularly low oil content.

6 The tracks in the gear selector drum, with which the selector forks engage, should not show any undue signs of wear unless neglect has led to under lubrication of the gearbox. Check that

Chapter 1: Engine, clutch and gearbox

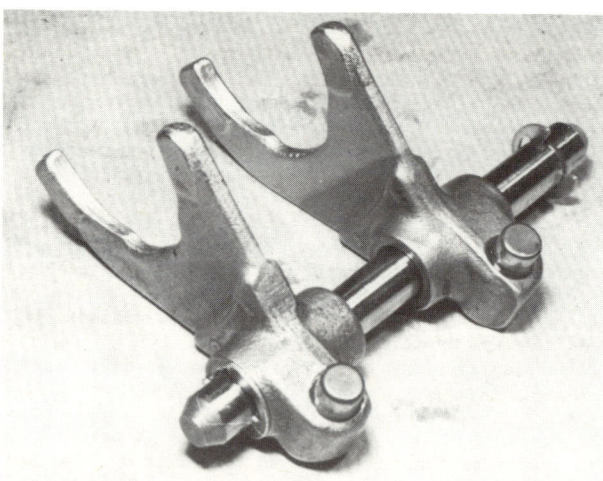

23.1a Check selector forks and ...

23.1b Cam tracks for wear

23.1c ... look for broken teeth and worn dogs on gears

the plunger spring bearing on the cam plate plunger has not lost its action and that the springs of the gearchange lever pawl assembly have good tension. Any damage to, or weakness of, the gearchange lever return spring will be self-evident.

7 If the kickstart has shown a tendency to slip, it will be necessary to examine the kickstart gear and shaft. The kickstart assembly can be inspected without dismantling, the most likely cause of failure being a broken kickstart spring clip.

24 Clutch assembly: examination and renovation

1 After an extended period of use the clutch linings will wear and promote clutch slip. The clutch plates should be measured with a vernier gauge or pair of calipers to ascertain the extent of wear. The measurements of thickness of the inserted plates and the maximum wear limits are as follows:

Plate width   0.118 in (3.0 mm)
Wear limit   0.106 in (2.7 mm)

If the plate width is less than the specified minimum then the plate must be renewed.

2 The plain clutch plates should not show any evidence of overheating (blueing). If they do, check them for overall flatness by placing each plate on a flat surface. In the event of the plates being buckled they should be renewed.

3 Check the free length of the clutch springs which should be as follows:

Free length   0.433 in (36.4 mm)
Wear limit   0.04 in (1.0 mm)

If the springs have shortened by more than 0.04 inch (1 mm) they must be renewed.

4 A worn clutch spacer is responsible for clutch noise and should be renewed if the fit within the clutch centre is particularly slack. Check the inner and outer surfaces for scratches; these will impair clutch action if not smoothed away.

5 Check the condition of the slots in the outer surface of the clutch centre and the inner surfaces of the outer drum. In an extreme case, clutch chatter may have caused the tongues of the inserted plates to make indentations in the slots of the outer drum, or the tongues of the plain plates to indent the slots of the clutch centre. These indentations will trap the clutch plates as they are freed and impair clutch action. If the damage is only slight the indentations can be removed by careful work with a file and the burrs removed from the tongues of the clutch plates in similar fashion. More extensive damage will necessitate renewal of the parts concerned.

6 The clutch release mechanism attached to the inside of the left-hand crankcase cover does not normally require attention.

25 Crankcase covers: examination and renovation

1 The right and left-hand crankcase covers are unlikely to suffer damage unless the machine is dropped or damaged in an accident. If the right-hand cover is fractured, the kickstart will be rendered inoperative since the cover acts as the outer bearing for the kickstart shaft. Renewal is therefore essential.

2 On early models, the covers are highly polished when they leave the factory and can be restored by using a proprietary aluminium polish such as Solvol Autosol. Badly scratched covers can be refurbished using very light grade emery paper followed by a rubber compound and aluminium polish.

Late models have engine casings finished in matt black paint. Should scratches appear, the cases can be resprayed using one of the proprietary paints available in an aerosol can.

26 Engine reassembly: general

1 Before reassembly of the engine/gearbox unit is commenced,

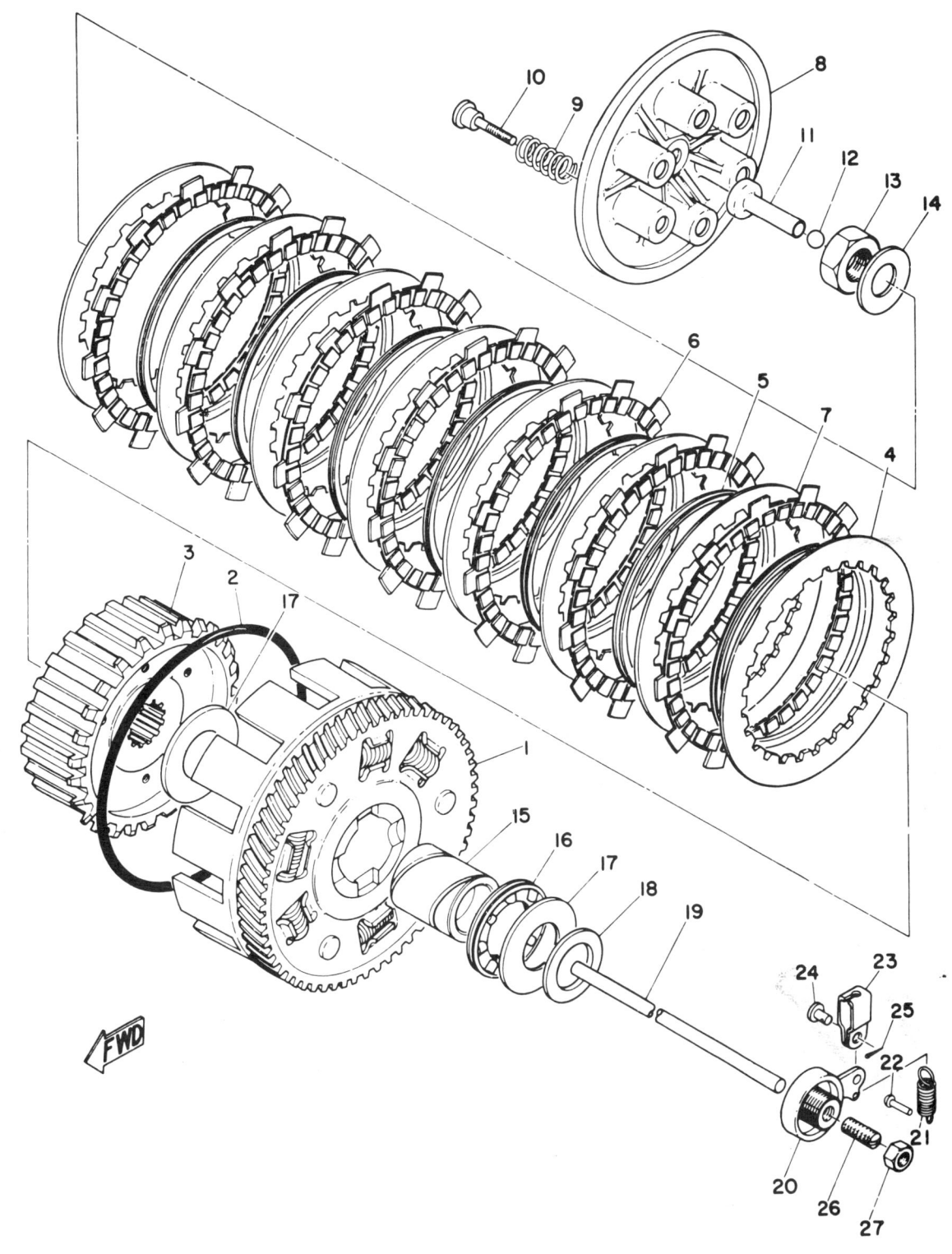

Fig. 1.6 Clutch assembly (Early models)

1 Clutch outer drum
2 'O' ring
3 Clutch centre boss
4 Plain base plate
5 Cushion ring - 7 off
6 Friction plate - inserted - 7 off
7 Plain plate - 7 off
8 Pressure plate
9 Clutch spring - 6 off
10 Clutch spring bolt - 6 off
11 Clutch pushrod end piece
12 Thrust ball bearing - 5/16"
13 Nut
14 Belville washer
15 Clutch spacer
16 Thrust bearing
17 Thrust plate - 1 - 2 off
18 Thrust plate - 2
19 Push rod
20 Quick-screw assembly
21 Return spring
22 Spring anchor pin
23 Cable anchor
24 Clevis pin
25 Split pin
26 Adjusting screw
27 Adusting nut

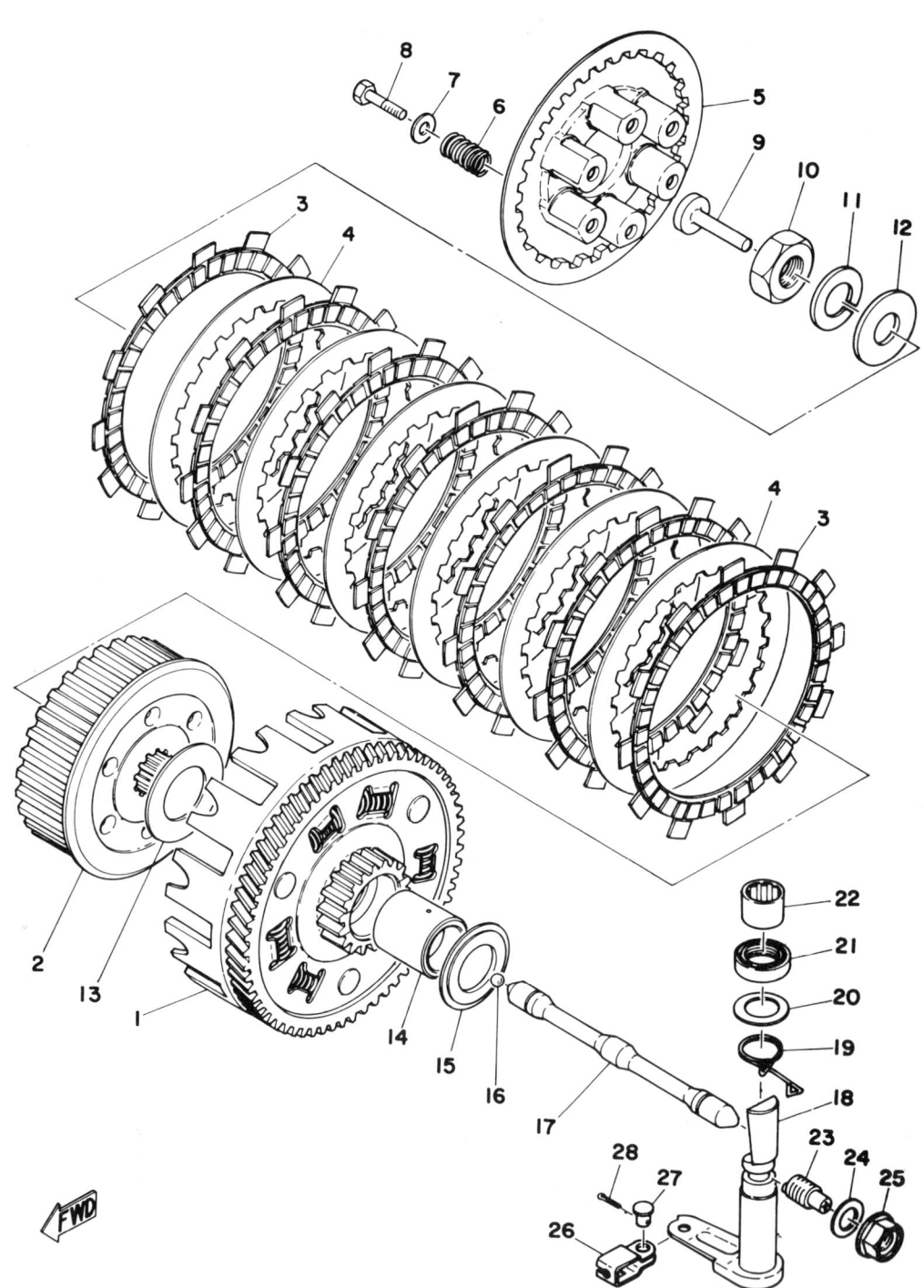

Fig. 1.7 Clutch assembly (Late models)

1 Clutch outer drum
2 Clutch centre boss
3 Friction plate (inserted) - 7 off
4 Plain plate - 6 off
5 Pressure plate
6 Clutch spring - 6 off
7 Plain washer - 6 off
8 Crosshead/hexagon screw - 6 off
9 Clutch pushrod end piece
10 Nut
11 Spring washer
12 Plain washer
13 Thrust washer
14 Clutch spacer
15 Thrust washer
16 Thrust ball bearing - 11/32"
17 Push rod
18 Operating cam arm
19 Return spring
20 Plain washer
21 Oil seal
22 Needle roller bearing
23 Adjusting screw
24 Plain washer
25 Adjusting nut
26 Cable anchor
27 Clevis pin
28 Split pin

Chapter 1: Engine, clutch and gearbox

the various component parts should be cleaned thoroughly and placed on a sheet of clean paper, close to the working area.

2 Make sure all traces of old gaskets have been removed and that the mating surfaces are clean and undamaged. One of the best ways to remove old gasket cement is to apply a rag soaked in methylated spirit. This acts as a solvent and will ensure that the cement is removed without resort to scraping and the consequent risk of damage.

3 Gather together all of the necessary tools and have available an oil can filled with clean engine oil. Make sure that all new gaskets and oil seals are to hand, also all replacement parts required. Nothing is more frustrating than having to stop in the middle of a reassembly sequence because a vital gasket or replacement has been overlooked.

4 Make sure that the reassembly area is clean and that there is adequate working space. Refer to the torque and clearance settings wherever they are given. Many of the smaller bolts are easily sheared if overtightened. Always use the correct size screwdriver bit for the crosshead screws and never an ordinary screwdriver or punch. If the existing screws show evidence of maltreatment in the past, it is advisable to renew them as a complete set.

27 Engine reassembly: replacing crankshaft

1 Check that the main bearing and oil seal in the left-hand crankcase are in their correct positions. The main bearing should be hard up against its retaining shoulder.

2 Insert the crankshaft assembly into position through the main bearing. If a special crank setting tool is not available to pull the crankshaft into its bearing, a rawhide mallet may be used to tap it home. It is imperative that the main crank pin be kept absolutely square with the bearing whilst it is being tapped home, to ensure that the two do not tie together and cause distortion. Remember to keep the connecting rod at TDC to prevent it fouling the crankcase edge.

28 Engine reassembly: replacing the gearbox assembly

1 Because the crankcase assembly and the gearbox components are effectively housed in the same casings it is necessary to replace them in consecutive operations. The gearbox assembly must therefore be replaced in the left-hand crankcase at this juncture.

2 The two gearbox shafts, complete with their pinions, should be replaced together as one unit. Place one endfloat shim over both the bosses in the gearbox wall. Note the split spacer on the mainshaft; the two collars should be placed so that the shouldered faces lies towards the inside of the gearbox. It will be found that the weight of the 2nd gear driven pinion will hold the spacer in situ and allow for easy replacement of the shaft. Before installing the layshaft in the casing, the clutch pushrod must be inserted in the hollow shaft from the right-hand end. Replacement of the pushrod at any time after layshaft installation is impossible.

3 Replace the gearchange drum followed by the drive shaft selector rod and forks and then the layshaft selector fork and rod. Replacement of the selector assemblies requires careful maneuvering in order that the fork ends lie in their respective channels in the pinions and that the selector roller pegs fit correctly in the gearchange drum.

4 Fit the kickstart return spring together with the guide sleeve (late models) into the recess in the crankcase. The turned end of the spring must be located on the anchor peg which is a splined fit in the casing wall. Replace the gear cam stopper assembly in the threaded aperture in the bottom of the gearbox casing.

29 Engine reassembly: jointing the crankcase

1 Check that the two crankcase locating dowels are firmly in position and coat the two inside mating surfaces of the crankcase

27.2 Tap crankshaft into place with rawhide mallet

28.1a Carefully position split spacer before shaft replacement

28.4 Kickstart return spring sits in recess

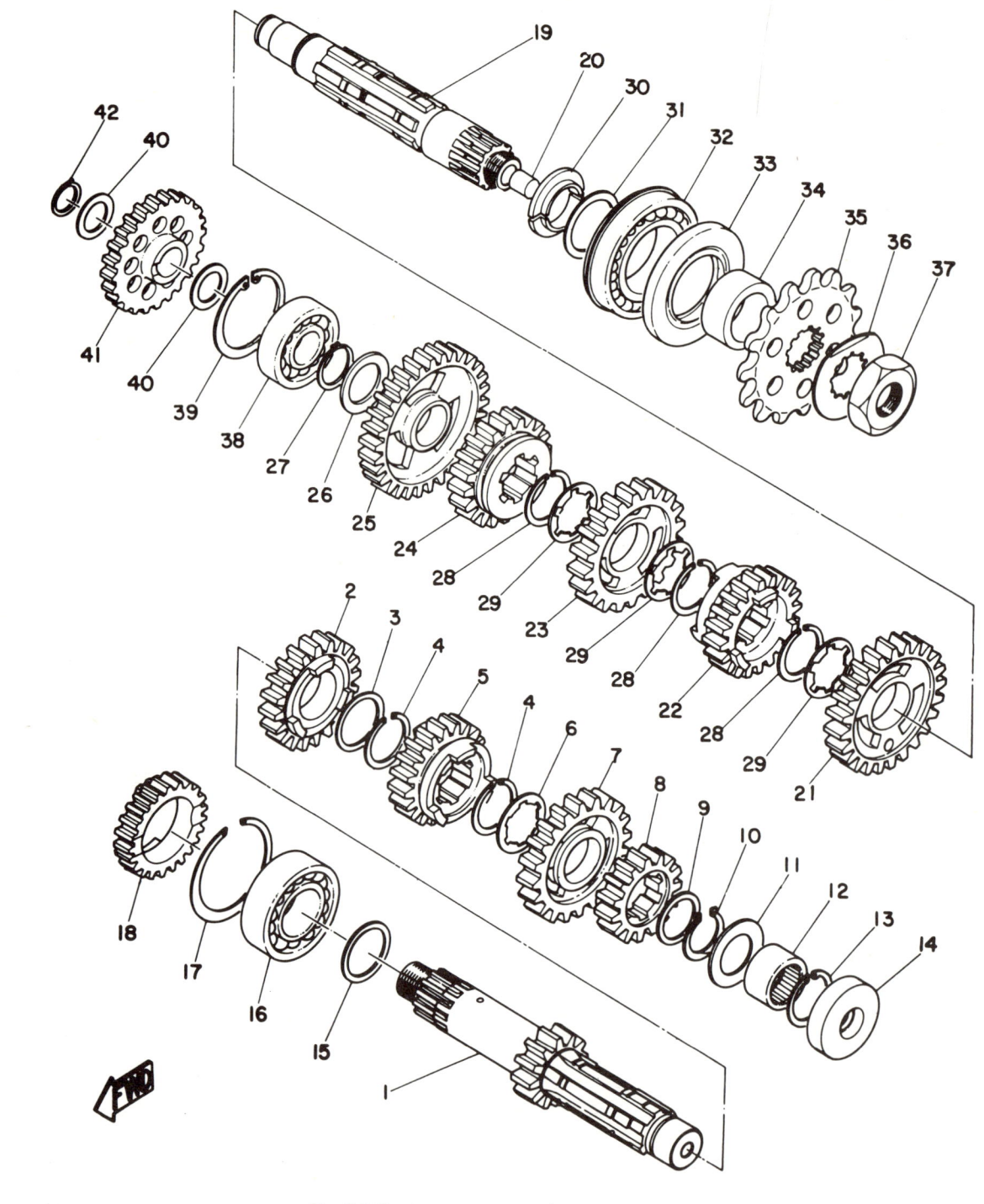

Fig. 1.8 Gearbox components (Early models)

1 Mainshaft - 15T or 16T
2 4th gear pinion - 26T
3 Shim
4 Circlip - 2 off
5 3rd gear pinion - 23T
6 Shim
7 3rd gear wheel - 30T
8 2nd gear pinion - 19T or 20T
9 Shim
10 Circlip
11 Shim
12 Bearing
13 Circlip
14 Oil seal
15 Shim
16 Bearing
17 Circlip
18 Kickstart driven gear - 18T
19 Layshaft
20 Blind plug
21 2nd gear wheel - 34T or 33T
22 3rd gear pinion - 23T
23 3rd gear wheel - 30T or 29T
24 4th gear wheel - 26T
25 1st gear wheel - 38T or 36T
26 Shim
27 Circlip
28 Circlip - 3 off
29 Shim - 3 off
30 Split spacer - 2 off
31 Shim
32 Bearing
33 Oil seal
34 Distance collar
35 Drive sprocket - 13T or 14T or 15T or 16T
36 Tab washer
37 Nut
38 Bearing
39 Circlip
40 Shim - 2 off
41 Kickstart idler gear - 23T
42 Circlip

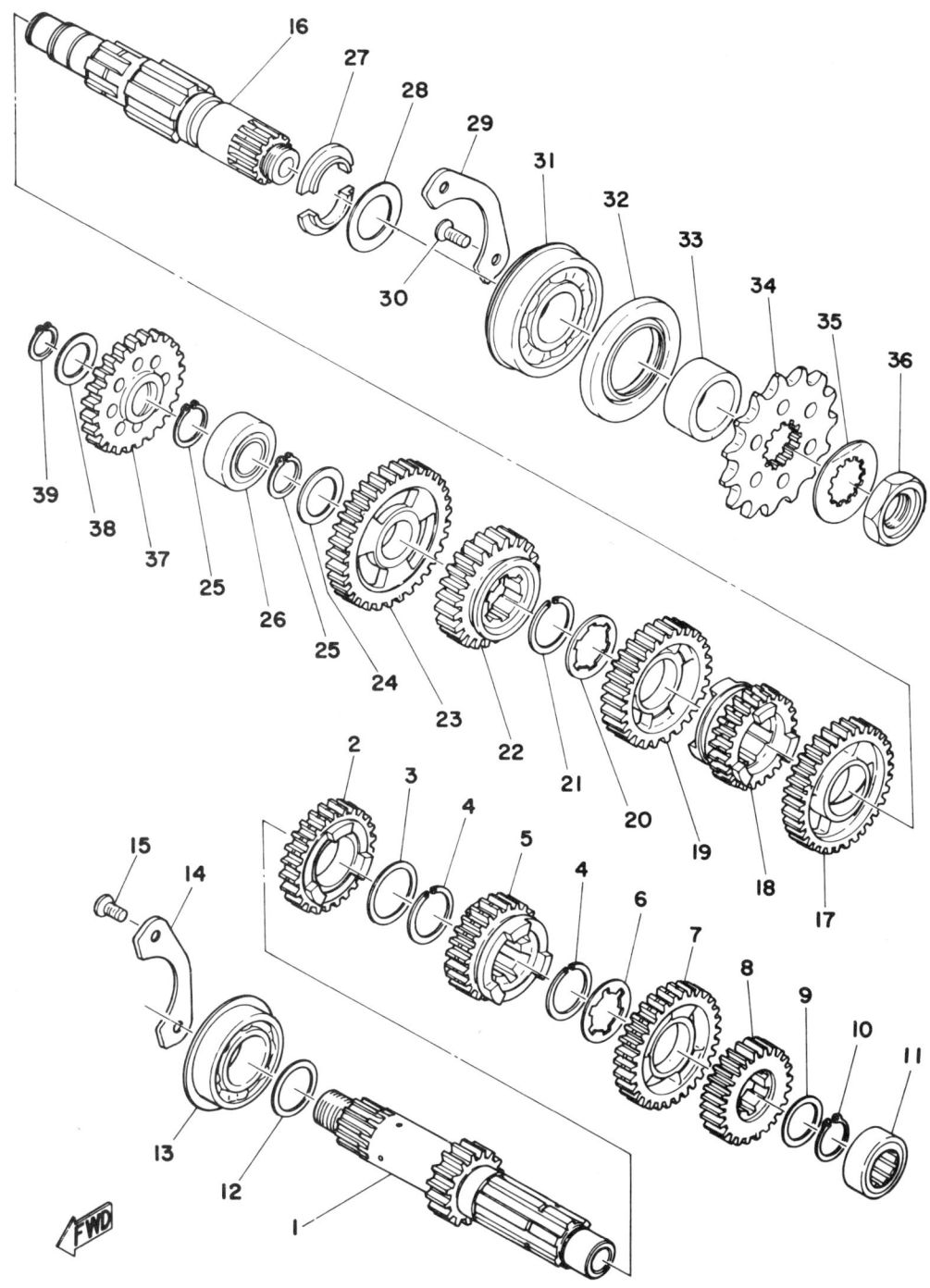

Fig. 1.9 Gearbox components (Late models)

1 Mainshaft - 16T
2 4th gear pinion - 26T
3 Plain washer
4 Circlip - 2 off
5 3rd gear pinion - 23T
6 Dog washer
7 5th gear pinion - 29T
8 2nd gear pinion - 19T
9 Shim
10 Circlip
11 Bearing
12 Shim
13 Bearing
14 Bearing retainer plate
15 Countersunk screw - 2 off
16 Layshaft
17 2nd gear wheel - 32T
18 5th gear wheel - 23T
19 3rd gear wheel - 29T
20 Washer
21 Circlip
22 4th gear wheel - 26T
23 1st gear wheel - 26T
24 Shim
25 Circlip - 2 off
26 Bearing
27 Split spacer - 2 off
28 Shim
29 Bearing retainer plate
30 Countersunk screw - 2 off
31 Bearing
32 Oil seal
33 Spacer collar
34 Drive sprocket - 13T or 14T or 15T
35 Tab washer
36 Nut
37 Kickstart idler gear - 23T
38 Shim
39 Circlip

halves with jointing compound. Ensure that the main pin O ring is positioned correctly in its seating groove.

2 Hold the connecting rod in the vertical position and feed the right-hand crankcase onto the main pin and gear shaft ends. It will be necessary to drive the main bearing over the right-hand main pin using the same method as prescribed for the left-hand main bearing and main crankpin, at the same time noting that the gear shafts enter their respective bearings square. DO NOT USE EXCESSIVE FORCE if the two crankcase halves will not mate up. Rotation of the gearbox shafts during assembly can sometimes ease any jamming. If, however, continued difficulty is encountered, remove the right-hand crankcase, re-align the shafts and gear assembly and then reassemble. On models the middle spacer must be replaced in the front top engine mounting lug before the cases come together.

3 Reinsert the crankcase retaining screws in the crankcase from the left and tighten in a diagonal sequence.

30 Engine reassembly: replacing the gearchange assembly

Late models

1 Lightly lubricate the end of the layshaft selector fork rod that issues through the crankcase wall next to the change drum pins.

2 Slide the gear change secondary quadrant onto the selector rod end, making sure that the change pawl engages correctly with the pins in the end of the change drum. With the assembly correctly positioned replace the locating circlip in the groove in the rod end.

3 Lightly grease the gearchange splined shaft and introduce it into the tunnel that runs through the two crankcase halves. Push the shaft home until the primary gearchange quadrant engages with the secondary quadrant. It may be necessary to gently prise the centraliser spring apart so that it slips easily over the peg in the crankcase wall. Note carefully that the two change quandrants must mesh with each other in a predetermined positon, ie; they are timed. The centre tooth on the secondary quadrant must engage with the gap between the two centre teeth on the primary quadrant.

4 With the gearchange shaft correctly positioned, turn the crankcase over so that the retaining washer and circlip can be replaced on the splined shaft end on the left of the engine.

30.2b Slide main change shaft into position so ...

30.3 ... that quadrants engage as show ...

30.2a Make certain change pawls engage with pins

30.4a Fit circlip and washer to retain shaft and ...

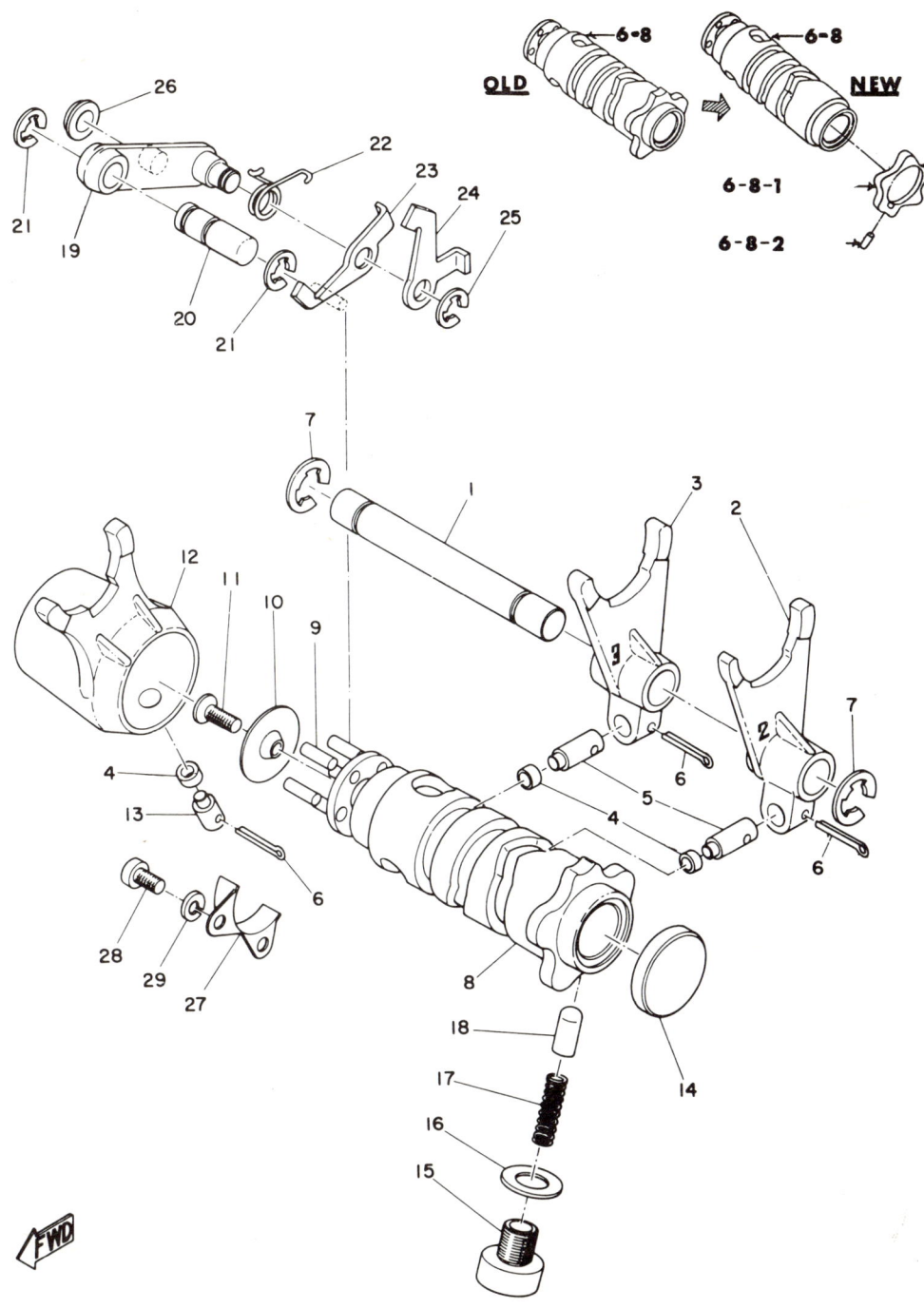

Fig. 1.10 Gearchange selector A (Early models)

1 Selector fork rod
2 Selector fork (2)
3 Selector fork (3)
4 Cam track roller - 3 off
5 Cam follower pin - 2 off
6 Split pin - 3 off
7 Circlip - 2 off
8 Gearchange drum
9 Dowel pin - 5 off
10 Pin plate
11 Counter sunk screw
12 Selector fork (1)
13 Cam follower pin
14 Blind plug
15 Detent housing
16 Washer
17 Detent spring
18 Plunger
19 Selector arm
20 Pivot
21 Circlip - 2 off
22 Spring
23 Change pawl
24 Change pawl
25 Circlip
26 Change arm roller
27 Change pawl guide
28 Pan head screw - 2 off
29 Spring washer - 2 off

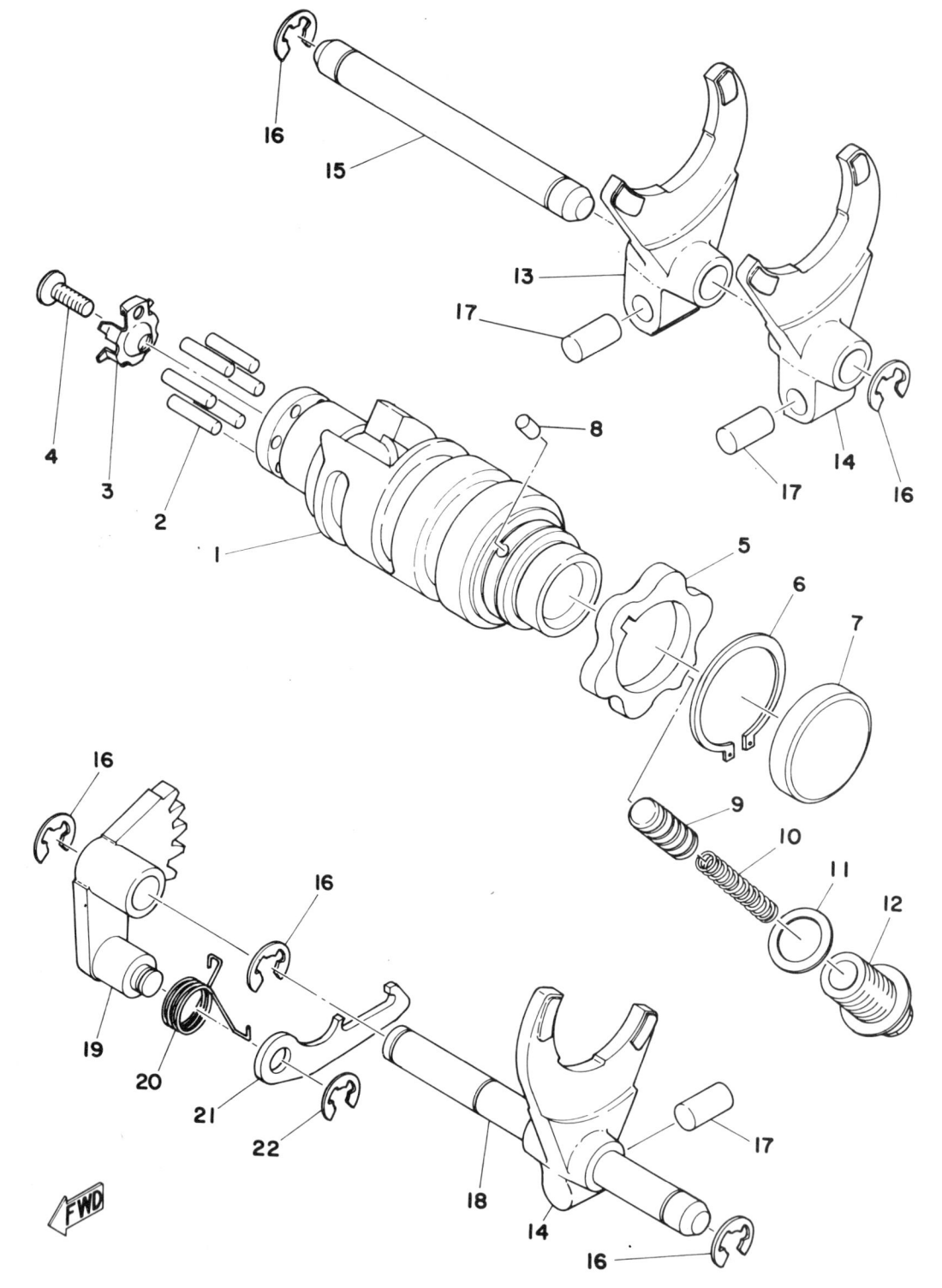

Fig. 1.11 Gearchange selector 1 (Late models)

1 Gearchange drum
2 Dowel pin - 6 off
3 Pin retainer
4 Counter sunk screw
5 Stopper plate
6 Circlip
7 Blind plug
8 Dowel pin
9 Cam plunger
10 Detent spring
11 Washer
12 Detent holder
13 Selector fork (1)
14 Selector fork (2) - 2 off
15 Selector fork rod (1)
16 Circlip - 5 off
17 Cam follower pin - 3 off
18 Selector fork rod (2)
19 Secondary gearchange quadrant
20 Return spring
21 Gear change pawl
22 Circlip

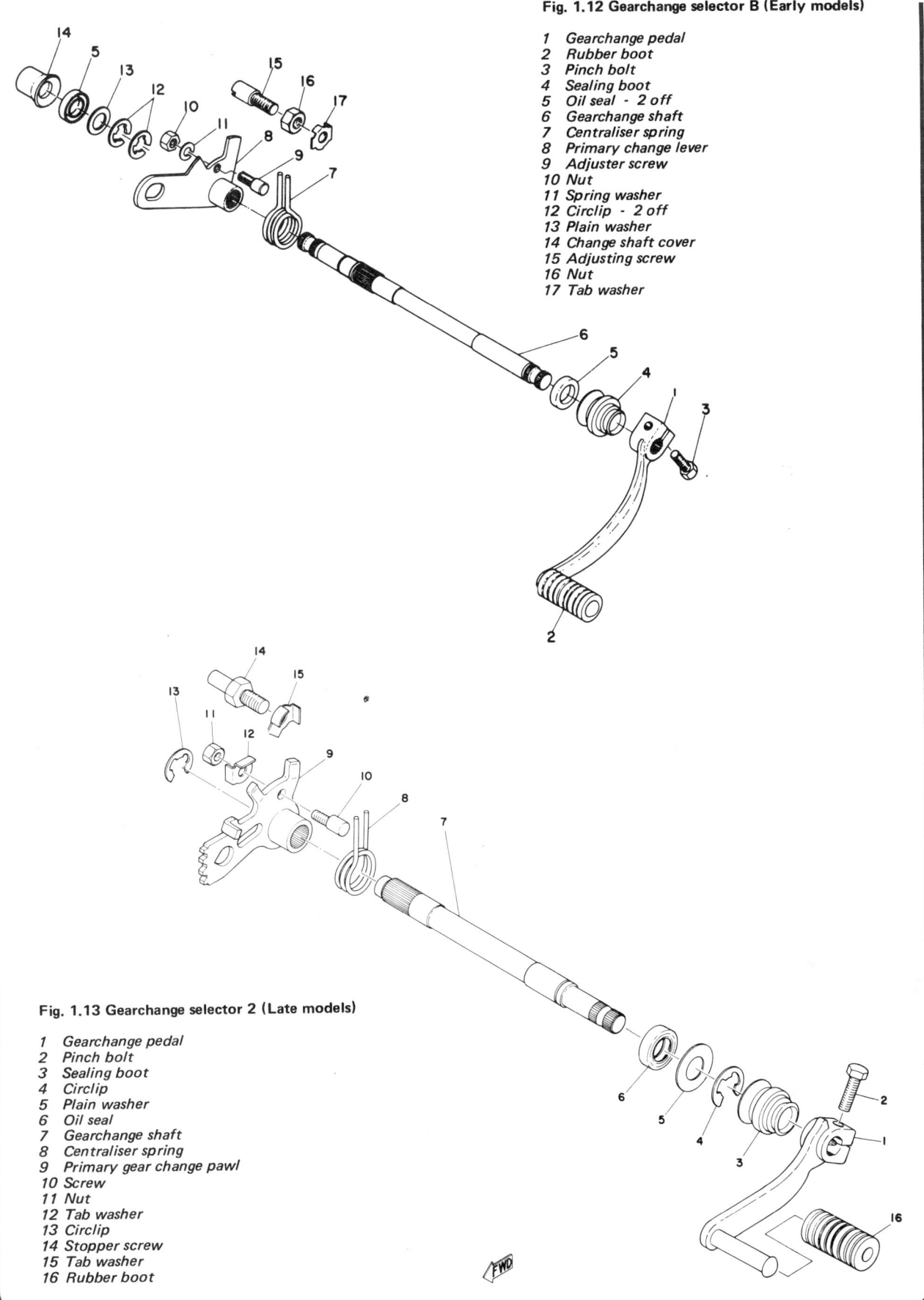

Fig. 1.12 Gearchange selector B (Early models)

1 Gearchange pedal
2 Rubber boot
3 Pinch bolt
4 Sealing boot
5 Oil seal - 2 off
6 Gearchange shaft
7 Centraliser spring
8 Primary change lever
9 Adjuster screw
10 Nut
11 Spring washer
12 Circlip - 2 off
13 Plain washer
14 Change shaft cover
15 Adjusting screw
16 Nut
17 Tab washer

Fig. 1.13 Gearchange selector 2 (Late models)

1 Gearchange pedal
2 Pinch bolt
3 Sealing boot
4 Circlip
5 Plain washer
6 Oil seal
7 Gearchange shaft
8 Centraliser spring
9 Primary gear change pawl
10 Screw
11 Nut
12 Tab washer
13 Circlip
14 Stopper screw
15 Tab washer
16 Rubber boot

31 Engine reassembly: replacing the gearchange assembly

Early models

1 Place the secondary change arm complete with the two spring loaded change pawls onto its pivot shaft. The change pawls must be prised apart so they lie each side of the change drum pins. Replace the retainer circlip.
2 Replace the change drum guide piece which is held by two cross-head screws and spring washers.
3 Lightly grease the change shaft and introduce it into the shaft tunnel that runs through the two crankcase halves. Push the shaft in until primary change arm return spring fouls the centraliser peg in the casing wall. Replace the roller on the peg of the secondary change arm. With the centralising return spring prised apart, the shaft assembly can be pushed fully home so that the roller on the secondary change arm engages in the elongated hole on the primary change arm. Finally replace the retainer circlip and washer (where fitted).

30.4b ... dust excluding boot

32 Engine reassembly: replacing the kickstart assembly

Early models

1 If the kickstart assembly has been dismantled, it must be reassembled as a complete unit prior to replacement in the casing. The accompanying illustration shows the correct sequence of assembly. When the ratchet wheel is replaced on the kickstart shaft the two components must be in the correct relationship to each other. Punch marks on the respective components must be aligned to ensure correct positioning.
2 If the ratchet wheel stopper plate and guide plate have been removed from the casing they should be replaced with the guide plate covering the stopper plate and the tongue on the stopper plate facing inwards. The plates are retained by two hexagon set screws which are located by a common tab washer, the ears of which should be knocked up against the screw heads after they have been tightened.
3 Oil the kickstart shaft where it enters the crankcase boss and slip the end float shim onto the shaft. Introduced the shaft into the crankcase boss and slide the ratchet wheel pawl over the ratchet wheel guide toward the stopper tongue. Make sure that the pawl is in close contact with the stopper. Pull the kickstart return spring round in a clockwise direction and hook it over the retainer projection on the casing.
4 The kickstart idler gear can now be replaced. Lightly lubricate the shaft and fit the gear, boss side inwards, preceeded by the plain washer and wave washer. Finally fit the outer washer and the circlip.

33.1a Dogs on kickstart shaft end engage with ...

33 Engine reassembly: replacing the kickstart assembly

Late models

1 The kickstart assembly on late models is similar to the early type except that the kickstart spring is located within the gearbox. When the kickstart shaft is introduced through the spring it should be placed so that the ratchet pawl is facing downwards. The shaft must be rotated against the pressure of the return spring in an anti-clockwise direction for one full turn before the ratchet pawl is pushed down past the pawl stop. The return spring so tensioned ensures that the kickstart lever returns to the top of its stroke.
2 Replace the kickstart idler gear, boss side inwards, followed by the plain washer and circlip. The tachometer nylon drive gear should be replaced with the collar on the outside.

33.1b ... turned end of kickstarter return spring

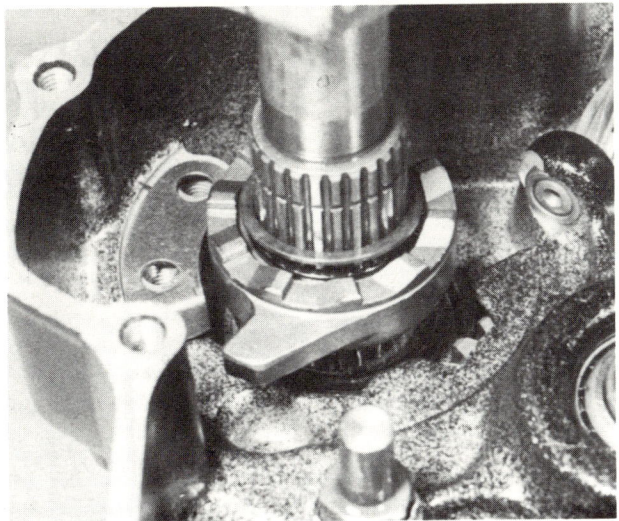
33.1c Refit pawl stop plate and ...

33.1d ... guide plate which are held by three bolts

33.2a Replace kickstart gear, circlip and washers followed by ...

33.2b ... idler and tachometer drive gears

34.1 Push pinion onto shaft over Woodruff key or splines

34.2 Replace washer and tighten centre nut

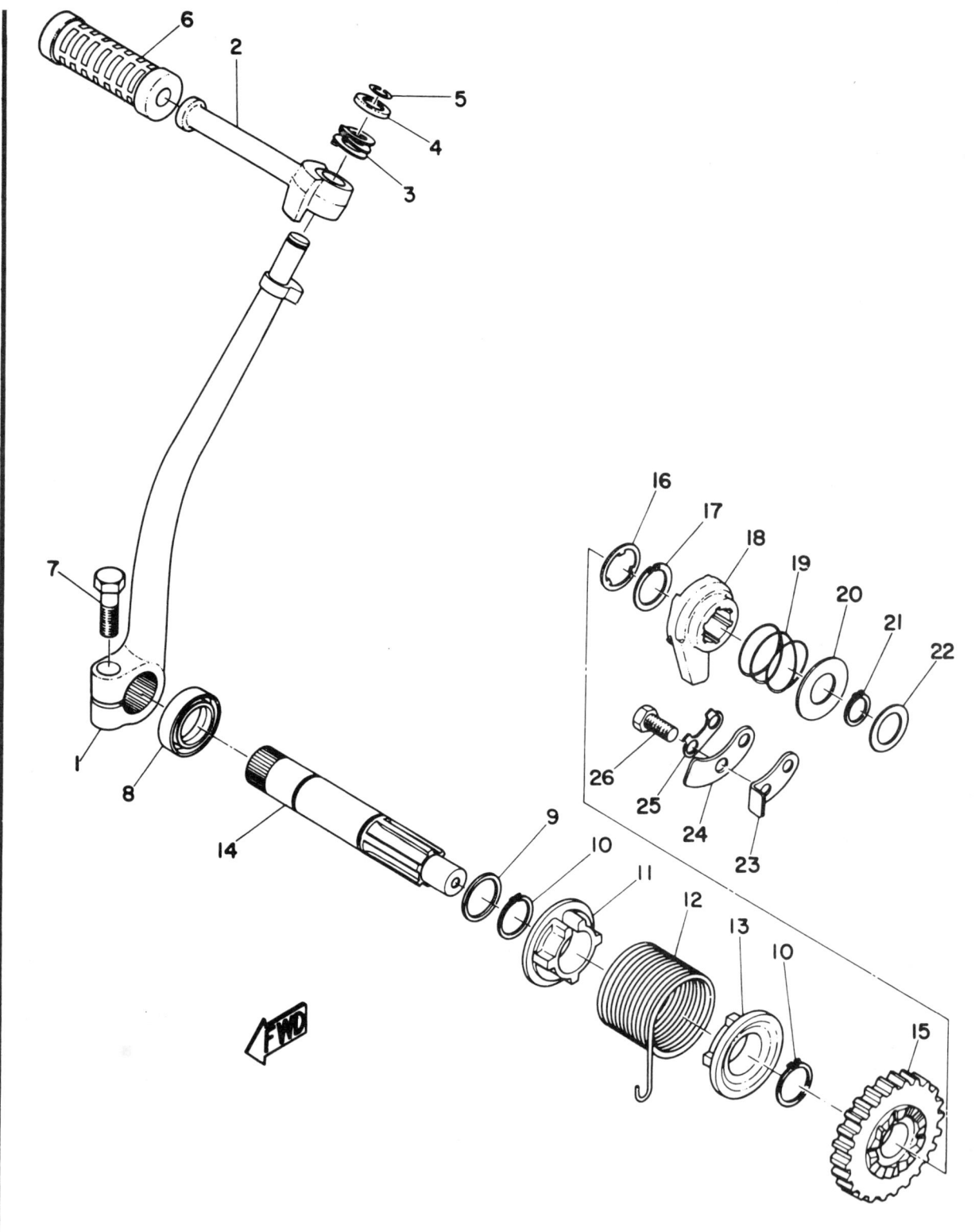

Fig. 1.14 Kickstart assembly (Early models)

1 Kickstart lever
2 Kickstart crank
3 Double spring washer
4 Plain washer
5 Circlip
6 Rubber
7 Pinch bolt
8 Oil seal
9 Shim
10 Circlip - 2 off
11 Spring guide - outer
12 Return spring
13 Spring guide - inner
14 Kickstart shaft
15 Kickstart gear
16 Washer - 2 off
17 Circlip
18 Ratchet wheel
19 Tension spring
20 Thrust washer
21 Circlip
22 Shim
23 Ratchet pawl stopper
24 Ratchet guide
25 Double tab washer
26 Bolt - 2 off

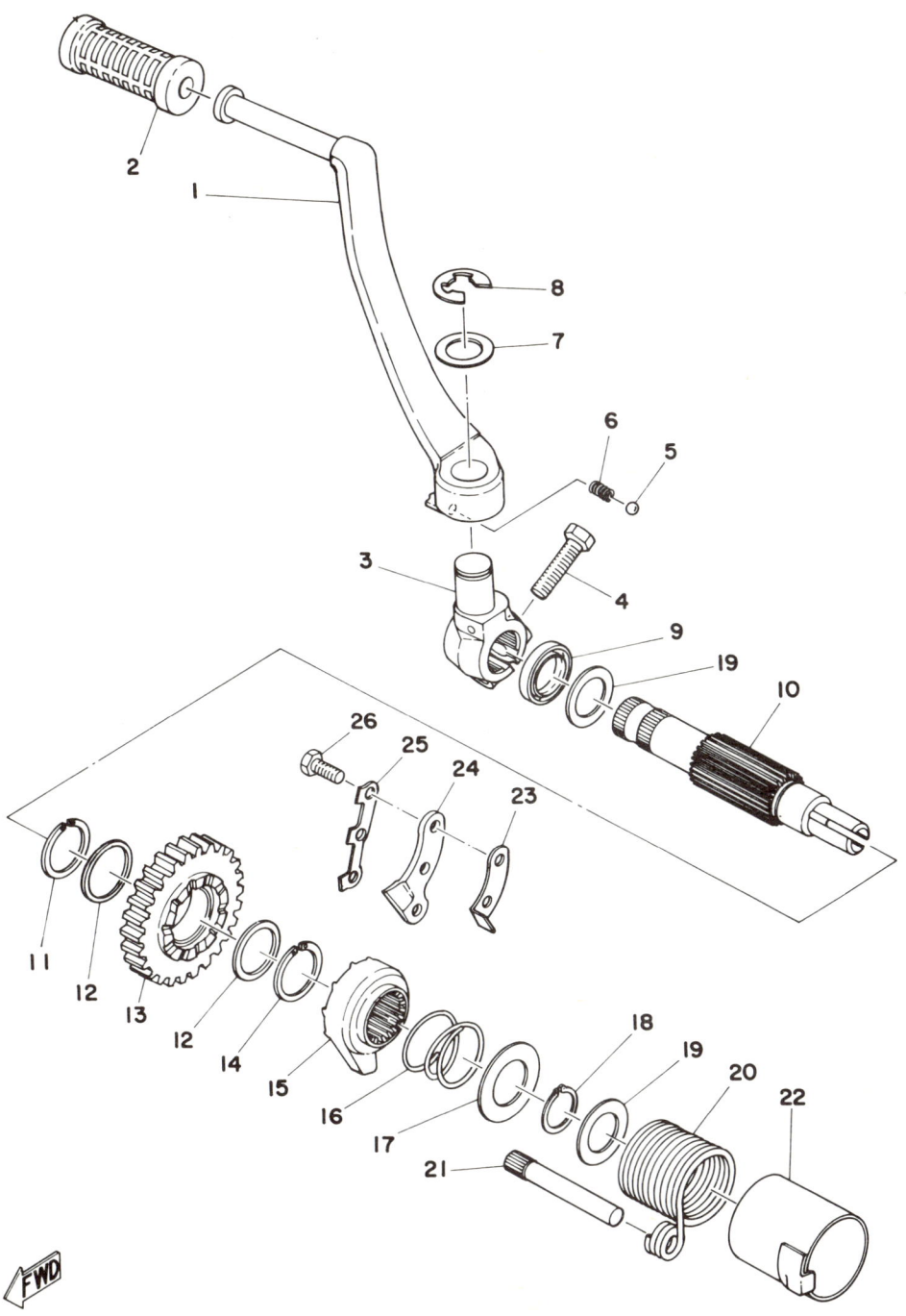

Fig. 1.15 Kickstart assembly (Late models)

1. Kickstart crank
2. Rubber
3. Kickstart crank boss
4. Pinch bolt
5. Detent ball - 7/32"
6. Detent spring
7. Washer
8. Circlip
9. Oil seal
10. Kickstart shaft
11. Circlip
12. Shim - 2 off
13. Kickstart gear - 26T
14. Circlip
15. Ratchet wheel
16. Tension spring
17. Thrust washer
18. Circlip
19. Plain washer - 2 off
20. Kickstart return spring
21. Return spring anchor
22. Spring guide
23. Pawl stopper
24. Ratchet guide
25. Triple tab washer
26. Bolt - 3 off

35.3a Replace the clutch spacer and thrust washers and ...

35.3b ... the outer drum ...

35.4a ... thrust washer and...

35.4b ... clutch centre boss

35.4c Replace plain washer, spring washer and tighten nut

35.5a Insert thrust ball bearing and ...

Chapter 1: Engine, clutch and gearbox

34 Engine reassembly: replacing the primary drive pinion

1 The primary drive pinion is located on the right-hand main crankpin either by parallel splines or a large Woodruff key depending on the model. In either case the pinion should be gently tapped into position, taking care not to damage the oil seal through which the pinion boss passes.

2 With the primary drive pinion in place, lock the crankshaft using two pieces of soft wood and a close fitting bar through the small end eye. Replace the belville or spring washer and then fully tighten the pinion retaining nut.

35 Engine reassembly: replacing the clutch assembly

Early models

1 Place the narrow thrust washer over the clutch shaft followed by the wide thrust washer and the thrust bearing. The thrust bearing should be placed with the plain side facing outwards. Lightly lubricate the clutch spacer collar and fit it on the shaft, followed by the kickstart drive gear. The clutch spacer collar is non-reversible and should be positoned so that the oil hole is furthest away from the thrust washer and will therefore line up with the oil hole in the clutch shaft.

2 Check that the noise damper ring is in place between the primary driven gear and clutch housing rear face. This rubber ring is designed to reduce gear noise at low engine speeds.

3 Replace the outer clutch drum on the clutch shaft making sure that the gear ring engages with the primary drive pinion and that the dogs in the rear of the gear ring engage with the dogs on the kickstart driven pinion.

4 Replace the thrust washer that lies between the clutch outer drum and the inner boss. The clutch inner boss may now be positioned on the shaft, followed by the spring washer and centre nut. Tighten the clutch centre nut by using the same method as described for dismantling. Alternatively the final drive sprocket may be replaced and the gearbox placed in a high gear. A chain wrapped round the sprocket will give sufficient purchase for the clutch sprocket to be fully tightened.

5 Replace the clutch plate backing plate which is similar to the plain clutch plates but of slightly different dimensions, followed by the clutch plate spacer ring.

6 The clutch plates may now be inserted one by one, commencing with a plain plate. Note that a rubber ring is interposed between each following set of plain and inserted (friction) plates to ensure smooth clutch action and easy disengagement. The sequence of assembly is therefore plain plate, rubber ring, inserted plate, plain plate, rubber ring etc. Make certain the rubber rings are not twisted once finally in position. Grease the mushroom headed clutch pushrod and install it through the opening in the gearbox mainshaft. The pressure plate may now be replaced with the six springs and retaining screws done up tight.

36 Engine reassembly: replacing the clutch assembly

Late models

1 Place the thrust washer on the clutch shaft with the raised face of the washer facing inwards, followed by the clutch spacer collar. As with the early models, the spacer collar should be placed so that the oil hole aligns with the oil hole in the clutch shaft.

2 Replace the clutch outer drum on the shaft making sure that the kickstart driven gear and the primary driven gear engage with their respective meshing pinions.

3 Place the thrust washer on the clutch shaft followed by the clutch centre and then replace the plain washer, spring washer and locknut. Tighten the lock nut as described in the previous section.

35.5b Grease and replace mushroom pushrod

35.6a Align plain plate projection with punch marks ...

35.6b ... and pressure plate with arrow mark

4 The clutch plates may now be replaced, one by one, in an alternate order, starting with an inserted (friction) plate. Note that the plain plates are reduced in overall diameter at one small point on the plate edge, with a small projection indicating the centre of the reduction. The tongue on each plate should be aligned with a pock mark on the face of the clutch centre segments, so that each successive plate is aligned with the next pock mark. This will ensure that the clutch mass retains balance when in rotation.

5 Lightly grease the waisted clutch pushrod and insert it into the clutch shaft, followed by the 11/32 inch ball bearing and the mushroom head pushrod end.

6 The clutch pressure plate should now be replaced, making certain that the arrow mark on its circumference aligns with one of the arrow marks on the clutch centre. Replace the clutch springs, backing washers and screws and fully tighten each screw in an even and diagonal sequence.

37 Engine reassembly: replacing the magneto assembly

1 Place the engine with the left-hand crankcase facing upwards. Position the magneto stator plate over the main crankpin and align the three retaining holes. On contact breaker type magnetos the stator plate should be placed with the contact breaker assembly nearest the cylinder barrel and when the retaining screws are inserted and tightened, the stator will automatically be located in precisely the same position as it was in before removal. The stator on CDI instruments should be replaced with the coils pointing towards the rear of the machine. Insert the three locating screws through the stator plate and then rotate the plate so that the two scribe marks (which were made before dismantling) line up correctly. Tighten the screws fully.

2 Slide the wiring harness and grommet into the recess in the top edge of the crankcase and replace the spring clip which is retained by a single screw. Note that on some instruments an earth lead from the main harness is also held by the clip screw.

3 Before replacing the flywheel on contact breaker type instruments, recharge the cam lubricator with oil. The lubricator wick is held in a small bracket screwed to the stator plate. **Do not** over lubricate the wick as any excess oil will find its way to the points and cause ignition failure. A few drops of light oil is quite sufficient.

4 Replace the Woodruff key in the recess in the tapered crankpin with the belled surface facing inwards, making sure that it is as far into the recess as possible. Place the magneto flywheel over the main crankpin and align the keyway with the key. Then press the flywheel home. Replace the plain washer(s) and spring washer (where fitted) followed by the centre nut. Tighten the nut fully having locked the crankshaft in the usual manner.

38 Engine reassembly: replacing the final drive sprocket

1 The final drive sprocket may either be replaced when the

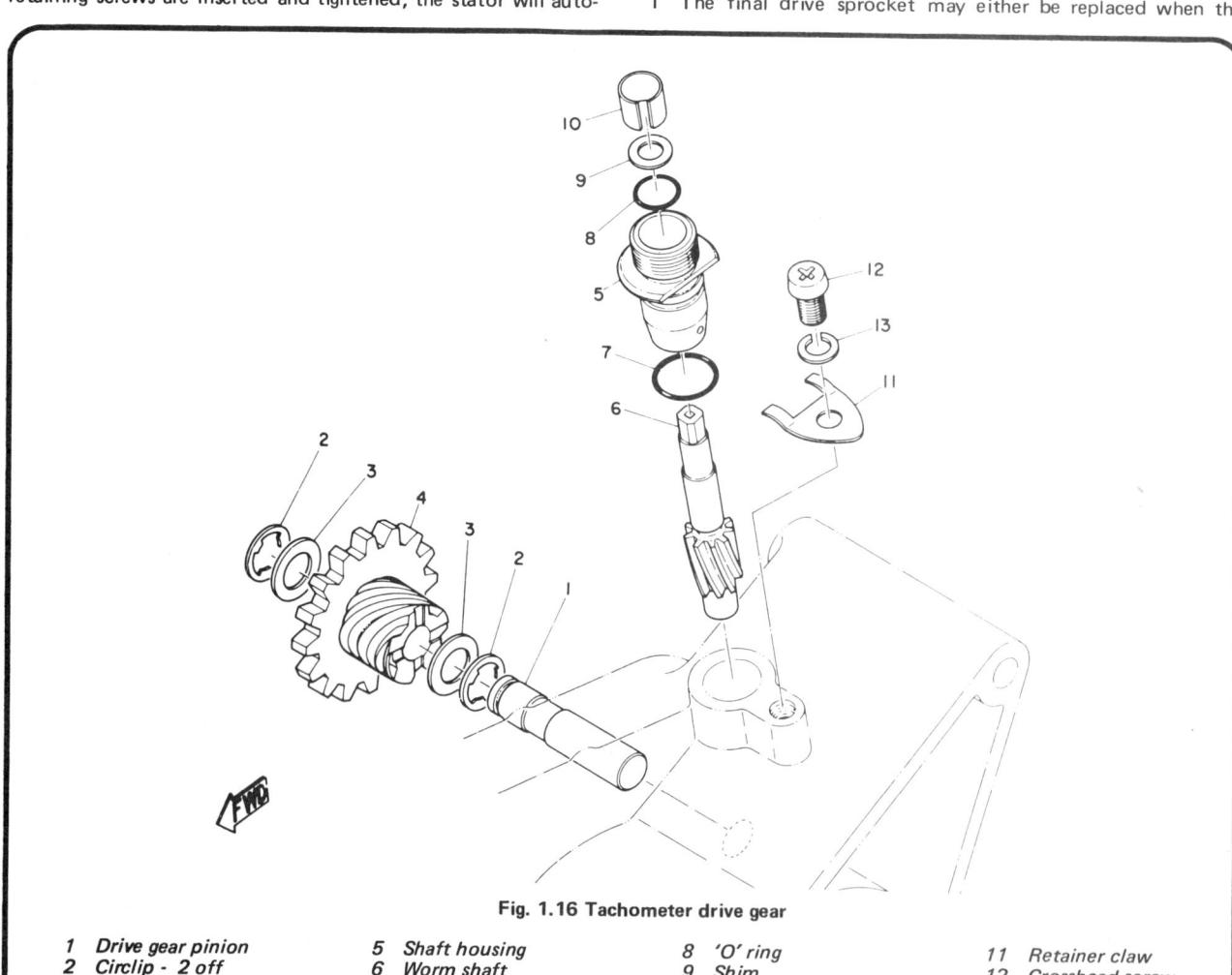

Fig. 1.16 Tachometer drive gear

1 Drive gear pinion
2 Circlip - 2 off
3 Shim - 2 off
4 Nylon drive pinion
5 Shaft housing
6 Worm shaft
7 'O' ring
8 'O' ring
9 Shim
10 Split bush
11 Retainer claw
12 Crosshead screw
13 Spring washer

Chapter 1: Engine, clutch and gearbox

engine is in the frame using the same method as for dismantling, or replaced with the engine out of the frame in the following manner.

2 Replace the drive sprocket distance collar on the shaft, followed by the drive sprocket and tab washer. The sprocket retaining nut is non-reversible as one side is recessed to take the spline ends which locate the drive sprocket. Make certain it is replaced correctly otherwise the tab washer will not function properly.

3 To tighten the retaining nut fully, wrap the drive chain around the drive sprocket and catch both ends of the chain in a vice. This will prevent the sprocket from rotating. When the centre nut is tightened fully knock the tab washer up against one face of the nut.

39 Engine reassembly: replacing the tachometer and oil pump drive shafts

1 If either the tachometer or oil pump drive shafts have been removed for inspection, they will have to be re-installed before the primary drive cover is replaced. On early models the oil pump is driven through a nylon reduction gear which should be replaced as follows:

2 Insert the oil pump worm drive through the bush and oil seal from the outside of the casing, having first lubricated it lightly. Replace the retaining circlip in its groove on the shaft end inside the casing, followed by the plain washer and the oil pump drive gear driving pin. Make certain that the driving pin is correctly positioned in the drive slots in the rear of the drive gear and then fit the toothed washer and retaining nut. The drive gear may be grasped more easily for tightening if a rag is placed around the teeth and then firmly held. Do not try to lock the pinion by inserting a screwdriver between the teeth as this will damage the soft material.

3 Lightly lubricate the blind end of the tachometer drive shaft and insert it through the top edge of the primary drive casing into its bush. Check that the shaft retaining housing cum bush has both O rings in position; the large outside ring should lie in the recessed groove on the lower part of the body, the smaller inner ring should lie in a recessed groove near the top of the shaft housing bore. Insert the shaft retaining housing over the drive shaft and into the crankcase recess and replace the top shim and bush, which should be lightly lubricated. The retaining claw plate may now be screwed onto the top of the primary drive casing. Make sure that its rotation stop tongue locates correctly with the machined edge on the shaft housing.

40 Engine reassembly: replacing the primary drive cover

1 Place the engine with the right-hand casing facing upwards. Smear a thin layer of jointing compound on both the right-hand crankcase outer face and the primary drive cover inner face. The new gasket should be placed on the primary drive cover where it will be located by the two dowels. On early models the primary drive nylon gear should be replaced preceeded by the plain washer and followed by the outer plain washer and the retaining circlip. It may be necessary to rotate the nylon gear to aid the meshing of the tachometer worm gears.

2 The casing can now be placed in position; the two dowels will hold it in position as the cross-head screws are inserted and tightened. Early models have (8) eight retaining screws and late models have (12) twelve screws.

3 Replace the oil pump making sure it meshes with the drive dog or the drive shaft worm (depending on the model) and replace and tighten the retaining screws. A new gasket should always be used to ensure oil tightness.

37.1 Replace the stator plate and tighten screws

37.4 Align mainshaft key with flywheel keyway

38.2a Replace sprocket spacer followed by ...

38.2b ... the final drive sprocket and ...

38.2c ... locking tab washer. Recessed nut will fit over splines

38.3a Carefully lock sprocket and tighten nut ...

38.3b Knock up tab washer to lock

40.1 Use new gasket to ensure oil tightness

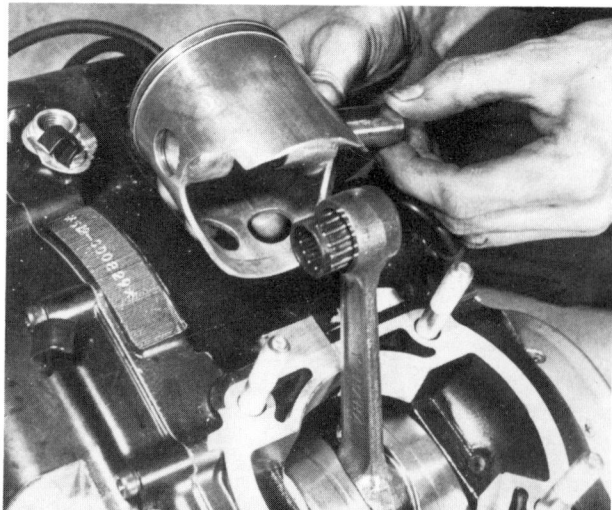
41.3a Refit the piston onto the connecting rod

Chapter 1: Engine, clutch and gearbox

41 Engine reassembly: replacing the piston and piston rings

1 Position the engine in an upright position on the crankcase base; a few small wooden blocks should help to steady it. Pad the crankcase mouth with clean rag prior to fitting the piston and rings so that any displaced parts will be prevented from entering.
2 Lubricate the small end caged needle roller bearing and replace it in the small end eye. Replace the piston and gudgeon pin, noting the small arrow mark on the piston crown, which should be facing forwards. If the gudgeon pin is a tight fit in the piston bosses, the piston may be heated with warm water to effect the necessary temporary expansion.
3 Oil the gudgeon pin and piston bosses before assembly and then fit the circlips, making quite certain that they are engaged fully with their retaining grooves. A good fit is essential, since a displaced circlip will cause extensive engine damage. ALWAYS fit new circlips, NEVER re-use old ones.
4 Check that the piston rings are fitted correctly with their ends either side of the locating pegs. Rings should always be replaced from the top of the piston, the second or bottom ring being put on first. If ring expanders were fitted they must be replaced in their correct position behind the main ring.

41.3b Arrow mark on piston must face forward

42 Engine reassembly: replacing the cylinder barrel

1 Place a new cylinder base gasket over the retaining studs, having first lightly greased both surfaces to aid sealing. Lubricate the cylinder bore with clean engine oil and with the piston at TDC, slide the barrel onto the retaining studs until it comes in contact with the piston. The rings may now be squeezed in, one at a time, to enable the cylinder barrel to slide over the piston. Check that the ring ends remain each side of their retaining pegs. Great care is necessary during this operation as piston rings are very brittle and will break easily.
2 Although the cylinder barrel has a good lead-in, to facilitate entry of the piston rings, a piston ring clamp can be used as an alternative to the hand feed method. Here again, care must be taken to ensure that the rings are correctly positioned in relation to the piston ring pegs.
3 When the rings have engaged fully with the cylinder bore, withdraw the rag packing from the crankcase mouth and slide the cylinder barrel down the retaining studs, so that it seats on the new base gasket (no gasket cement).
4 On late models the four or six sleeve bolts and washers must be replaced and tightened fully before the cylinder head is replaced as the cylinder barrel retaining studs are separate. The retaining nuts should be tightened in an even and diagonal sequence to a torque setting of 4.2 - 4.5 kg m) (30 - 35 lb ft).
5 Place a clean rag in both inlet and exhaust ports to exclude foreign matter.

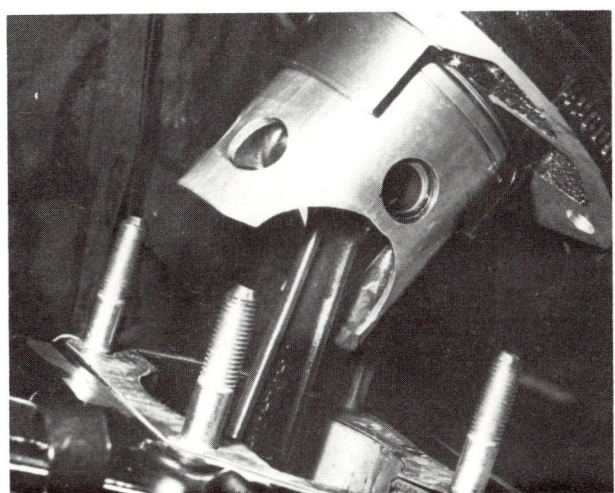
42.2a Carefully ease barrel over piston making ...

43 Engine reassembly: replacing the cylinder head

1 Place a new copper cylinder head gasket on the top of the cylinder barrel, lightly greasing it beforehand to aid sealing (jointing compound should not be used).
2 Fit the cylinder head, taking care that the gasket is not displaced or distorted during the initial tightening down.
3 The cylinder head nuts should be tightened down in an even and diagonal sequence. This is important as distortion will occur if this precaution is not observed.
4 Use a torque wrench for the final tightening down, at the following settings.

8 mm bolts	2.0 kg m - 2.5 kg m (15 - 18 ft lb)
10 mm bolts	4.2 kg m - 4.5 kg m (25 - 30 ft lb)

42.2b ... sure that rings are fitted correctly

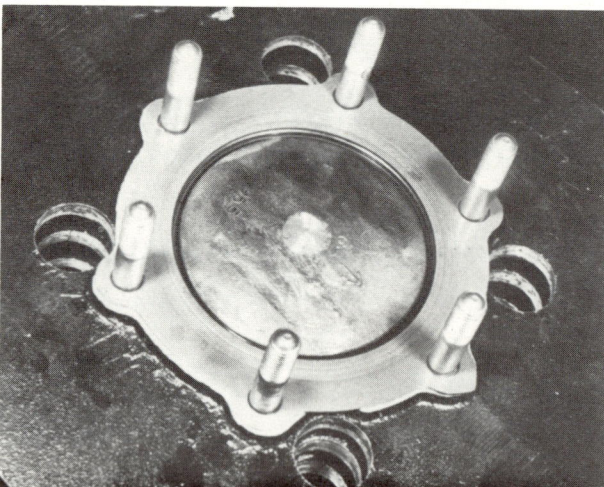

43.1 Alway fit new copper gasket

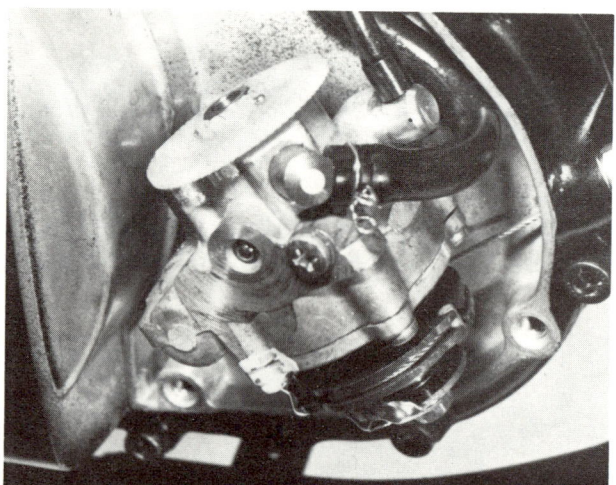

47.1a Refit oil pump cable and pipes

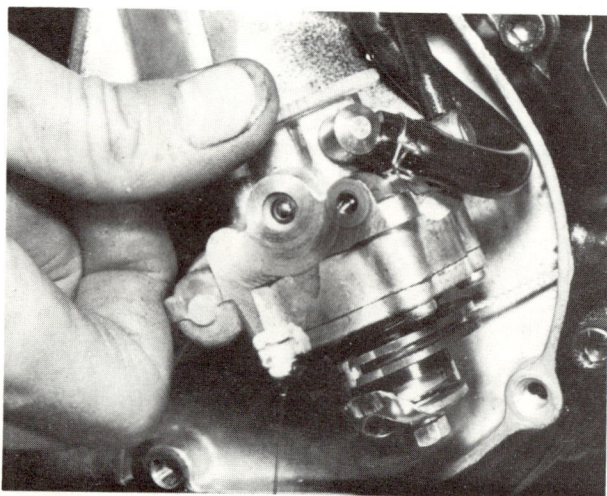

47.1b Remove bleed screw and bleed pump

44 Engine reassembly: replacing the decompressor unit

1 If the decompressor unit has been dismantled for cleaning it should be reassembled as a unit before it is replaced in the cylinder barrel.
2 Slide the decompressor valve stem into the main body from the threaded end. Make certain that the stem sealing 'O' ring is correctly located before insertion of the stem. Place the inner cover on the face of the main body, followed by the lever holder, return spring and the main lever. With the main lever clipped onto the groove in the end of the valve stem the pivot pin and retaining circlip may be replaced.
3 Place a new sealing washer over the threaded portion of the main decompressor body and screw the unit into the cylinder barrel.

45 Refitting the engine/gearbox unit into the frame

1 If the blocks holding the frame in an upright position have been removed they should be replaced in their original positions while the engine is fitted to the frame.
2 The engine may now be lifted into the frame from either side and while it is possible to accomplish this single handed, it is wise to have the aid of an assistant to steady the engine.
3 Lift the engine to clear the mounting plate as it goes in and let it down so that it lies in approximately the correct position. The final positioning can be done with the aid of a rawhide mallet. Insert the engine mounting bolts into their respective brackets. Do not tap the bolts through unless their progress is completely unhampered, as the threads are easily damaged.

46 Engine reassembly: reconnecting the oil pipes and the carburettor

1 Reconnect the main oil feed pipe to the oil pump inlet after threading the pipe through the rubber grommet at the top of the right-hand crankcase cover. The pipe is held in position by a small wire clip.
2 Reconnect the oil delivery pipe to the inlet port using new fibre washers for the banjo union. Insert the tachometer drive cable and tighten up the knurled union nut.
3 Replace the carburettor assembly on 7 port models as follows: Refit the reed valve 'sandwich' using new gaskets, followed by the Bakelite heat sink block and the carburettor. It is important that no leaks occur around the inlet manifold, as this will cause a weak mixture leading to bad starting and overheating. Tighten the four reed valve retaining bolts evenly, in a diagonal sequence. This will avoid distortion. 5 port models which are not fitted with a reed valve 'sandwich' have the carburettor attached to the barrel in the normal manner by two studs and nuts. A Bakelite heat sink lies between the carburettor flange and the barrel; new gaskets should be used on the heat sink to ensure perfect sealing.
4 Refit the throttle slide assembly into the carburettor body. There is a longitudinal slit in the throttle slide which locates with a peg in the carburettor bore. The slide will not push home unless these locate correctly. Take care when screwing the carburettor top onto the carburettor body as the fine thread is always prone to stripping or cross-threading.
5 Replace the air filter hose on the carburettor mouth and tighten up the screw clip.

47 Engine reassembly: reconnecting, bleeding and setting the oil pump

1 Reconnect the wire control cable linking the oil pump with the twist grip throttle. It is best to arrange the wire in a loop and

Chapter 1: Engine, clutch and gearbox

engage the nipple with the oil pump pulley, before the cable is seated in the pulley groove.

2 Because the oil feed pipe now contains air, it is necessary to bleed the oil pump until all the air bubbles are removed. Check that the oil tank is filled with oil, then unscrew and remove the small crosshead screw, which has a fibre washer beneath the head, from the oil pump body. Rotate the plastic wheel with the milled edge at the rear of the oil pump, in a CLOCKWISE direction (as denoted by the arrow marking) and continue turning until the oil commences to flow from the outlet which the bleed screw normally seals. Continue turning until all air bubbles have been eliminated from the main feed, then replace the screw and washer.

3 To check whether the pump opening is correct, follow the procedure given in Chapter 2, Section 15. If the pump was set up correctly initially, it is improbable that significant changes in setting will be required. DO NOT OMIT THIS CHECK UNDER THE ASSUMPTION IT MUST BE CORRECT.

4 Replace the semicircular cover over the oil pump, which is retained by three crosshead screws.

48 Engine reassembly: replacing the left-hand crankcase cover

Early models

1 Grease the clutch operating rod and insert it into the aperture in the mainshaft end. Remember to precede this by inserting the 5/16 inch ball bearing that lies between the two pushrods.

2 Loop the final drive chain around the final drive sprocket and reconnect it around the rear sprocket. This can be done most easily when the two chain ends are positioned correctly meshed onto the sprocket. The sprocket will then hold the chain ends at precisely the right distance from each other while the master link is replaced. The spring clip for the master link should always be replaced so that the closed end is travelling in a forward direction on the upper run of the chain. Grease the clutch operating mechanism.

3 Rest the left-hand crankcase cover on the footrest while the clutch operating cable is threaded into the outer cable holding aperture in the casing top edge, and the inner cable is connected to the operating arm. This must be done whilst the clutch cable is disconnected from the handlebar lever.

4 The outer casing can now be positioned and screwed up, taking care that the clutch operating rod locates correctly with the clutch operating adjustment screw.

5 Before replacing the final casing which covers the magneto flywheel and the clutch adjusting screw it is worthwhile to check the contact breaker gap and the clutch adjustment. All relevant details appertaining to points adjustment may be found in Chapter 3.3.

6 The clutch should be adjusted as follows. Reconnect the clutch cable at the handlebar lever, making sure that the cable is properly tracked and there are no excessive bends. Screw the cable end adjuster back until there is maximum adjustment available. Screw in the clutch adjusting screw on the crankcase cover until it can be felt to meet with the clutch operating rod and then unscrew it approximately ½ of a turn to give it the required clearance. Adjust the cable adjusting bolt on the handlebar lever until there is free play of 1/6 - 1/8 inch (2 - 3 mm). Tighten up the locking nut.

49 Engine reassembly: replacing the left-hand crankcase covers

Late models

1 Provided that the magneto stator plate was marked with a scribe line before it was removed from the crankcase, and that it was replaced in exactly the same position it may be assumed that the ignition timing is correct. Note the less, a check is available. The magneto cover plate may then be replaced. The cover plate is held by four cross-head screws of equal length.

2 Before replacing the final drive sprocket cover, the chain must be replaced as described in the previous section. Remember also to fit the rubber boot over the gear change shaft in order to exclude foriegn matter.

50 Engine reassembly: replacing the exhaust system

1 Position the exhaust system so that it is located in approximately the correct place and insert the various bracket bolts. On late models the exhaust pipe passes from the right of the machine, above the carburettor and through the rubber mud excluder under the seat. The exhaust flange gasket should be new and correctly placed in the exhaust port before the flange is bolted up. Replace the pipe/flange gasket (where fitted) and push the pipe into the flange boss. Replace the retainer springs.

2 Bolt the brackets up tightly, making certain that the rubber washers (where fitted) are correctly placed in relation to the washers.

51 Engine reassembly: completion and final adjustments

1 On late models reconnect the clutch cable with the clutch arm beneath the crankcase and replace the crankcase guard. This will necessitate removal of the blocks which are holding the machine in the upright position. Make certain that the rubber boot is correctly replaced on the short length of inner cable between the outer cable anchor and the clutch arm.

2 Remake the electrical connection from the magneto and contact breaker assembly with the main harness. Reconnection is very simple as the block type connectors are neither interchangeable nor reversable.

3 Reconnect the battery terminals, the earth lead being screwed to the frame adjacent to the battery and the 'live' lead having a torpedo connector.

4 Replace the kickstart and gearchange levers. Both fit on splines and are retained by a pinch bolt. Check that the levers are at the correct operating angle before tightening the pinch bolts.

5 Replace the petrol tank in precisely the reverse manner used for removal. The seat should be detached from the machine or at the least hinged in the most upright position. Position the tank so that the cups on the upper frame tube align with the rubber buffers on the underside of the tank and knock the tank forward using the flat of the hand. Having made sure that the throttle cable and electrical leads are correctly made the rear of the tank may be fixed. Connect the fuel pipe to the tap union and the carburettor, remembering to position the two spring clips.

6 Check the oil tank and top up if necessary with oil. SAE 30 two-stroke grade or recommended lubricant as available. Remove the filler cap from the rear of the right-hand crankcase cover and add the correct quantity of SAE 10W30 oil. This is 1 litre (1.06 qt) for all models. Leave the oil to settle for a few minutes and then check the level with the dipstick.

52 Starting and running the rebuilt engine

1 When the initial start-up is made, run the engine slowly for the first few minutes, especially if the engine has been rebored or a new crankshaft fitted. Check that all the controls function correctly and that there are no oil leaks before taking the machine on the road. The exhaust will emit a high proportion of white smoke during the first few miles, as the excess oil used whilst the engine was reassembled is burnt away. The volume of smoke should gradually diminish until only the customary light blue haze is observed during normal running. It is wise to carry a spare spark plug during the first run since the existing plug may oil up due to the temporary excess oil.

2 Remember that a good seal between the piston and the

50.1 Always use new exhaust gasket

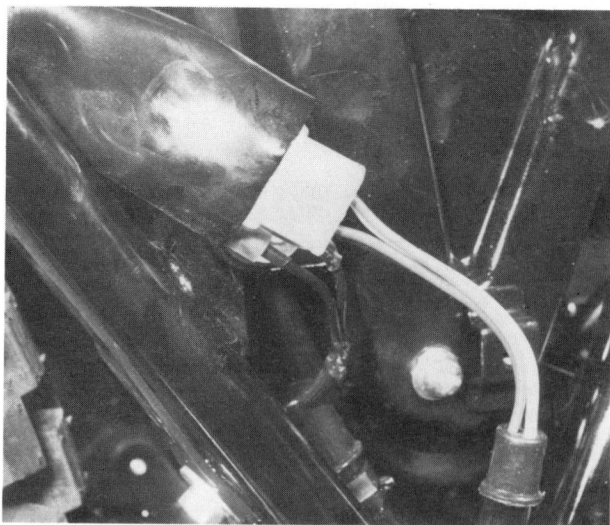
51.2a Remake electrical connections and ...

51.2b ... reconnect the battery

51.6a Replace transmission oil and ...

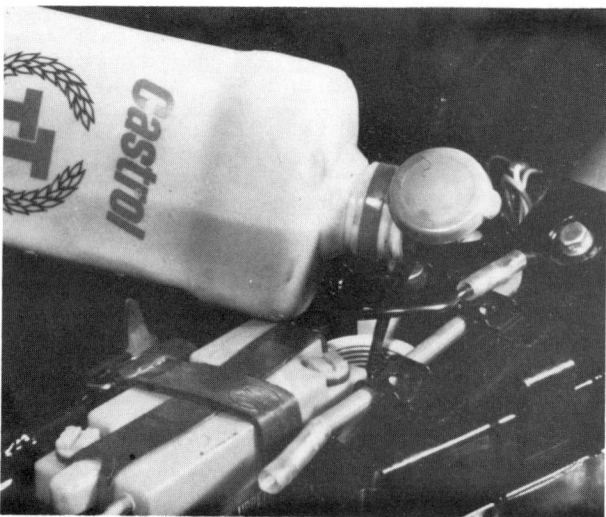
51.6b ... replenish oil pump reservoir

Chapter 1: Engine, clutch and gearbox

cylinder barrel is essential for the correct functioning of the engine. A rebored two-stroke will require more careful running-in, over a longer period, than its four-stroke counterpart. There is a far greater risk of engine seizure during the first one hundred miles if the engine is permitted to work hard.

3 Do not tamper with the exhaust system, or run the engine without the baffles fitted to the silencer. Unwarranted changes in the exhaust system will have a very marked effect on engine performance, invariably for the worst. The same advice to dispensing with the air cleaner or the air cleaner element.

4 Do not on any account add oil to the petrol under the mistaken belief that a little extra oil will improve the engine lubrication. Apart from creating smoke, the addition of oil will make the mixture weaker, with the consequent risk of overheating and engine seizure. The oil pump alone should provide full engine lubrication.

53 Fault diagnosis - engine

Symptom	Cause	Remedy
Engine will not start	Defective spark plug	Remove plug and lay on cylinder head. Check whether spark occurs when engine is kicked over.
	Dirty or closed contact breaker points	Check condition of points and whether gap is correct.
	Air leak at crankcase or worn crankshaft oil seals	Flood carburettor and check whether petrol is reaching the plugs.
Engine runs unevenly	Ignition and/or fuel system fault	Check as though engine will not start.
	Blowing cylinder head gasket	Oil leak should provide evidence. Replace gasket.
	Incorrect ignition timing	Check and if necessary adjust.
	Choked silencer	Remove baffles and clean.
Lack of power	Incorrect ignition timing	See above.
	Fault in fuel system	Check system and vent in filler cap.
	Choke silencer	See above.
White smoke from exhaust	Too much oil	Check oil pump setting.
	Engine needs rebore	Rebore and fit oversize piston.
	Tank contains two-stroke petroil and not straight petrol	Drain and refill with straight petrol.
Engine overheats	Pre-ignition and/or weak mixture	Check carburettor settings, also grade of plug fitted.
	Lubrication failure	Stop engine and check oil pump setting. Is oil tank dry?

54 Fault diagnosis - gearbox

Symptom	Cause	Remedy
Difficulty in engaging gears	Selector forks or rods bent	Replace.
	Broken springs in gear slector mechanism	Check and replace.
	Clutch drag	See next Section.
Machine jumps out of gear	Worn dogs on ends of gear pinions	Strip gearbox and replace worn parts.
	Sticking camplate plunger	Remove plunger cap and free plunger assembly.
Kickstart does not return	Broken return spring	Remove right-hand crankcase cover and replace spring.
Kickstart slips or jams	Worn ratchet assembly	Remove right-hand crankcase cover, dismantle kickstart assembly and replace worn parts.
Gearchange lever does not return to normal position	Broken return spring	Remove right-hand crankcase cover and replace spring.

Chapter 1: Engine, clutch and gearbox

55 Fault diagnosis - clutch

Symptom	Case	Remedy
Engine speed increases but machine does not respond	Clutch slip	Check whether clutch adjustment still has free play. Check thickness of linings and replace if near wear limit.
Difficulty in engaging gears, gear changes jerky and machine creeps forward, even when clutch is withdrawn fully	Clutch drag	Check clutch adjustment to eliminate excess play. Check whether clutch centre and outer drum have indented slots.
Operating action stiff	Clutch assembly loose Bent pushrod Dry pushrod Damaged, trapped or frayed control cable	Check tightness of retaining nut. Renew. Lubricate. Check cable and renew if necessary. Make sure cable is lubricated.

Chapter 2 Fuel system and lubrication

Contents

General description ... 1	Crankcase drain plug ... 10
Petrol tank: removal and replacement ... 2	Exhaust pipe and silencer: examining and cleaning the exhaust system ... 11
Petrol tap: removal, dismantling and replacement ... 3	The lubrication system ... 12
Petrol feed pipe: examination ... 4	Removing and replacing the oil pump ... 13
Carburettor: removal ... 5	Bleeding the oil pump ... 14
Carburettor: dismantling and examination ... 6	Checking the oil pump setting ... 15
Carburettor: checking the settings ... 7	Removing and replacing the oil tank ... 16
Reed valve assembly: removal, examination and replacement ... 8	Fault diagnosis: fuel system ... 17
Air cleaner: removing, cleaning and replacing the element ... 9	Fault diagnosis: lubrication system ... 18

Specifications

Petrol tank capacity ... All models 2.5 US gals. / 2.0 Imp. gals. approx. / 9.5 litres

Gearbox oil capacity ... All models 1.75 Imp. pints, 2 US pints, 1 litre

Oil tank capacity ... All models 1.7 US qts. 2¾ Imp. pints / 1.6 litres

Carburettor

	DT-1	DT2 and DT3
Make	Mikuni	Mikuni
Type	VM26SH	VM26SH
Main jet	150	160
Jet needle	5D1-3	5DP7-3
Needle jet	0-2	N-8
Throttle valve cutaway	2.5	1.5
Pilot jet	35	30
Air screw	1 - 1½	1¼
Starter jet	60	60

Carburettor

	DT1-B, DT1-C and DT1-E
Make	Mikuni
Type	VM26SH
Main jet	160
Jet needle	5D1-3
Needle jet	0-2
Throttle valve cutaway	2.5
Pilot jet	35
Air screw	1½
Starter jet	60

Carburettor

	RT1	RT1-B	RT2 and RT3
Make	Mikuni	Mikuni	Mikuni
Type	VM32SH	VM32SH	VM32SH

Main jet	220	240	230
Jet needle	6CF1-2	6CF1-2	6DH3-3
Needle jet	0.4	0.4	P.0
Throttle valve cutaway	1.5	1.5	3.0
Pilot jet	30	30	45
Air screw	1¼	1¾	1½
Starter jet	60	60	60

1 General description

The fuel system comprises a petrol tank from which petrol is fed by gravity, via a petrol tap with a built-in bowl-type filter, to the float chamber of the Mikuni carburettor.

For cold starting the carburettor is fitted with a hand-operated choke, either push-button or lever actuated. This provides the rich mixture necessary for a cold start and can be opened as soon as the engine will accept full air under normal running conditions.

Unlike many two-stroke, the Yamaha singles do not require a petrol/oil mix for lubrication. Oil for lubricating the engine is contained within a separate, side mounted oil tank, from which it is fed to an engine-driven pump, attached to the right-hand crankcase cover. Oil from the pump is fed to a drilling in the cylinder barrel inlet passage, and is drawn into the engine with the incoming mixture. The two-stroke engine depends on the compression of the incoming mixture before it is transferred to the combustion chamber via the transfer ports. Thorough lubrication of the bottom end of the engine as well as the piston and cylinder is therefore essential.

An added refinement is a direct link between the oil pump and the throttle so that the oil pump opening varies according to the engine demand.

2 Petrol tank: removal and replacement

1 Although it is not necessary to remove the petrol tank when the engine unit is removed from the frame, better access is gained and there is less risk of damage to the painted surface if the tank is out of harms way. Apart from occasions such as these, there is rarely any need to remove the tank unless rust has formed inside as the result of long storage or if it needs re-painting.

2 On early models the tank is not rigidly attached to the frame in any way. It is retained by rubber buffers at the front and rear, which are compressed when the tank is pushed into position over the top frame tube. The forward mounted rubbers engage with retaining cups attached to each side of the gusset at the rear of the steering head. The rear of the tank is retained by a rubber strap which passes over a hook on the rear of the tank. The tanks on later models fit on the frame in a similar manner but are retained at the rear by a nut and large grommet.

3 Before the petrol tank is removed it is necessary to detach the fuel line from the tap union, by releasing the small retaining clip. Providing the tank is not more than approximately half full, and that no work is to be carried out on the fuel tap, it is not necessary to drain the tank before removal.

4 To remove the tank, lift the dual seat (this may be removed if desired) and release the tank rear fixing. The tank can now be pulled back as far as necessary to clear the front mounting buffers and cups and then lifted upwards and forwards away from the machine. When replacing the tank check that the mounting rubbers are correctly located and are in good condition. The rear retaining strap is particularly prone to perishing and breakage.

3 Petrol tap: removal, dismantling and replacement

1 The petrol tap is secured to the left-hand underside of the petrol tank by two pan-head screws, one either side of the main tap body, a good seal between the tap and the tank being maintained by a rubber sealing ring. The detachable filter bowl is held on to the main tap body by a knurled union ring which must be unscrewed in an anticlockwise direction to release the bowl wire filter that is retained within.

2 There is seldom need to disturb the main body of the petrol tap. In the event of a leak at the operating lever, the complete lever assembly can be dismantled (provided the petrol tank is drained first) with the main body undisturbed. Remove the two crosshead screws that retain the tap lever plate in position and withdraw the lever complete with plate, crinkle washer and the valve insert behind the lever. The valve is the item to be replaced if leakage occurs; it is composed of a synthetic rubber material which may commence to disintegrate after an extended period of service.

3 Before reassembling the petrol tap, check that all parts are clean, especially the two tubes (short tube reserve, long tube main feed) which extend into the tank, the filter and filter bowl assembly. New gaskets should be fitted to both the filter bowl and the tab where it joins with the tank.

4 Do not overtighten any of the petrol tap components during reassembly. The castings are in a zinc-based alloy, which will fracture easily if overstressed. Most leakages occur as the result of defective seals.

5 There is no necessity to drain the tank when the filter bowl is removed for cleaning, provided the tap is turned to the stop position.

4 Petrol feed pipe: examination

The single petrol feed pipe is made from thin-walled plastic, and is of the push-on type, retained by a wire clip. Renewal is seldom required unless the plastic becomes hard or splits. Always replace the pipe in the same position from which it was removed, as the plastic sometimes takes a permanent form of the fitting over which it is connected. It is unlikely that the wire retaining clips will need renewal due to fatigue as the main seal between the pipe and union is effected by an interference fit.

5 Carburettor: removal

1 Detach the petrol feed pipe from its union with the carburettor float chamber by removing the spring clip and pulling the pipe off. The air cleaner hose is attached to the carburettor by a screw clip around the carburettor mouth and by a wire spring band around the air cleaner outlet duct. With the screw clip loosened off the hose can be pulled from both.

2 Unscrew the top of the mixing chamber and remove the knurled ring and cap, complete with cable, throttle slide and the needle assembly. It is a wise precaution to tape these parts to the frame crosstube so that they are not damaged as dismantling continues.

3 Those engines which employ the 'torque induction' system have the carburettor attached to the mouth of the rubber induction stub by a screw clip. Having loosened the clip the carburettor may be pulled from place.

4 The carburettor on those machines with 5 port cylinder barrels is fixed directly to the barrel on two studs which pass through the carburettor flange. A heat sink and gasket is interposed between the two.

3.1 Filter is housed in tap union body

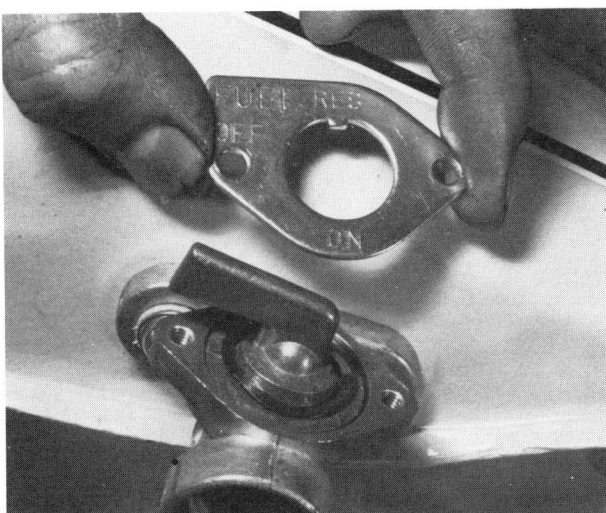

3.3a Remove plate to allow access to ...

3.3b ... rubber diaphragm for replacement

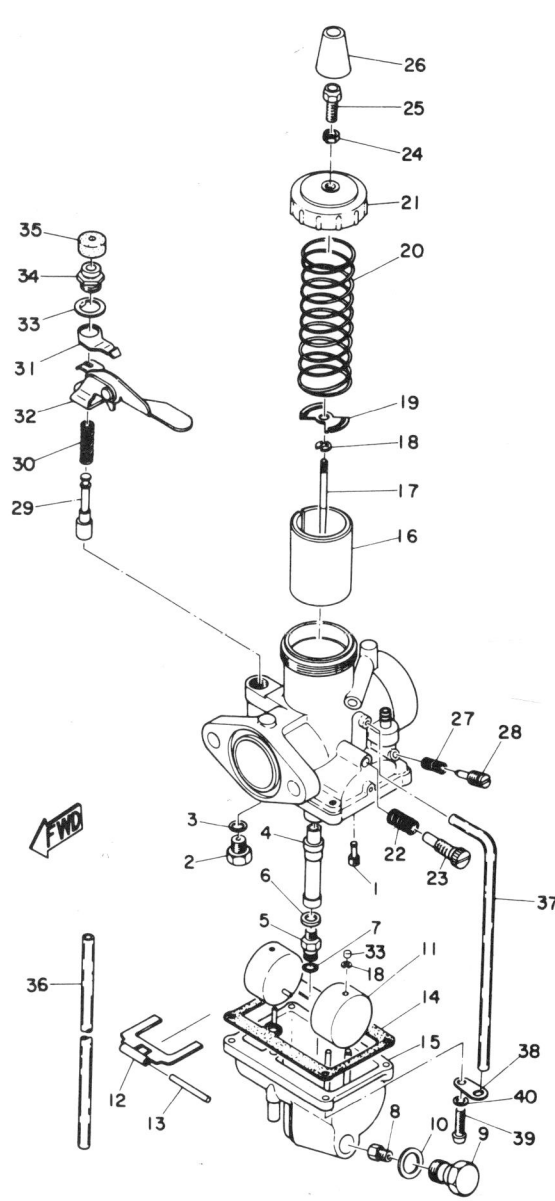

Fig. 2.1 Carburettor

1 Pilot jet
2 Valve seat
3 Valve seat washer
4 Needle jet nozzle
5 Needle jet
6 Main jet washer
7 'O' ring
8 Main jet
9 Banjo bolt
10 Gasket
11 Float - 2 off
12 Float pivot arm
13 Float pivot pin
14 Float chamber gasket
15 Float chamber body
16 Throttle valve
17 Needle
18 Needle clip
19 Spring seat
20 Throttle valve return spring
21 Mixing chamber cap
22 Throttle stop spring
23 Throttle adjuster screw
24 Cable adjuster lock nut
24 Cable adjuster screw
26 Rubber boot
27 Air screw spring
28 Air screw spring
29 Starter plunger (choke)
30 Return spring
31 Stop plate
32 Lever
33 Washer - 2 off
34 Plunger cap
35 Cover
36 Overflow pipe
37 Breather pipe
38 Holder plate
39 Screw - 4 off
40 Spring washer - 4 off
41 'O' ring

6 Carburettor: dismantling and examination

1 To separate the float chamber, invert the carburettor and remove the four small screws and spring washers holding the float chamber in position. There is a gasket between the float chamber body and the mixing chamber, to maintain a petrol-tight joint. The old gasket should be discarded.

2 The twin plastic floats which fit over the two metal rods projecting from the base of the mixing chamber will lift out once the pivot pin has been slid out of position. The floats are rebated to clear various parts of the mixing chamber and float chamber interiors; they are not reversible, and on reassembly should be replaced with the single rebate on the left-hand float facing downwards.

3 The float valve needle is operated by the centre tongue on the float assembly and is a sprung two-piece construction. Persistent flooding is invariably caused by a dirty valve needle or valve seating, or by a worn needle. The floats are of a solid plastic material and therefore rarely suffer from leakage. Dirt on the valve seat can be removed most effectively by the use of a compressed air jet; however flushing the seat with petrol will usually effect a cure.

4 The main jet is housed within a banjo-type bolt which is screwed into a recess in the base of float chamber. The banjo bolt and jet can be removed for cleaning without disturbing the float chamber.

5 Depending on the carburettor type utilised, the needle jet and main nozzle is a one-piece assembly which screws into the mixing chamber body from below, being concentrically placed with the throttle slide housing, or is a two-piece unit, the main nozzle screwing in from above (within the throttle slide housing) and the needle jet screwing into the mixing chamber from below. The needle jet is subject to considerable wear, as nearly all the fuel used by the engine passes through it. It should be renewed, if the petrol consumption is unduly high.

6 The throttle valve is still attached to the top of the mixing chamber by means of the throttle cable and return spring. To release the throttle valve, lift the return spring and remove the metal seating that fits over the needle. This serves the dual function of providing a seating for the spring and by a bent tab which forms a locking device to prevent the throttle cable from being detached. When the seating is removed, the throttle cable nipple can be slipped out of the throttle valve and the throttle valve detached. The needle will lift out, with the retaining clip which holds it in the correct notch. When the needle jet is renewed, the needle should be renewed too since they work in conjunction with one another.

7 Before reassembling the carburettor in the reverse order of that given for dismantling, make sure all the component parts are clean. Check that the needle is not bent, by rolling it on a sheet of plain glass. Examine the throttle slide; signs of wear will be evident on the polished outer surface.

8 Never use wire or any pointed instrument to clear a blocked jet or any of the internal air passages in the mixing chamber body. It is only too easy to enlarge the small precision drilled orifices and cause carburation changes which will prove very difficult to rectify. Always use compressed air; even a jet of air from a tyre pump should suffice.

9 When replacing the throttle valve, make sure the slot in the base of the valve registers with the projection inside the mixing chamber, so that the valve will seat correctly. It is also important to check that the needle suspended from the throttle valve has entered the needle valve, otherwise there is risk of damaging both the needle and the jet.

10 When replacing the carburettor a new fibre gasket must be used. Note also that there is a back up O ring installed in the locating groove on the carburettor flange face. This O ring should be discarded if it shows any signs of compression or roughness.

6.1a Carburettor, showing mixture screw

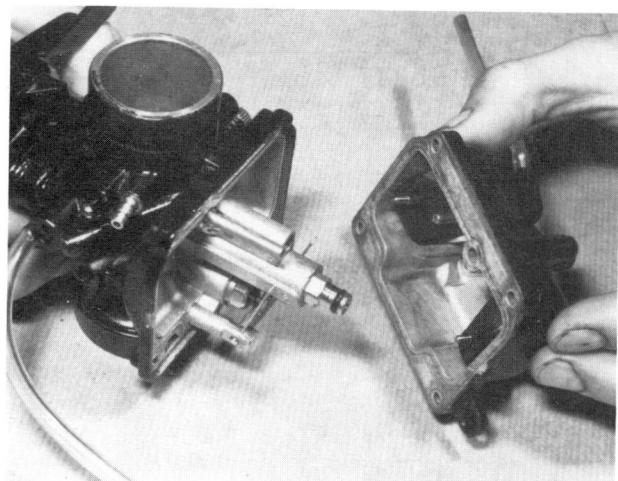

6.1b Float bowl held by four screws

6.2a Floats fit on seperate posts

6.2b Slide out pivot pin for tongue removal and ...

6.2c ... access to the two piece needle

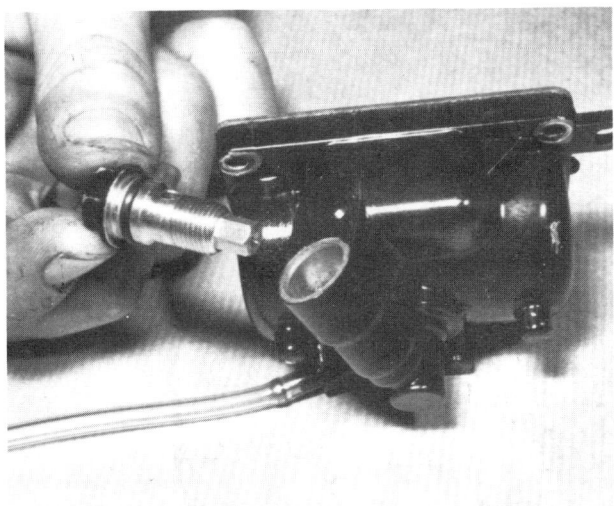
6.4 Main jet housed in base of float chamber

6.5a Remove mixing nozzle to allow ...

6.5b ... removal of needle jet from above

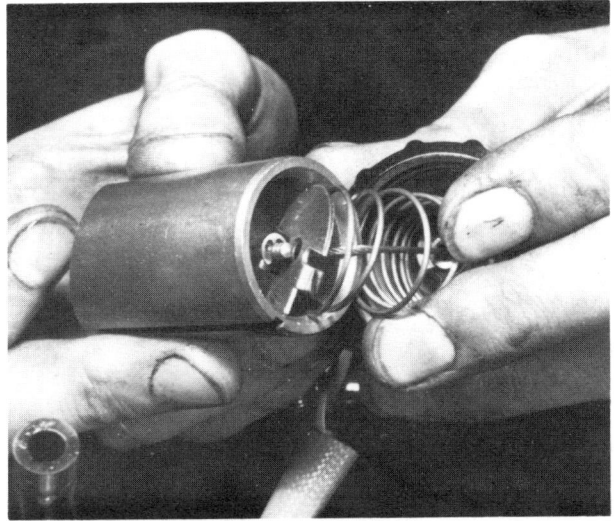
6.6 Throttle cable assembly removal

Chapter 2: Fuel system and lubrication

7 Carburettor: checking the settings

1 The various jet sizes, throttle valve cutaway and needle position are predetermined by the manufacturer and should not require modification. Check with the specifications list at the beginning of this Chapter if there is any doubt about the values fitted.

2 Slow running is controlled by a combination of the throttle stop and pilot jet settings. Adjustment should be carried out as explained in the following Section. Remember that the characteristics of the two-stroke engine are such that it is extremely difficult to obtain a slow, reliable tick-over at low rpm. If desired, there is no objection to arranging the throttle stop so that the engine will shut off completely when the throttle is closed. Unlike a petroil lubricated engine, the oil used for engine lubrication is injected into the inlet passage of each cylinder barrel, behind the closed throttle slide. In consequence there is no risk of the engine 'drying up' when the machine is coasted down a long incline, if the throttle is closed.

3 As a rough guide, up to 1/8 throttle is controlled by the pilot jet, 1/8 to 1/4 by the throttle valve cutaway, 1/4 to 3/4 throttle by the needle position and from 3/4 to full by the size of the main jet. These are only approximate divisions, which are by no means clear cut. There is a certain amount of overlap between the various stages.

4 Guard against the possibility of incorrect carburettor adjustments which wil result in a weak mixture. Two-stroke engines are very susceptible to this type of fault, causing rapid overheating and often subsequent engine seizure. Changes in carburation leading to a weak mixture will occur if the air cleaner is removed or disconnected, or if the silencer is tampered with in any way. Above all, do not add oil to the petrol, in the mistaken belief that it will aid lubrication. The extra oil will only reduce the petrol content by the ratio of oil added, and therefore cause the engine to run with a permanently weakened mixture.

5 In order that an even idling speed be obtained, the pilot jet screw (air screw) should be adjusted in conjunction with the throttle stop screw. As defined in the specifications for each model at the beginning of this Chapter the engine tick-over at normal running temperature should be between 1200 and 1500 rpm and the pilot jet screw should be screwed out between 1½ and 2 turns depending on the particular model. With the air screw adjusted as specified, unscrew the throttle stop screw until the engine runs evenly at the slowest possible speed. The pilot jet scerw can now be screwed in or out within the range of about half a turn, the optimum position being where the engine runs most evenly. With the carburettor correct set, adjust the throttle cable screw until all slack is taken up. This will give more positive action at the twist-grip.

8 Reed valve assembly: removal, examination and replacement

1 The reed valve 'sandwich' is secured to the cylinder barrel by four bolts and spring washers, and comprises the carburettor mounting stub, reed valve case and the gasket. Before removing the reed valve assembly mark the relative positions of the mounting stub and reed casing with the barrel in order that they may be correctly replaced. Separate the components and discard the old gasket, as it is essential that an airtight seal be made on replacement. The mounting stub is made from a rubber material which should be closely inspected for cracks.

2 It is unlikely that the reed valve assembly will have deteriorated during normal usage. However the valves and valve stoppers should be checked for cracks and distortion. After a considerable mileage it is possible for the valves to develop fatigue and cease seating properly. If this is the case they should be renewed. If the valve case seats have become pitted or scored, the whole unit must be renewed. When replacing valves and stoppers the setscrews should not be tightened to more than 8.0 kg cm or distortion will develop. No gasket jointing compound should be used for assembly as the gaskets are designed to vulcanise by the heat of the engine.

9 Air cleaner: removing, cleaning and replacing the element

1 The air cleaner box is located below the dual seat and contains either an oil-impregnated foam element or a corrugated paper element.

2 On early models the element may be removed after the four retaining screws on the lid are removed. The dual seat must be raised to allow access to the air box lid.

3 Later models are fitted with the air box lid on the right of the machine where it is located by three screws or bolts. Here again once the lid has been removed the element may be withdrawn.

4 Oil-impregnated foam elements should be cleansed by washing thoroughly in the recommended solvent supplied by a Yamaha service agent. If this solution is not available methylated spirits may be used in the same manner. **Do not** use petrol or allied solvents as this may reduce the plastic based foam to a sticky mass. Squeeze out the cleaning agent from the element until it is quite dry, and recharge with 10W 30 grade oil. The element should be completely impregnated with oil, but not dripping with it.

5 If the foam has hardened through age, or has disintigrated a new element should be fitted.

6 Corrugated paper elements should be cleaned with the use of an air hose inside or by tapping so that the loose dust on the surface is displaced. If the element is damp or badly contaminated it should be discarded and in any event should be renewed at 3,000 mile intervals. Where a machine is exclusively used in dusty or muddy conditions the element should be renewed more frequently.

10 Crankcase drain plug

Unlike most two-strokes, the crankcase is not fitted with a drain plug with which to drain the contents in the event of flooding. If flooding occurs, any excess fuel/oil mixture can be blown from the engine by removing the spark plug and kicking the engine over the throttle wide open until the engine is thoroughly vented.

11 Exhaust pipe and silencer: examining and cleaning the exhaust system

1 The exhaust pipe and silencer is manufactured as a complete unit on most models, the exhaust pipe being inseparable from the silencer. On the late models, where the exhaust system runs under the fuel tank and the seat, a short tail pipe is fitted for ease of maintenance.

2 The component most likely to cause trouble and therefore require attention is the silencer baffle which will block up with a sludge composed of carbon and oil if not cleaned out at regular intervals. A two-stroke is very susceptible to this fault, which is caused by the oily nature of the exhaust gases. As sludge builds up, back pressure will increase, with a resultant fall-off in power.

3 On early models it is not necessary to remove the exhaust system in order to gain access to the baffle. It is retained by a small bolt passing through a reinforced plate which is positioned about an inch from the end of the silencer tail pipe. With this bolt removed the baffle can be eased from position.

4 If the build up of carbon and oil is not too great, a wash with a petrol/paraffin mix will probably suffice as a cleaning medium. Otherwise more drastic action will be necessary, such as the application of a blow lamp flame to burn away the accumulated deposits. Before the baffle is refitted it must be completely clean with none of the holes in the baffle obstructed.

Chapter 2: Fuel system and lubrication

8.1 Reed valve assembly held by four screws

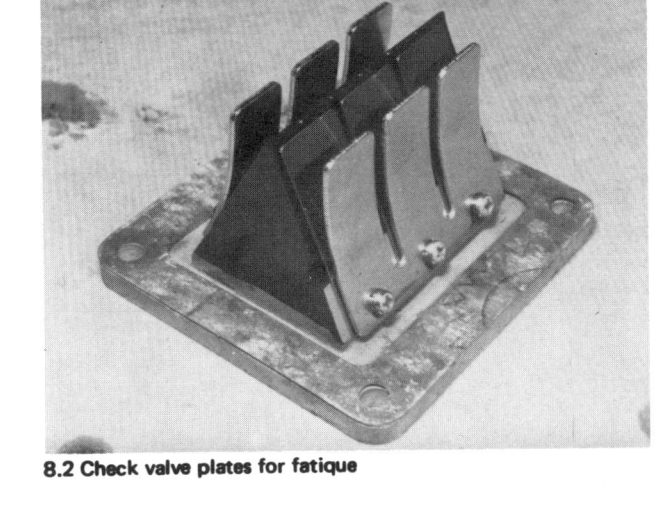

8.2 Check valve plates for fatigue

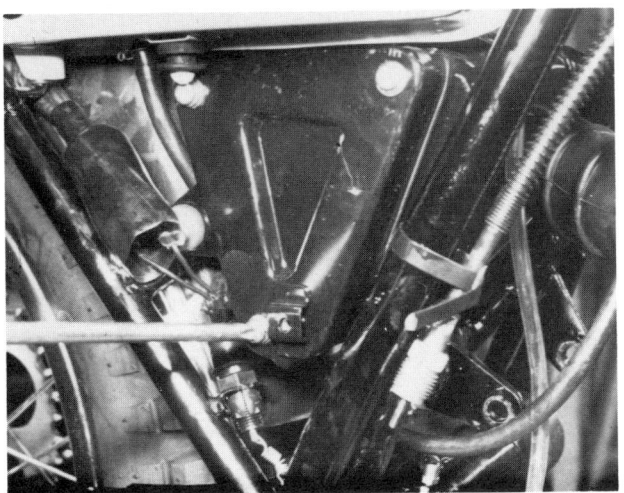

9.3a Air cleaner cover held by three screws ...

9.3b ... allowing removal of element

11.1 Renew exhaust pipe 'O' ring when perished

5 When replacing the baffle, make sure that retaining bolt is located correctly and fully tightened. If the baffle bolt falls out, the baffle will work loose, creating excessive exhaust noise accompanied by a marked fall-off in performance.

6 Do not run the machine without the baffles in the silencer or modify the baffle in any way. Although the changed exhaust note may give the illusion of increased power, the chances are that the performance will be reduced, accompanied by a noticeable lack of acceleration. There is also a risk of prosecution by causing an excessive noise. The carburettor is jetted to take into account the fitting of a silencer of a certain design and if this balance is disturbed, the carburation will suffer accordingly.

12 The lubrication system

1 Unlike many two-strokes, the Yamaha singles have an independent lubrication system for the engine and do not require the mixture of a measured quantity of oil to the petrol content of the fuel tank in order to utilise the so-called 'petroil' method. Oil of the correct viscosity (SAE 30) is contained in a separate oil tank mounted on the left-hand side of the machine

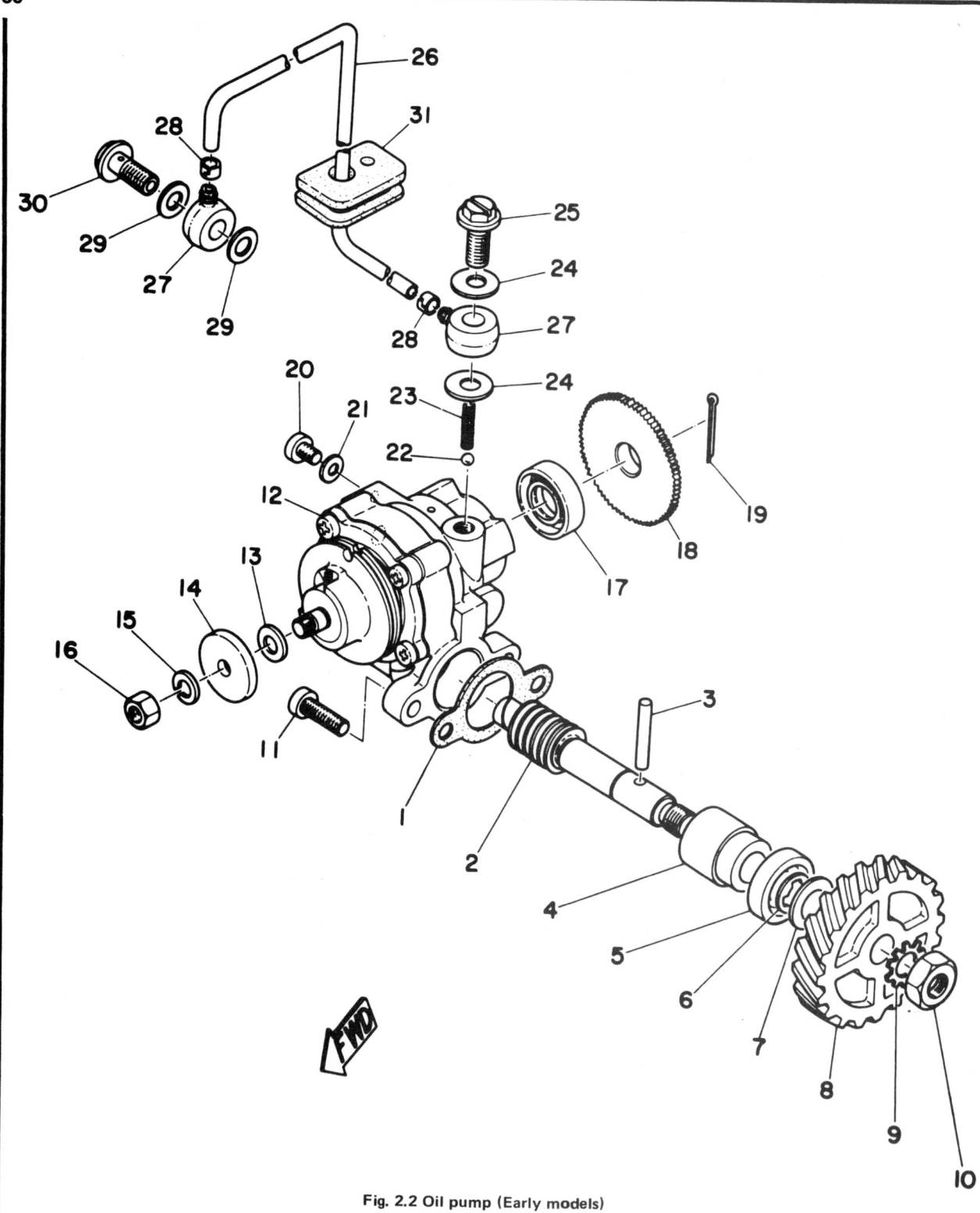

Fig. 2.2 Oil pump (Early models)

1 Gasket
2 Worm shaft
3 Dowel pin
4 Outer shaft bush
5 Oil seal
6 Circlip
7 Plain washer
8 Nylon drive gear
9 Tooth washer
10 Nut
11 Pan head screw - 2 off
12 Oil pump assembly
13 Plunger shim
14 Adjuster plate
15 Spring washer
16 Nut
17 Oil seal
18 Bleed wheel
19 Split pin
20 Bleed screw
21 Bleed screw washer
22 Non-return ball - 5/32"
23 Non-return ball spring
24 Banjo bolt gasket
25 Banjo bolt gasket
26 Delivery pipe
27 Banjo union
28 Delivery pipe clip
29 Banjo bolt gasket
30 Banjo bolt
31 Oil pipe holder

Note: Late models utilise a similar pump driven by simple dog system.

Chapter 2: Fuel system and lubrication

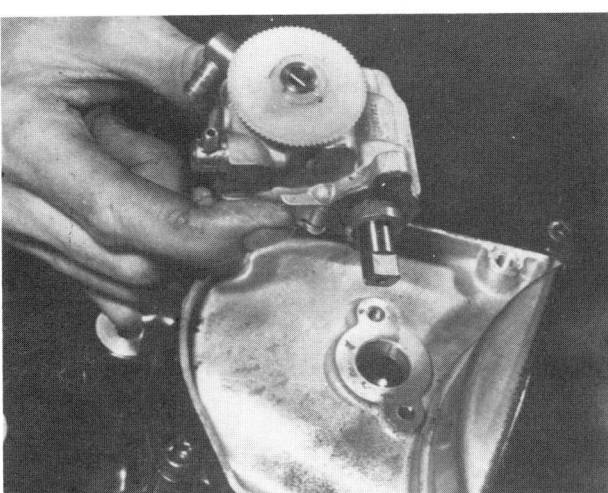

13.4 Fit new gasket when replacing pump

15.4a Oil pump cable adjuster allows ...

15.4b ... guide pin and pulley mark alignment

and is fed to a mechanical oil pump on the right-hand side of the engine which is driven from the crankshaft by reduction gear. The pump delivers oil at a predetermined rate via a plastic feed pipe to an oilway drilled into the inlet manifold of the cylinder. In consequence, the oil is carried into the engine by an incoming charge of petrol vapour, when the inlet port opens.

2 The oil pump is also interconnected to the twist grip throttle, so that when the throttle is opened, the oil pump setting is increased a similar amount. This technique, pioneered by a British two-stroke manufacturer in the early 1930's, ensures that the lubrication requirements of the engine are always directly related to the degree of throttle opening. This facility is arranged by means of a control cable looped around a pulley on the end of the pump; the cable is joined to the throttle cable junction box.

13 Removing and replacing the oil pump

1 There is no necessity to remove the oil pump assembly unless the cover itself is damaged and has to be replaced. Under these circumstances the oil pump must be removed from the crankcase cover and the worm drive shaft and pinion removed from the inside. In the unlikely event of the pump itself failing mechanically, it is probable that the engine will need overhauling at least in part, due to the damage caused by lubrication deficiency.

2 To remove the right-hand crankcase cover follow the procedure given in Chapter 1, Section 9. There is no necessity to remove the engine from the frame in order to carry out this operation, but the oil delivery pipe must be detached from the cylinder barrel.

3 The oil pump is secured to the cover by two pan-head screws which must be removed before the crankcase cover forward retaining screw can be reached for loosening. Follow the procedure in Chapter 1, Section 15.3, to remove the oil pump worm drive shaft and nylon drive pinion.

4 Refit the oil pump to the replacement crankcase cover, using a new gasket at the oil pump/crankcase cover joint and a new oil seal behind the ddrive pinion. Replace and tighten the two crosshead oil pump mounting screws after the crankcase cover has been replaced and screwed down. **Do not** replace the oil pump cover plate as the oil pump must be bled to ensure the oil lines are completely free from air bubbles.

14 Bleeding the oil pump

1 It is necessary to bleed the oil pump every time the main feed pipe from the oil tank is removed and replaced. This is because air will be trapped in the oil line, no matter what care is taken when the pipe is removed.

2 Check that the oil pipe is connected correctly, with the retaining wire clip in position. Then remove the crosshead screw in the outer face at the pump body with the fibre washer beneath the head. This is the oil bleed screw.

3 Check that the oil tank is not close to the refill level, then place a container below the oil bleed hole to collect the oil that is expelled as the pump is bled. Rotate the white plastic pinion at the base of the oil pump in a clockwise direction; this is the pinion with a milled edge with arrows showing the direction of rotation stamped on the face. Continue rotating the pinion until the oil expelled from the bleed hole is completely free from air bubbles, then replace the bleed screw and fibre washer. **Do not** replace the front portion of the crankcase cover until the pump setting has been checked, as described in the next Section.

15 Checking the oil pump setting

1 Make sure the twist grip is fully closed, then rotate the white plastic pinion used for bleeding the oil pump until the gap

between the oil pump pulley at the opposite end of the of the casing and the body of the oil pump is at its maximum. It will be found that the pulley rises and falls as the pinion is turned, if light pressure is applied with the fingers to the end of the pulley.

2 Check the gap with a feeler gauge. It must be within the range 0.20 - 0.25 mm (0.008 - 0.012 inch) if the pump stroke is correct. To make adjustments, remove the locknut above the plate in the centre of the pulley and lift off the plate. If the clearance was too small, place the appropriate number of 0.1 mm (0.004 inch) shims below the plate before replacing the plate and locknut. If the clearance is too great, remove the appropriate number of shims four below the plate. Always recheck after replacing the plate and tightening down the locknut.

3 Adjust the throttle cable so that when the throttle is fully closed there is 0.5 - 1.0 mm play. The adjuster is located close to the twist grip.

4 If the pump adjustment is now correct, the mark on the outer face of the oil pump pulley will be directly in line with the guide pin passing through the pulley boss, when the throttle is closed.

5 Check that the pump pulley moves quite freely in each direction as the throttle is opened and closed. Replace the pump inspection cover.

16 Removing and replacing the oil tank

1 The oil tank is secured to the frame by bolts screwed through lugs on the tank and into threaded brackets on the frame. Note the rubber buffers which are located between the tank and frame lugs.

2 Before the tank is removed it must either be drained of oil, by removing the oil pump feed pipe from the union on the oil tank base, or sealed off by blocking the oil feed pipe at the pump end with a suitable bolt. Note that the oil tank breather pipe must be tracked correctly, so that it does not foul the rear chain, rear tyre or any other moving part.

3 The oil pipe union is of the banjo type, with a hollow bolt passing through it into the tank. A filter is fitted to the end of the hollow bolt which should be removed and checked at intervals. Always renew the two fibre washers on the banjo union to avoid oil leaks.

17 Fault diagnosis - fuel system

Symptom	Cause	Remedy
Excessive fuel consumption	Air cleaner choked or restricted	Clean or replace element.
	Fuel leaking from carburettor	Check all unions and gaskets.
	Badly worn or distorted carburettor	Replace.
	Carburettor settings incorrect	Readjust. Check settings with Specifications.
Idling speed too high	Throttle stop screw in too far	Adjust screw.
	Carburettor top loose	Tighten.
Engine sluggish. Does not respond to throttle	Back pressure in silencer	Check baffles and clean if necessary.
Engine dies after running for a short while	Blocked vent hole in filler cap	Clean.
	Dirt or water in carburettor	Remove and clean.
General lack of performance	Weak mixture; float needle sticking in seat	Remove float chamber and check needle seating.
	Air leak at carburettor or leaking crankcase seals	Check for air leaks or worn seals.

18 Fault diagnosis - lubrication system

Symptom	Cause	Remedy
White smoke from exhaust	Too much oil	Check oil pump setting and reduce if necessary.
Engine runs hot and gets sluggish when warm	Too little oil	Check oil pump setting and increase if necessary.
Engine runs unevenly, not particularly responsive to throttle openings	Intermittent oil supply	Bleed oil pump to displace air in feed pipes.
Engine dries up and seizes	Complete lubrication failure	Check for blockages in feed pipes, also whether oil pump drive has sheared.

Note:
Lubrication failures will occur if a change is made from mineral oil to vegetable-base oils of the 'R' type (or vice-versa) if the engine is not stripped completely and all traces of the original oil removed. Mineral and vegetable oils do not mix but under the action of heat from a rubber-like sludge that will quickly block the internal oilways.

Chapter 3 Ignition system

Contents

General description ... 1
Checking the ignition source coil or exciter coil ... 2
Contact breaker: adjustment ... 3
Contact breaker points: removal, renovation and replacement ... 4
Condenser: location, removal and replacement ... 5
Condenser: testing ... 6
CDI (capacitor discharge ignition) unit: location and testing ... 7
Ignition coil: checking ... 8
Ignition timing: checking and setting (contact breaker models) ... 9
Ignition timing: checking and setting (CDI models) ... 10
Ignition switch ... 11
Spark plug: checking and resetting the gap ... 12
Fault diagnosis: ignition system ... 13

Specifications

	DTI and DTI-C	DTI-B and DTI-E	DT2 and DT3
Flywheel magneto			
Make	Mitsubishi	Mitsubishi	Mitsubishi
Model	FZA-1BL	FZC-IAIL	FZA-IBL
Rectifier			
Make	Mitsubishi	Mitsubishi	Mitsubishi
Model	DS10HJ-1	DS10HJ-1	DS10HJ-8
Ignition coil			
Make	Mitsubishi	Mitsubishi	Mitsubishi
Model	HP-E	HP-E	HD-A4
Spark plug			
Make	NGK	NGK	NGK
Type	B-7E	B-8ES	B-8ES
Reach	¾" (19 mm)	¾" (19 mm)	¾" (19 mm)
Gap	0.5 - 0.6 mm (0.023 inch)	0.5 - 0.6 mm (0.023 inch)	0.5 - 0.6 mm (0.023 inch)

	RT1 & RT1B	RT2 and RT3
Flywheel magneto		
Make	Mitsubishi	Mitsubishi
Model	FZC-IAIL	FZA-IBL
Rectifier		
Make	Mitsubishi	Mitsubishi
Model	DS10HJ-1	DS10HJ-8
Ignition coil		
Make	Mitsubishi	Mitsubishi
Model	HP-E	HD-A4
Spark plug		
Make	NGK	NGK
Type	B-9ES	B-9ES
Reach	¾" (19 mm)	¾" (19 mm)
Gap	0.5 - 0.6 mm (0.023 inch)	0.5 - 0.6 mm (0.023 inch)

Chapter 3: Ignition system

1 General description

1 Two different types of ignition system are utilised on this range of Yamaha trail bikes, depending on the model. All early models and the late 250 cc machine utilise a flywheel-magneto mounted on the left-hand crankshaft, the timing being controlled by the traditional contact breaker mechanism. The late 400 cc machine also utlises a crankshaft-mounted flywheel magneto, but in this system the contact breaker is replaced by a capacitor. This system is generally referred to as a CDI (Capacitor Discharge Ignition) system. Although the two types of ignition utilise the same principle of power production ie., the flywheel magneto; the principles of operation are different. This being so, separate descriptions for each system are outlined below.

2 Early models and late 250 cc

The ignition system comprises a flywheel magneto, contact-breaker assembly, condenser, ignition coil and spark plug.

As the flywheel rotates, the contact-breaker points open and close alternately by means of a cam, mounted integrally on the inside of the flywheel centre. The make and break operation develops an electromotive force in the ignition power source coil (housed within the flywheel assembly) and produces a low voltage in the ignition coil primary windings. The voltage (150 - 300v) which is produced in the ignition coil primary windings is stepped up to 12,000 - 14,000 volts by mutual induction in the ignition coil secondary windings and the electricity is led to the spark plug where it arcs across the electrodes, igniting the mixture under compression.

Both the ignition power source coil and the two lighting circuit charging coils are housed within the flywheel magneto, mounted on the stator plate. The charging citcuit does not require or utilise any excess current from the ignition source coil, and is therefore not interconnected in any way.

3 400 cc machine

As the ignition system utilised with these models is not yet widely used and may not generally be understood a short glossary of those components used, preceeds the description of the principles of operation as follows:

Exciter coil

This unit is housed within the flywheel assembly and generates the voltage and current that serves to produce the spark.

Diode

The voltage generated by the exciter coil is rectified by this component, from A.C. (alternating current) to D.C. (direct current) in order that the condenser (capacitor) may be charged.

Condenser

This component stores the current (100-300v) rectified by the diode and discharges it rapidly at the pre-set ignition time to the primary side of the ignition coil.

Thyristor

This component has the special property that in order to make the current flow in a forward direction, a specified voltage must be impressed on the 'gate', otherwise the current will not start flowing. This is the same as a switch that works by 'signal voltage'.

Pulser coil

This component generates the correct valve signal voltage for opening the thyristor 'gate'.

Phase inversion circuit

This circuit consists essentially of a silicon control rectifier, a Zener diode which works as a breaker and condenser, which serves to store the current generated by the pulser coil. Enough current flows to open the thyristor 'gate' when the voltage generated by the pulser coil reaches the Zener diode passage voltage. At this time, the condenser storing the exciter voltage starts to discharge and causes current to flow rapidly to the ignition coil primary windings.

Zener diode

This component has the same properties as an ordinary diode, but has the additional property of allowing the required current to flow in the reverse direction when the voltage impressed in the reverse direction, reaches a certain value (Zener voltage).

Principles of operation

4 When the magneto flywheel rotates, alternating current is generated in the exciter coil. This current is rectified by the diode and charges the condenser to 100 - 300 volts. At this time, the thyristor is in the OFF state. Alternating current is also generated simultaneously in the pulser coil and this flows through a second diode and the phase inversion circuit, this current differing in phase to that charging the condenser. When this current reaches the voltage (Zener voltage) that will actuate the phase inversion circuit, the thyristor 'gate' is opened, switching the thyristor from the OFF state to the ON state so that the current charged in the condenser discharges rapidly through the thyristor to the ignition coil primary windings. This discharge current produces mutual induction in the secondary windings of the ignition coil, thereby producing 12,000 - 14,000 volts which causes arcing at the spark plug electrodes, igniting the mixture under compression. When the plug has sparked, a signal current flows through the thyristor gate for a very short time in order to return the thyristor to the OFF state.

2 Checking the ignition source coil or exciter coil

1 The performance and output of both the source coils for the charging circuit and the ignition source coil, can only be efficiently checked with specialised test equipment of the multi-meter type. It is unlikely that the average owner/rider will have access to this type of equipment or the instruction in its use. In consequence, if the performance is suspect it should be checked by a Yamaha service agent or auto-electrician.

2 Diminished performance or complete failure of the charging system may be caused by faults other than in the coil windings. Check that the coil mounting bolts are tight, as poor earthing results in low or erratic output, and check that all main wiring connections are firm and bright. Total output failure on all the coils may be due to the flywheel having sheared its drive key on the crankshaft drive taper. This fault will be self-evident on inspection.

3 Contact-breaker: adjustment

1 Remove the magneto cover from the left-hand crankcase cover, and remove the spark plug from the head. The contact-breaker assembly is housed beneath the magneto flywheel rotor which must remain in position for contact-breaker adjustment, as the points cam is an integral part of the flywheel. Apertures in the face of the rotor permit access for inspection and adjustment.

2 Rotate the flywheel until the points are in the fully open position. Examine the faces of the contacts. If they are dirty, pitted or burnt it will be necessary to remove them for further attention, as described in Section 4 of this Chapter.

3 The correct contact-breaker gap when the points are fully open, is within the range 0.012 - 0.016 inch (0.3 - 0.4 mm).

Adjustment is effected by slackening the screw holding the fixed contact point in position, and using a screwdriver to move the points either closer together or further apart as required.

Chapter 3: Ignition system

It is essential that the points are in the fully open position when adjustment is made, or a false reading will result. When the gap is correct, retighten the holding screw and recheck for accuracy.

4 Contact-breaker points: removal, renovation and replacement

1 If the contact-breaker points are burnt, pitted or badly worn they should be removed for dressing. If it is necessary to remove a substantial amount of material before the faces can be restored, new contacts should be fitted.

Before the contact-breaker assembly can be removed, it will be necessary to remove the magneto flywheel rotor as described in Chapter 1, Section 8.

2 To remove the moving contact, slacken the screw and nut at the end of the return spring and remove the circlip from the post on which the contact pivots. The moving contact can now be lifted away complete with the return spring and the fibre heel bearing on the contact-breaker cam.

3 To remove the fixed contact, remove the screw and nut that has already been slackened, so that the wires can be detached from the end of the mounting plate. Remove the screw that holds the mounting plate in position and lift away the plate complete with fixed contact.

4 When removing the wires from the fixed contact mounting plate, take particular note of the arrangement of the insulating washers. If they are replaced incorrectly, the points will be isolated electrically, causing the ignition circuit to fail completely.

5 The points should be dressed with an oilstone or fine emery cloth. Keep them absolutely square during the dressing operation, otherwise they will make angular contact when they are replaced and will burn away rapidly as a result.

6 Replace the contact by reversing the dismantling procedure, taking care to position the insulating washers in the correct sequence. Lightly grease the pivot post before replacing the moving contact and check that there is no oil or grease on the points faces. Place a few drops of oil on the lubricating wick that bears on the contact-breaker cam, so that the surface is kept lubricated.

7 Readjust the contact-breaker gap to the recommended setting after verifying that the points are in the fully open position.

5 Condenser: location, removal and replacement (early models and late 250)

1 The condenser is included in the contact breaker circuit to prevent arcing across the contact-breaker points as they separate. It does this by storing electricity from the points when the points are open, and discharging the electricity when the points close. The condenser is connected in parallel with the contact-breaker circuit and if a fault develops in this component, ignition failure is liable to occur.

2 If the engine is difficult to start, or if misfiring occurs, it is possible that the condenser is at fault. To check whether the condenser has failed, observe the points whilst the engine is running. If any excess sparking across the points is visible through the blur caused by the fast rotating flywheel, and the points are badly burned and blackened, then it can be assumed that the condenser is no longer serviceable. In theory there should be absolutely no sparking visible between the oscillating contact points whilst the engine is running. However, a small amount of irregular sparking can often be observed. This may be considered quite normal even for a condenser in good condition.

3 The condenser is located on the contact breaker assembly mounting plate, directly below the main crankpin and is retained by a single screw through a small bracket soldered to the condenser body. In the event of the condenser needing renewal, it will be necessary to unsolder the three wires at the condenser terminal which run to the ignition source coil, the

3.1 Point faces must be clean and parallel

3.3 Adjust points through window in flywheel

6.1 Condenser is screwed to stator plate

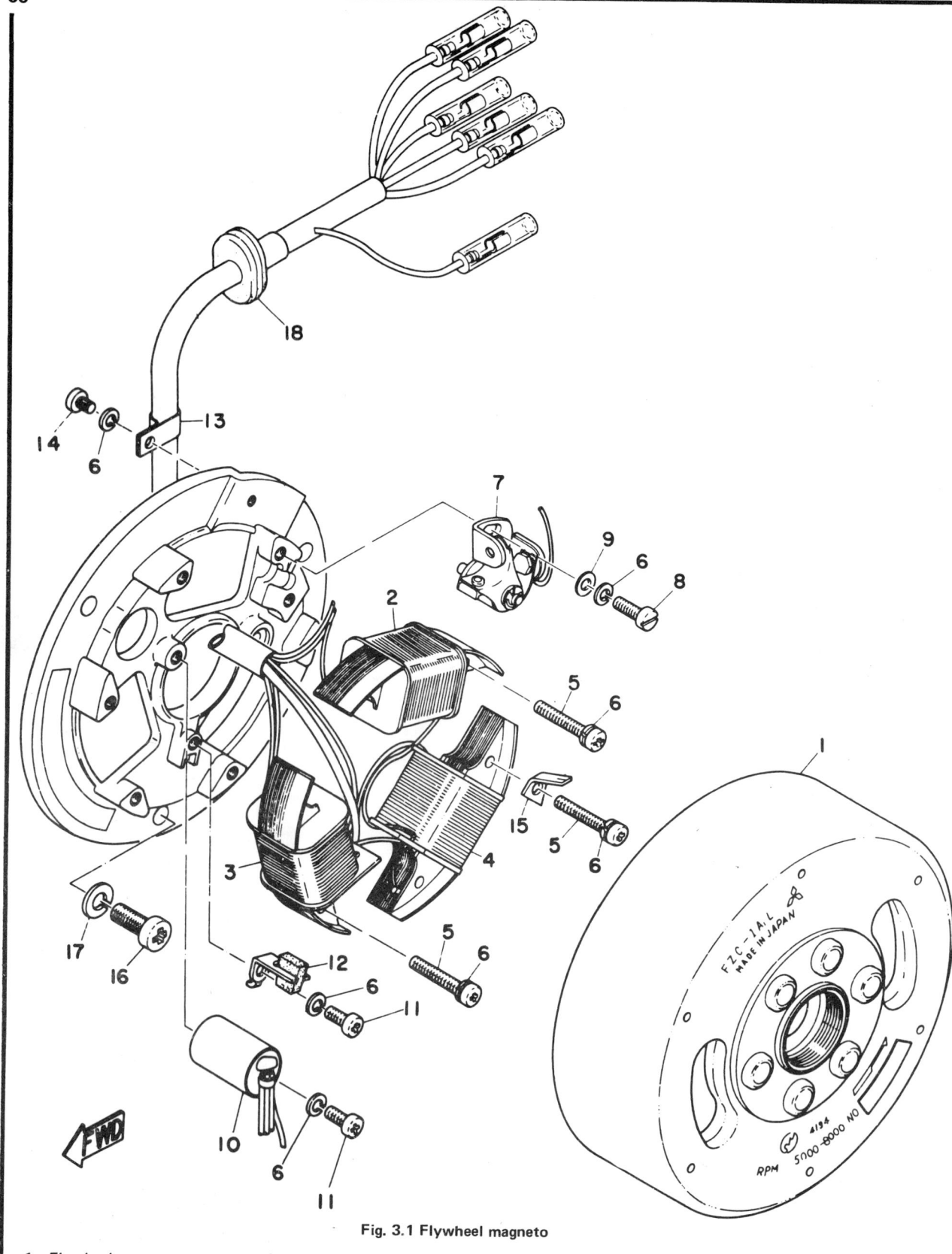

Fig. 3.1 Flywheel magneto

1 Flywheel
2 Ignition source coil
3 Lighting coil (1)
4 Lighting coil (2)
5 Pan head screw - 6 off
6 Spring washer - 10 off
7 Contact breaker assembly
8 Screw
9 Plain washer
10 Condenser (capacitor)
11 Screw - 2 off
12 Lubricator assembly
13 Lead clip
14 Screw
15 Timing plate
16 Pan head screw - 3 off
17 Spring washer - 3 off
18 Cable grommet

Spark plug maintenance: Checking plug gap with feeler gauges

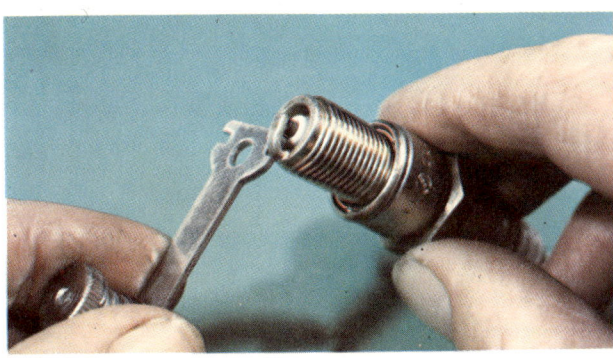

Altering the plug gap. Note use of correct tool

Spark plug conditions: A brown, tan or grey firing end is indicative of correct engine running conditions and the selection of the appropriate heat rating plug

White deposits have accumulated from excessive amounts of oil in the combustion chamber or through the use of low quality oil. Remove deposits or a hot spot may form

Black sooty deposits indicate an over-rich fuel/air mixture, or a malfunctioning ignition system. If no improvement is obtained, try one grade hotter plug

Wet, oily carbon deposits form an electrical leakage path along the insulator nose, resulting in a misfire. The cause may be a badly worn engine or a malfunctioning ignition system

A blistered white insulator or melted electrode indicates over-advanced ignition timing or a malfunctioning cooling system. If correction does not prove effective, try a colder grade plug

A worn spark plug not only wastes fuel but also overloads the whole ignition system because the increased gap requires higher voltage to initiate the spark. This condition can also affect air pollution

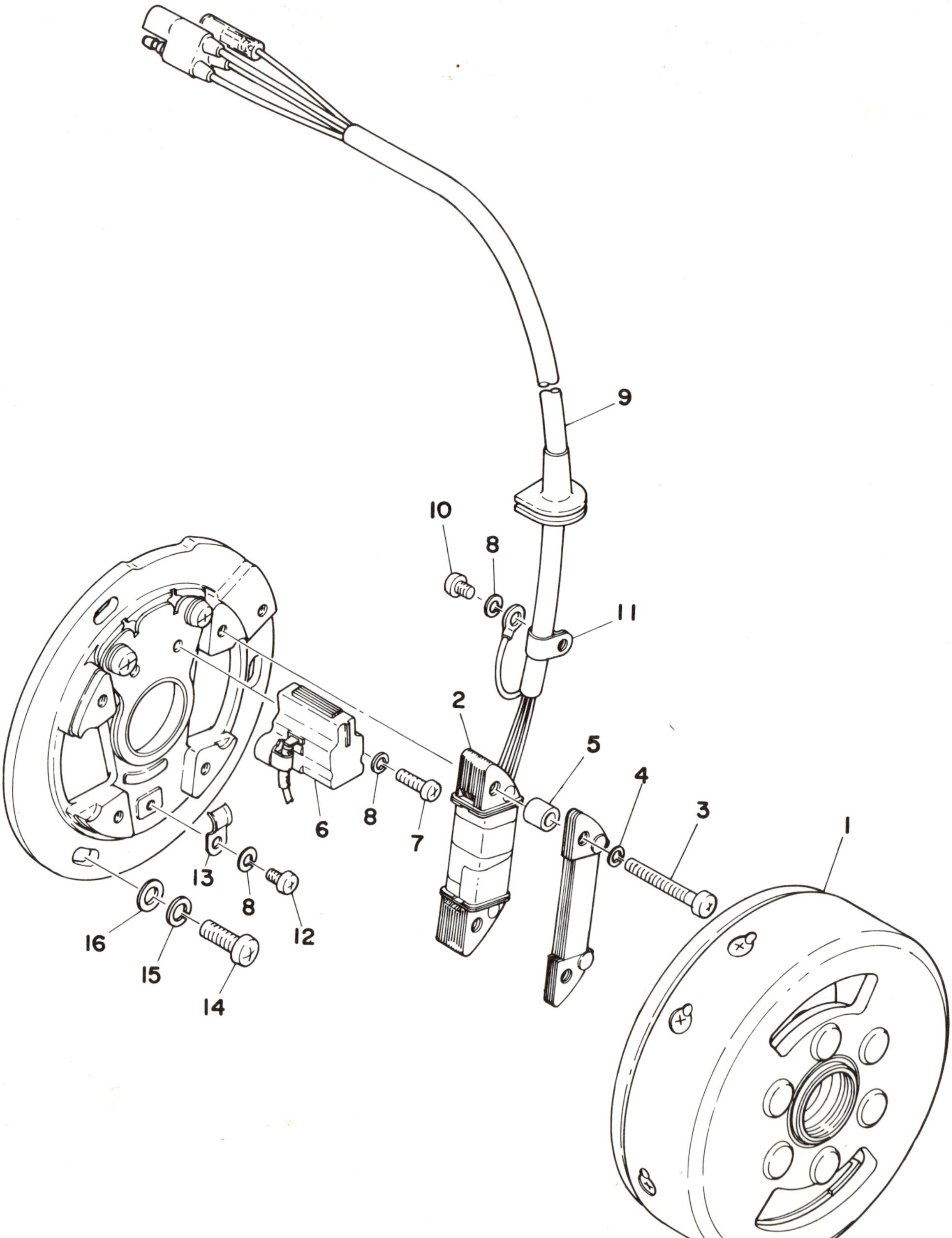

Fig. 3.2 CDI magneto (DT 400B model)

1 Flywheel
2 Ignition source coil
3 Screw - 2 off
4 Spring washer - 2 off
5 Spacer - 2 off
6 Pulser coil
7 Screw - 2 off
8 Spring washer - 4 off
9 Harness assembly
10 Screw
11 Lead clip
12 Screw
13 Clamp
14 Pan head screw - 3 off
15 Spring washer - 3 off
16 Plain washer - 3 off

Chapter 3: Ignition system

contact-breaker assembly and the ignition coil. Although the connection at the contact-breaker is detachable, the remaining wires are permanently fixed. Those motorcycles (AT series) fitted with starter generator units have a condenser with a single wire connection which runs to the contact-breaker unit. This wire is easily detachable as it is fixed in the normal way by a screw and nut.

4 CDI systems work on an entirely different principle and do not have replaceable condensers.

6 Condenser - testing

Without the appropriate test equipment (resistance meter) there is no means of verifying whether a condenser is still serviceable. Bearing in mind the low cost of a condenser it is far more satisfactory to check whether it is malfunctioning by direct replacement.

7 CDI (Capacitor Discharge Ignition) unit: location and testing

1 The CDI unit is attached to the frame below the dual seat by two screws. This unit contains the phase inversion circuit, exciter coil diode, thyristor, condenser (capacitor) and diode. If the efficiency of any component within this unit is suspect, it must be tested using a special Yamaha pocket tester. As the average owner/rider is unlikely to have access to this specialised equipment, it is recommended that the machine be checked by a Yamaha service agent or auto-electrical expert.

8 Ignition coil: checking

1 The ignition coil is a sealed unit, designed to give long service without need of attention. It is mounted below the frame top-tube and attached to a bracket, access to which is obscured by the fuel tank. If a weak spark and difficult starting indicate suspect performance of the ignition coil, it should be tested by a Yamaha service agent or an auto-electrical expert, who will have the necessary test equipment. A quick test of the coil condition may be made without test equipment, as follows: With the ignition switched on, hold the HT lead between 5 mm and 7 mm away from the cylinder head. If the spark jumps the gap when the engine is turned over quickly it may be assumed that the ignition coil is in good condition. The HT lead suppressor cap **must be removed for this test, a small pin or nail can be pressed** into the end of the HT lead, to allow the spark to jump more effectively.

2 As the ignition coil is a sealed unit, it is not possible to effect a satisfactory repair. In the event of coil failure a new unit must be fitted.

9 Ignition timing: checking and setting (contact-breaker models)

1 If the ignition timing is correct the contact-breaker points must be on the verge of opening when the piston's relationship with TDC is as follows for each model:

250 cc $3.2 {}^{+0.2}_{-0.5}$ *mm BTDC*

360 cc $2.9 {}^{+0.2}_{-0.5}$ *mm BTDC*

2 Before carrying out any ignition timing checks, make certain that the contact-breaker is adjusted to its recommended setting within the range 0.012 - 0.016 inch (0.3 - 0.4 mm).

3 Remove the spark plug from the cylinder head and fit a 14 mm dial gauge adaptor. Install the dial gauge and set it so that a zero reading shows, when the piston is **exactly** at TDC. Rotate the crankshaft backwards until it reaches precisely the recommended piston position. The contact breaker points must be just about to separate in this position for correct ignition timing.

4 The RT1-B is fitted with a governor which must be jammed in the fully opened position to ensure correct ignition timing.

5 If the ignition timing is found to be incorrect, it can be adjusted only by altering the contact breaker points gap. Badly worn or overdressed points will preclude accurate ignition timing. If this is the case they must be renewed.

10 Ignition timing: checking and setting (CDI models)

1 On those machines using CDI systems, the ignition timing is set by the pulser coil generated voltage, so that the ignition timing cannot be checked accurately in a static state. However, during manufacture, a line will have been stamped adjacent to the stator top mounting screw, which when aligned with a similar mark on the casing, will give accurate timing.

2 For guaranteed accuracy, the timing should be checked using a strobe system. It is recommended that the machine be taken to a service agent for this operation.

11 Ignition switch

1 The ignition switch is a multipoint switch which also controls the lighting circuits. The switch will be found either between the speedometer and rev-counter or on the left-hand side of the machine, attached to the frame below the fuel tank.

2 The switch is unlikely to malfunction during the normal serviceable life of the machine and does not require any maintenance. If an ignition failure occurs and the switch appears to be responsible, a voltmeter or testing bulb may be used to check correct current flow through switch. If the switch is at fault, it must be renewed as a complete unit as it is sealed and cannot be repaired.

12 Spark plug: checking and resetting the gap

1 A single 14 mm long-reach spark plug is fitted to all models. The correct reach is ¾ in. (19 mm).

8.1 Ignition coil mounted on top tube

2 All models are fitted as standard with NGK spark plugs, the correct type for each model being as follows:

DTI and DTI-C	B-7E
DTI-B and DTI-E	B-8ES
DT2 and DT3	B-8ES
RTI-B, RT2 and RT3 and DT400	B-9ES

3 Certain operating conditions may dictate a change in spark plug grade. If riding conditions are mild, the engine may require a slightly hotter plug than is supplied as standard. Unusually severe riding conditions may require a slightly colder plug.

4 Always carry a spare spark plug of the correct type. The plug in a two-stroke engine lead a particularly hard life and is liable to fail more readily than when fitted to a four-stroke.

5 Never overtighten a spark plug, otherwise there is risk of stripping the threads from the cylinder head, especially as it is cast in light alloy. A stripped thread can be repaired without having to scrap the cylinder head by using a 'Helicoil' thread insert. This is a low cost service operated by a number of dealers.

6 Use the correct size spanner when tightening a plug, otherwise the spanner may slip and damage the ceramic insulation. The plug should be tightened sufficiently to seat firmly on its sealing washer and no more.

7 Make sure that the plug insulation cap is a good fit and free from cracks. Apart from acting as an insulator from water and road dirt, it contains the suppressor for eliminating radio and TV interference.

The correct plug gap for all models is 0.020 - 0.024 inch (0.5 - 0.6 mm.

13 Fault diagnosis - ignition system

Symptom	Cause	Remedy
Engine will not start	No spark at plug	Faulty ignition switch. Check whether current is reaching ignition coil.
	Weak spark at plug	Dirty contact breaker points require cleaning. Contact breaker gap has closed up. Re-set.
Engine starts but runs erratically	Intermittent or weak spark	Renew plug. If no improvement check whether points are arcing. If so replace condenser.
	Ignition over-advanced	Check ignition timing and if necessary reset.
	Plug lead insulation breaking down	Check for breaks in outer covering, especially near frame.
Engine difficult to start and runs sluggishly. Overheats	Ignition timing retarded	Check ignition timing and advance to correct setting.

Chapter 4 Frame and forks

Contents

General description ... 1	Foot rests: examination and removal ... 12
Front forks: removal from the frame ... 2	Rear brake pedal: examination and renovation ... 13
Front forks: dismantling ... 3	Kickstarter lever: examination and renovation ... 14
Steering head bearings: examination and renovation ... 4	Dual seat: removal and replacement ... 15
Front forks: examination and renovation ... 5	Speedometer and tachometer heads: removal and replacement ... 16
Front forks: replacement ... 6	
Steering damper: function and replacement ... 7	Speedometer and tachometer drive cables: examination and maintenance ... 17
Frame: examination and renovation ... 8	
Swinging arm rear fork: dismantling, examination and renovation ... 9	Speedometer and tachometer drive: location and examination ... 18
Rear suspension units: examination ... 10	Cleaning the machine ... 19
Prop stand: examination ... 11	Fault diagnosis: frame and forks ... 20

1 General description

The Yamaha Enduro trail bikes employ a common frame and fork assembly of conventional design. The front forks are telescopic, oil-damped units. The frame is of the full cradle type, employing duplex tubes. Rear suspension is provided by a swinging arm fork, with replaceable bushes, controlled by hydraulically damped, adjustable rear suspension units.

2 Front forks: removal from the frame

1 It is unlikely that the front forks will need to be removed from the frame as a complete unit unless the steering head bearings require attention or the forks are damaged in an accident.
2 If the forks or front wheel are to be removed it will be necessary to block the motorcycle up until the front wheel is clear of the ground; this may be done by putting wooden blocks under the flatest portion of the crankcase guard. With the front wheel clear, place a small block in front of the rear wheel to prevent the machine accidentally rolling forward.
3 Start by removing either the control cables from the handle bar control levers or the levers complete with cables. The shape of the handlebars and the length of the control cables will probably dictate which method is used.
4 Detach the handlebars from their mountings. The mountings are split clamps which are retained by two chromed bolts each. Once the upper clamp halves are removed the handlebars will be free, except for the indicator wiring and the lighting dipswitch wiring which can be disconnected on removal of the headlamp.
5 Remove the tachometer and speedometer drive cables from the meter heads and their respective take-off points. The tachometer drive is taken from the forward portion of the right-hand crankcase, the cable being retained by a knurled union ring. The speedometer drive is taken from the front wheel brake plate where the cable is retained by a circlip lying recessed in the drive take-off boss.
6 Remove the meter mounting plate complete with the tachometer and the speedometer heads. It is held onto the top fork yoke by two bolts and spring washer running through rubber antivibration bushes in the mounting plate. Detach the headlamp rim, which is retained by a single self-tapping screw which passes through the headlamp shell directly below the right-hand headlamp mounting bolt, and disconnect the wiring from the main frame. The wiring system inside the headlamp will appear confusing but is colour coded for easy replacement. The headlamp shell is secured to the lugs on the fork shrouds by two chrome bolts. With these removed the headlamp shell and the two meters may be removed.
7 Detach the front brake cable from the front brake operating lever by pulling the barrel nipple over the lever end. Pull the outer cable stop from its housing and slide the inner cable through the retainer slit. The cable is now free to be pulled through from under the mudguard stay.
8 The front wheel can be released by withdrawing the spindle, which passes through the left-hand fork leg and is retained by a nut and washer. Note that it will be necessary to slacken the two nuts which secure the clamp around the head of the spindle, at the extreme end of the right-hand fork leg. Between the clamp and spindle is a collar which should be removed after the spindle is withdrawn. The spindle head is drilled to make a tommy bar which may be inserted to aid removal. The wheel will pull clear after the anchorage slot on the brake plate has disengaged from the abutment on the left-hand fork leg. If desired, the front mudguard can be removed at this stage. It is secured to the inside of each fork leg by three bolts and washers which, when removed, will release the stays and the mudguard as a complete unit.
9 Unscrew the large nut in the centre of the fork top yoke and remove it along with the large chamfered washer. Slacken the three fork top yoke pinch bolts, two of which clamp the inner

2.4 Handlebars clamped by four bolts

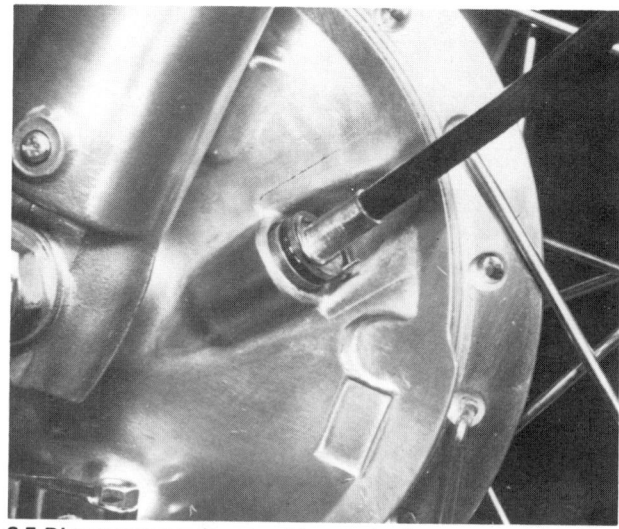
2.5 Disconnect speedometer drive at wheel

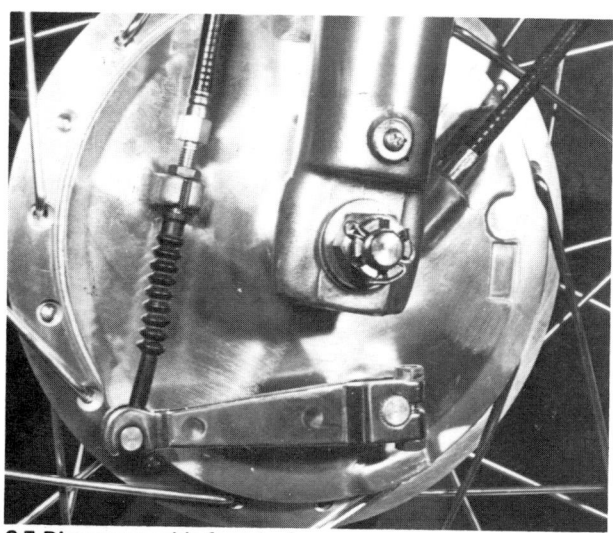
2.7 Disconnect cable from brake arm

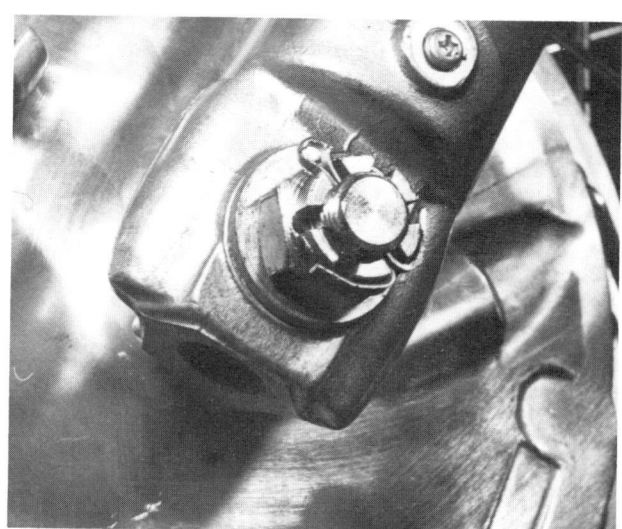
2.8a Remove split pin and remove nut

2.8b Spindle held by clamp

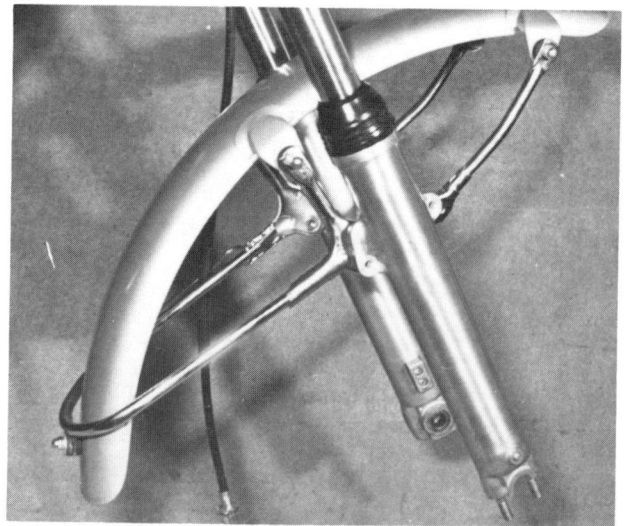
2.8c Mudguard retained by four bolts and ...

Chapter 4: Frame and forks

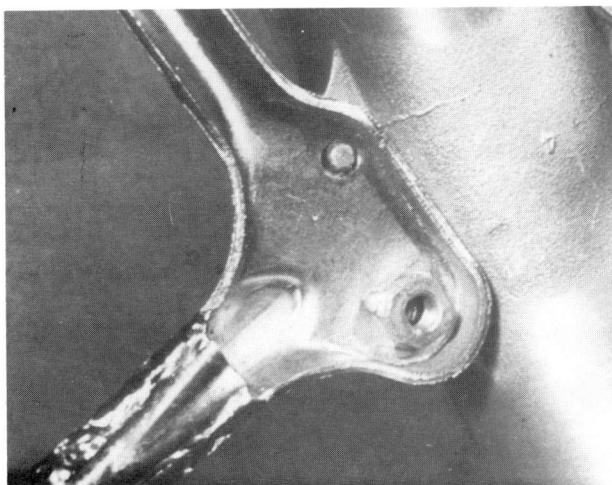
2.8d ... located by dowel pins

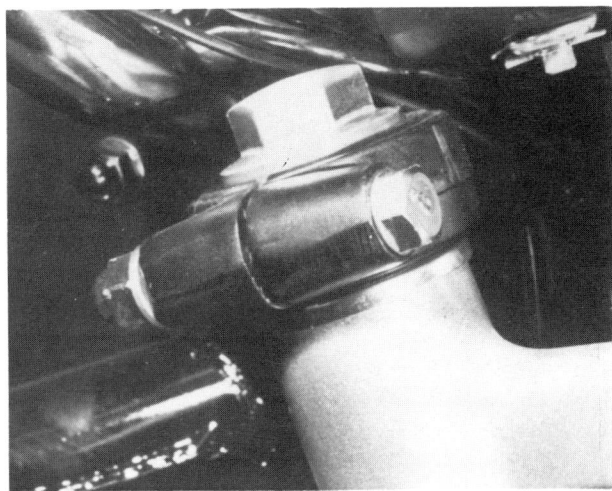
2.12a Loosen top clamp pinch bolt and ...

2.12b ... the two lower clamp pinch bolts

2.12c Fork leg will pull free

3.1 Drain fork leg before dismantling

fork legs, the other clamping the yoke to the steering column. The top yoke can now be lifted away, if necessary, by lightly tapping the underside with a rawhide mallet to free it initially.

10 Unscrew the slotted nut at the head of the steering column, using a C spanner of the correct shape. As the nut is slackened, the forks will gradually ease away from the steering head, uncovering the uncaged ball bearings of the steering head races. Make provision to catch the ball bearings as they are released; only the lower bearings will drop free since the upper bearings will most probably remain seated in the cup retaining them.

11 When the slotted nut has been removed from the steering column completely, the fork can be withdrawn from the lower end of the steering head as a complete unit. It may be necessary to raise the machine even higher during this operation, so that the fork stem will clear the steering head.

3 Front forks: dismantling

1 The fork legs can be dismantled individually, without need to disturb the steering head bearings. The preliminary dismantling is accomplished by following the procedure detailed in paragraphs 5 - 8 of the preceding Section, then continuing with the instructions given in this Section, after removing the chromium plated

74

Chapter 4: Frame and forks

Fig. 4.1 Front forks

1 L.H. lower leg
2 R.H. lower leg
3 Circlip - 2 off
4 Damper piston - 2 off
5 Damper rod - 2 off
6 Fork spring - 2 off
7 Stanchion - 2 off
8 Spring seat - 2 off
9 Spacer - 2 off
10 Bush - 2 off
11 'O' ring - 2 off
12 Fork nut - 2 off
13 Oil seal - 2 off
14 Washer - 2 off
15 Oil seal clip - 2 off
16 Felt ring - 2 off
17 Washer - 2 off
18 Dust cover - 2 off
19 L.H. lower cover
20 L.H. lower cover
21 Packing washer - 2 off
22 Cover lower guide - 2 off
23 L.H. upper cover
24 R.H. upper cover
25 Cover upper guide - 2 off
26 'O' ring - 2 off
27 Cap washer - 2 off
28 Fork cap - 2 off
29 Steering head column
30 Pinch bolt - 2 off
31 Spring washer - 2 off
32 Cable holder
33 Bolt - 2 off
34 Washer - 2 off
35 Bolt
36 Spring washer
37 Dust excluder
38 Lower cup
39 Lower lone
40 Ball bearing ¼" - 19 off
41 Upper cup
42 Upper cone
43 Ball bearing 3/16" - 22 off
44 Race cover
45 Adjuster nut
46 Top yoke
47 Pinch bolt
48 Nut
49 Spring washer - 7 off
50 Pinch bolt - 2 off
51 Washer
52 Crown bolt
53 Spacer
54 Special washer
55 Damper shaft
56 Handlebar top clamp - 2 off
57 Handlebar lower clamp - 2 off
58 Nut - 2 off
59 Spring washer - 2 off
60 Bolt - 4 off
61 Damper plate (1)
62 Damper plate (2)
63 Damper plate (3)
64 Clip
65 Split pin
66 Mudguard complete
67 Rear stay assembly
68 L.H. front stay
69 R.H. front stay
70 Rubber buffer - 5 off
71 Spacer collar - 5 off
72 Bolt - 5 off
73 Nut - 5 off
74 Washer - 5 off
75 Bolt - 4 off
76 Spring washer - 9 off
77 Nut - 2 off
78 Bolt - 2 off
79 Spring washer - 2 off
80 Reflector - 2 off
81 Spring washer - 2 off
82 Plain washer - 2 off

bolts from the top of each fork leg and draining off the damping oil.

2 If both fork legs are to be dismantled, strip them separately, using an identical procedure. There is less chance of unwittingly interchanging parts if this approach is adopted.

3 Slacken the pinch bolts through the lower fork yoke and pull the complete fork leg from the assembly, leaving the upper fork shroud in position. Invert the fork with the spring still in position and using an hexagonal Allen key, remove the socket screw recessed into the curved portion of the lower fork end, through which the wheel spindle normally passes. The spring pressure is essential, to prevent the fork damper unit from rotating whilst this socket screw is removed. Remove the chromed spring retaining bolt from the top of the fork leg.

4 Remove the top split spacing collar and top spring seat along with the main spring. The chrome dust cover followed by the dust seal should be pulled upwards and out of position along the inner sliding tube. The operations described in the remainder of this paragraph differ, depending on the particular forks utilised for each model.

3.3a Remove damper assembly holding screw

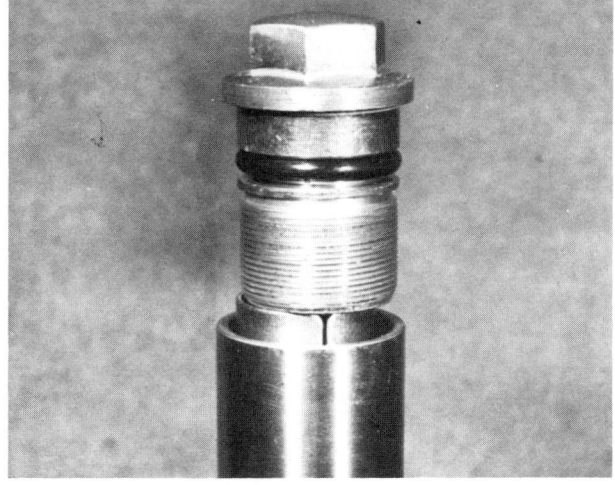

3.3b Unscrew fork tube cap and ...

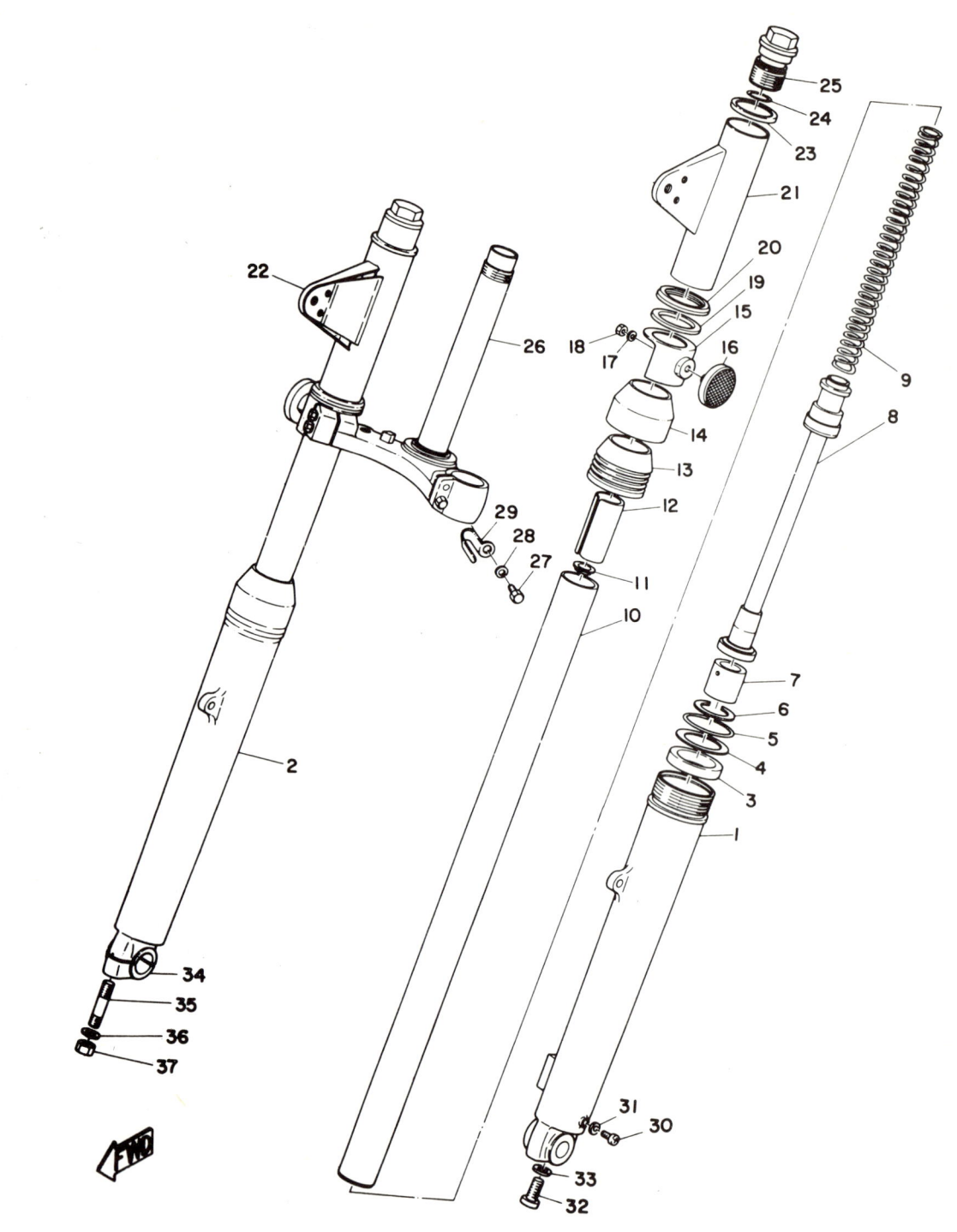

Fig. 4.2 Front forks

1. L.H. lower leg
2. R.H. lower leg
3. Oil seal - 2 off
4. Washer - 2 off
5. Oil seal retainer circlip - 2 off
6. Circlip - 2 off
7. Piston - 2 off
8. Damper rod - 2 off
9. Fork spring - 2 off
10. Stanchion - 2 off
11. Upper spring seat - 2 off
12. Spacer - 2 off
13. Dust cover - 2 off
14. Dust seal cover - 2 off
15. Lower cover - 2 off
16. Reflector - 2 off
17. Spring washer - 2 off
18. Nut - 2 off
19. Upper cover packing - 2 off
20. Upper cover lower guide - 2 off
21. L.H. upper cover
22. R.H. upper cover
23. Upper cover upper guide - 2 off
24. Packing - 2 off
25. Cap bolt - 2 off
26. Lower yoke
27. Pinch bolt - 4 off
28. Spring washer - 4 off
29. Cable holder
30. Drain plug - 2 off
31. Drain plug gasket - 2 off
32. Bolt - 2 off
33. Washer - 2 off
34. Spindle clamp
35. Stud - 2 off
36. Spring washer - 2 off
37. Nut - 2 off

3.3c ... remove spacer and spring guide

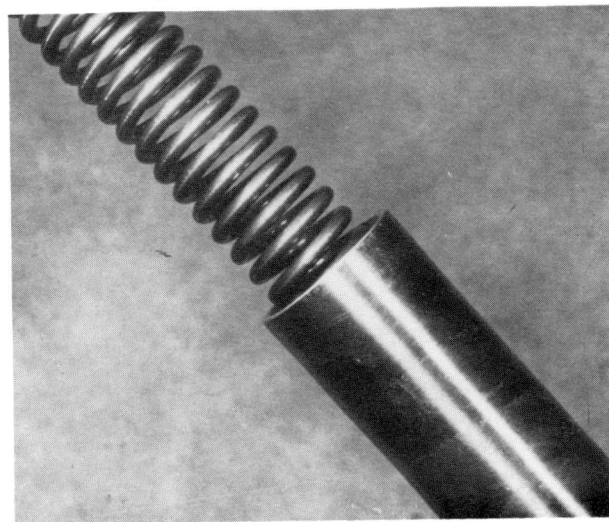
3.3d Pull out main spring

3.4 Prise off dust cap and ...

3.5a ... pull the fork tube out

3.5b Remove seating spacer

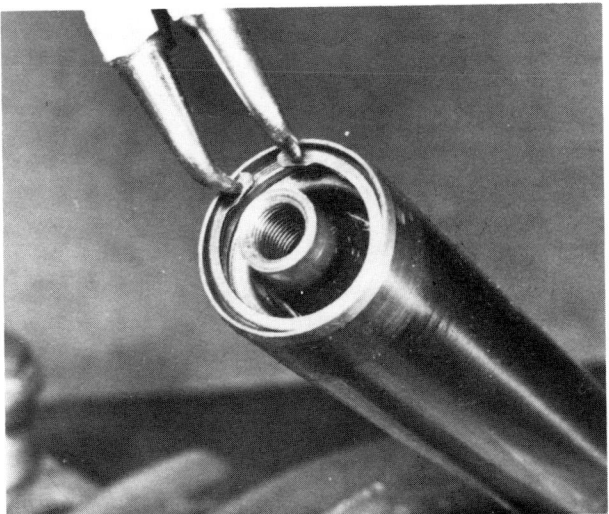
3.5c Removal of the circlip will allow ...

Chapter 4: Frame and forks

For one piece fork lower legs

5 At this stage the fork tube (stanchion) may be withdrawn from the outer fork leg, the damper unit being withdrawn at the same time. To remove the damper unit from the inner fork tube, invert the fork leg and detach the circlip inside the tapered bottom end. The damper assembly, complete with piston, can now be drawn out as a complete assembly unit. No further dismantling is necessary.

For two piece fork lower legs

6 Before the fork tube (stanchion) can be withdrawn from the lower fork leg, it will be necessary to unscrew the outer fork nut which houses the fork slider oil seal and O ring and which retains the bush and spacer. It is very easy to damage the finish of the chromed outer nut during dismantling, the operation should be carried out as follows. Place a double thickness of tyre inner tubing between the opened jaws of a bench vice. Position the fork leg between the jaws, and gently tighten the vice against the outer nut. Using a strap wrench or close fitting tommy bar through the lower fork leg spindle eye, turn the fork leg in an anticlockwise direction until the nut is free. The outer nut can be easily deformed by applying too much pressure with the vice. This will have the effect of locking the threads. The rubber inner tubing will give a high degree of grip without the vice having to be locked up too tightly.

7 With the nut removed the fork tube (stanchion) can be withdrawn along with the damper unit. Invert the lower fork leg and shake out the short sub-spring which lies below the spacer. The damper unit can be withdrawn once its retaining circlip, housed in the tapered end of the fork tube (stanchion), is removed.

4 Steering head bearings: examination and renovation

1 Before reassembly of the forks is commenced, examine the steering head races. The ball bearing tracks of the respective cup and cone bearings should be polished and free from indentations or cracks. If wear or damage is evident, the cups and cones must be renewed as a complete set. They are a tight press fit and should be drifted out of position.

2 Ball bearings are cheap. If the originals are marked or discoloured, they should be renewed. To hold the steel balls in position during reassembly, pack the bearings with grease.

3 Note that the top ball race contains twenty two 3/16 inch ball bearings and the lower race contains nineteen ¼ inch ball bearings. There is space for the addition of one extra ball, but this must be left empty to prevent the ball bearings from skidding on one another, a situation that would greatly accelerate the rate of wear.

5 Front forks: examination and renovation

1 The parts most likely to wear over an extended period of service are the slider bush (if fitted), the fork tube (stanchion) and damper assembly and the fork oil seal. Wear is normally accompanied by a tendency for the forks to judder when the front brake is applied and it should be possible to detect the increased amount of play by pulling and pushing on the handlebars when the front brake is on fully. This type of wear should not be confused with slack steering head bearings, which can give identical results. A worn or damaged oil seal may produce oil leakage at the top of the lower fork leg; this fault will be self-evident.

2 Renewal of the worn parts is quite straightforward. Particular care is necessary when renewing the oil seal. Do not try and remove the oil seal retaining circlip unless a new seal is needed as it is almost impossible to move the circlip without damaging the seal. In order to avoid damage to the feather edge of a new oil seal, grease the seal and the fork tube before assembly.

3 After a long period of time, particularly if sludge has developed within the fork legs, the damper unit valve holes may become partially blocked, they may be cleared either with an air line or by the use of a pipe cleaner as used by pipe smokers.

4 It is possible after an extended period of service for the fork springs to take a permanent set, ie become fatigued until they no longer return to their correct length after each fork movement. If the fork springs are suspect, take them to your local Yamaha agent and compare their length with that of new springs. Always replace fork springs as a pair, never individually as this will upset the roadholding and produce rapid wear in the new spring.

5 Check the outer surface of the fork tube for scratches or roughness. It is only too easy to damage the oil seal during reassembly, if these high spots are not eased down. The fork tubes are unlikely to bend unless the machine is damaged in an accident. Any significant bend will be detected by eye, but if there is any doubt about straightness, roll the tubes on a flat surface. If the tubes are bent, they must be renewed. Unless specialised repair equipment is available, it is rarely practicable to straighten them to the necessary standard.

6 The dust seals must be in good order if they are to fulfill their proper function. Replace any that are split or damaged.

7 Damping is effected by the damper units contained within each fork tube. The damping action can be controlled within certain limits by changing the viscosity of the oil used as the damping medium, although a change is unlikely to prove necessary except in extremes of climate.

6 Front forks: replacement

1 Replace the front forks by reversing either of the dismantling procedures described in Sections 2 and 3 of this Chapter, whichever the more appropriate. Make sure the abutment of the brake plate align correctly with the retaining slot cast in the left-hand lower fork leg.

2 Before fully tightening the front wheel spindle, right-hand spindle clamp, fork yoke pinch bolts and the chromium plated bolts in the top of each fork leg, bounce the forks several times to ensure that they work freely and settle down in their original positions. Complete the final tightening from the front wheel spindle upward.

3 Do not forget to add the correct quantity of damping oil to each fork leg before the bolts in the top are replaced and tightened. Each fork should be filled with 175 cc (5.85 fl. oz) of 10W30 grade oil, with the exception of the RT1 model which should have 210 cc (7.1 fl. oz) of the same viscosity oil.

4 Check the adjustment of the steering head bearings before the machine is used on the road and again shortly afterwards, when they settle down. If the bearings are too slack, fork judder will occur. There should be no play at the headraces when the handlebars are pulled and pushed hard, with the front brake applied hard.

5 Overtight headraces are equally undesirable. It is possible to place a pressure of several tons on the head bearings by overtightening, even though the handlebars may seem to turn quite freely. Overtight bearings will cause the machine to roll at low speeds and give imprecise steering. Adjustment is correct if there is no play in the bearings and the handlebars swing to full lock either side when the machine is on the centre stand with the front wheel clear of the ground. Only a light tap on each end should cause the handlebars to swing.

7 Steering damper: function and replacement

1 A steering damper is fitted to the Yamaha trail bikes to aid control over very rough ground and improve steering stability at high speeds. The steering damper acts on the steering head as added friction which means that the front wheel is less easily deflected by uneven ground and rocks etc.

2 The non-adjustable damper is of the vane type, comprising a moving paddle, which rotates in a damping medium of oil, when the handlebars are moved.

Chapter 4: Frame and forks

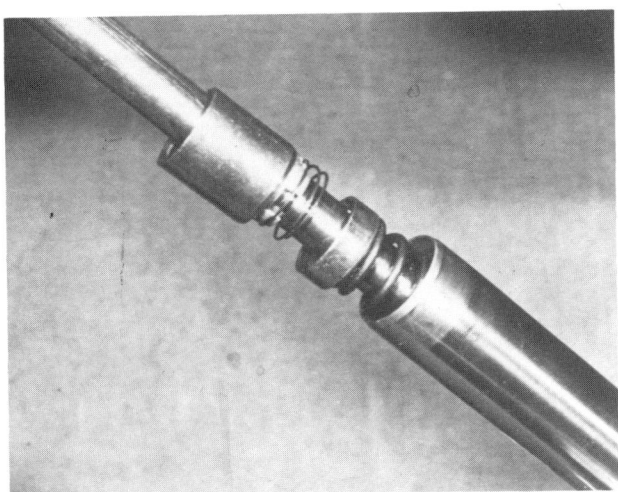

3.5d ... complete damper unit to be pulled free

5.5 Oil seal retained by circlip and washer

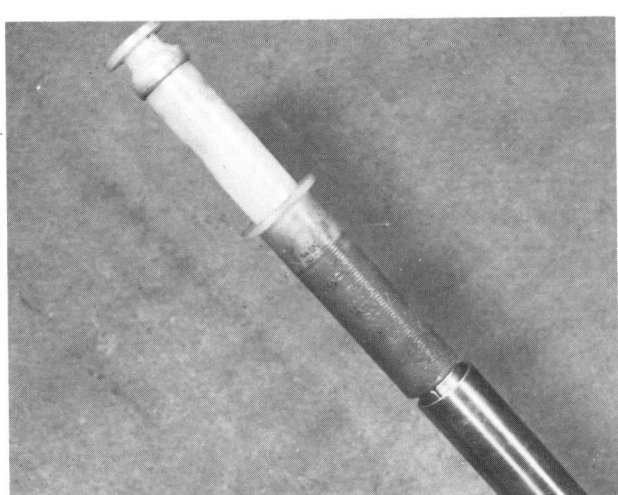

6.3 Fill fork leg with correct quantity of oil

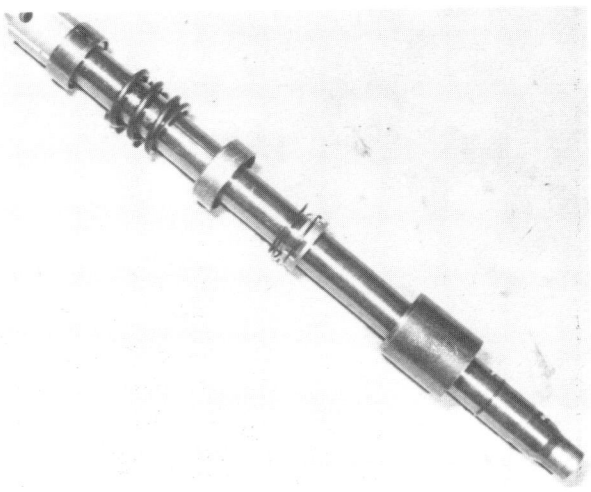

5.3 Assembly sequence of damper unit

3 If any faults develop in the damper assembly it should be removed as described below and returned to a Yamaha service agent who will advise either servicing or replacement of the unit.
4 The main damper case is retained in position by a lug which locates with an abutment on the frame, directly behind the lower fork yoke. At right angles to the internal paddle is the splined damper shaft, which locates the bottom of the steering head column, and which is retained by a small bolt and spring washer from the rear of the bottom fork yoke. With the splined shaft retaining bolt loosened, the damper assembly may be pulled from position as a complete unit.
5 When replacing the damper unit make certain that the splined shaft is in the centre of its maximum travel, otherwise the steering lock will diminish when turning right or left, depending on the incorrect positioning of the internal paddle. The locating lug must be correctly positioned with the abutment on the frame during replacement, or the damper unit will not function correctly and may cause dangerous irregularities in the steering.

8 Frame: examination and renovation

1 The frame is unlikely to require attention unless it is damaged as the result of an accident. In many cases, replacement of the frame is the only satisfactory course of action, if it is badly out of alignment. Comparatively few frame repair specialists have the necessary mandrels and jigs essential for the accurate resetting of the frame and, even then there is no means of assessing to what extent the frame may have been overstressed such that a later fatigue failure may occur.
2 After a machine has covered an extensive mileage, it is advisable to keep a close watch for signs of cracking or splitting at any of the welded joints. Rust can cause weakness at these joints, particularly if they are unpainted. Minor repairs can be effected by welding or brazing, depending on the extent of the damage found.
3 A frame out of alignment will cause handling problems and may even promote 'speed wobbles' in a particular speed range. If misalignment is suspected as the result of an accident, it will be necessary to strip the machine so that the frame can be checked, and if needs be, renewed.

9 Swinging arm rear fork: dismantling, examination and renovation

1 The rear fork of the frame assembly pivots on a detachable bush within each end of the fork crossmember and a pivot shaft which passes through frame lugs and the centre of each of the

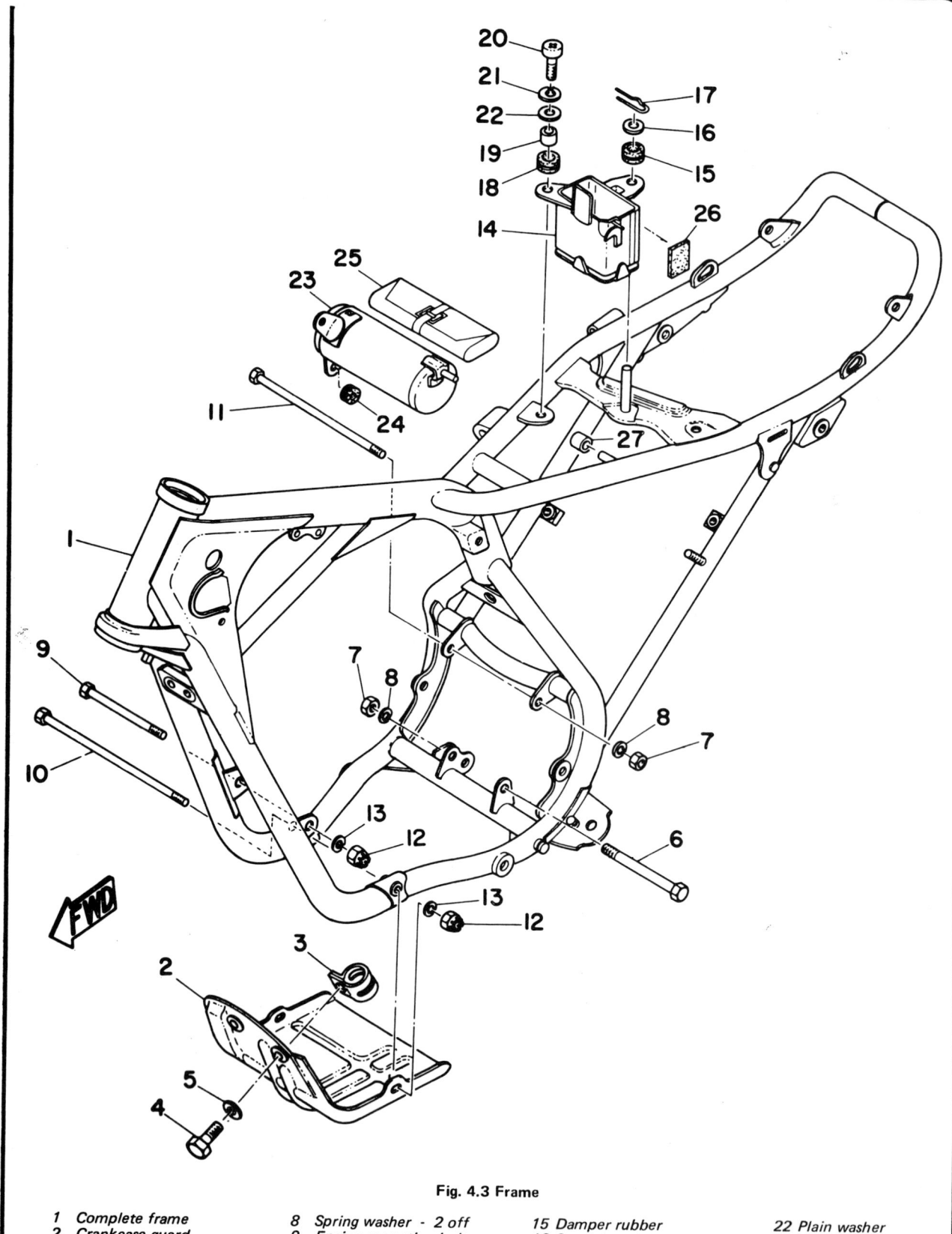

Fig. 4.3 Frame

1 Complete frame
2 Crankcase guard
3 Guard bracket - 2 off
4 Bolt - 2 off
5 Plain washer - 2 off
6 Engine mounting bolt
7 Nut - 2 off
8 Spring washer - 2 off
9 Engine mounting bolt
10 Engine mounting bolt
11 Engine mounting bolt
12 Nut - 2 off
13 Spring washer - 2 off
14 Battery box
15 Damper rubber
16 Special washer
17 Clip
18 Damper rubber
19 Spacer
20 Screw
21 Spring washer
22 Plain washer
23 Tool box
24 Damper rubber
25 Tool kit
26 Battery seating
27 Damper rubber

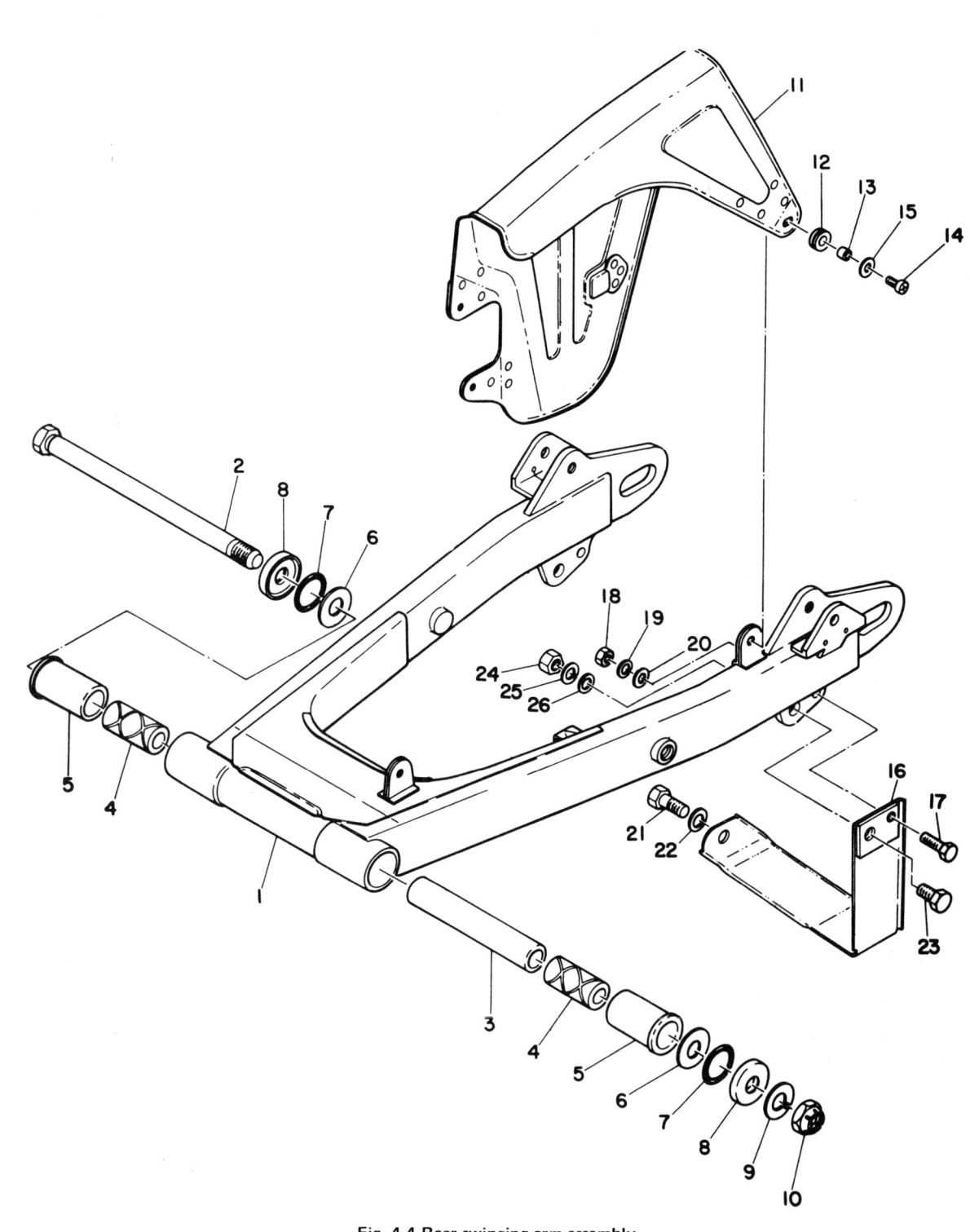

Fig. 4.4 Rear swinging arm assembly

1 Swinging arm fork
2 Pivot shaft
3 Distance piece
4 Inner bush - 2 off
5 Outer bush - 2 off
6 Shim - 2 off
7 'O' ring
8 Thrust cover - 2 off
9 Spring washer
10 Nut
11 Chain case
12 Grommet - 3 off
13 Spacer - 3 off
14 Screw - 3 off
15 Washer - 3 off
16 Damper unit - 2 off
17 Bolt - 4 off
18 Nut
19 Spring washer - 2 off
20 Washer
21 Bolt
22 Spring washer
23 Bolt
24 Nut
25 Spring washer
26 Plain washer

9.3a Disconnect brake rod at arm and ...

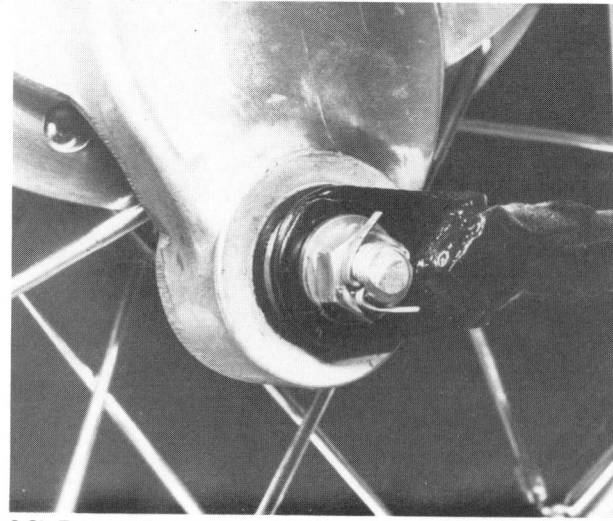
9.3b Remove the torque arm bolt

9.4a Remove spindle nut and washer and ...

9.4b ... pull spindle out to release rear wheel

9.5a Remove pivot shaft nut and knock out pivot

9.5b Disconnect the rear suspension units

Chapter 4: Frame and forks

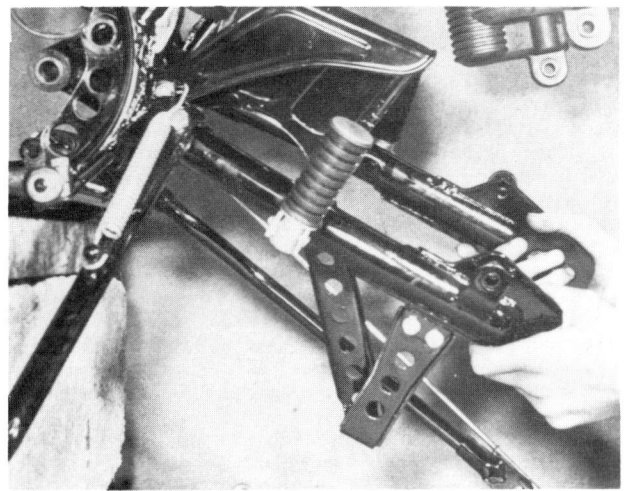
9.6 Pull swinging arm from frame

9.7a Prise rubber chain guard off followed by ...

9.7b ... the dust excluder cap

9.7c Centre bush will push out and ...

9.7d ... outer bush will knock out

two bushes. It is quite easy to renovate the swinging arm pivots when wear necessitates attention.

2 To remove the swinging arm fork, first place the machine on suitable blocks so that the rear wheel is clear of the ground. The blocks should be placed as far to the rear of the machine as possible so that the weight falls onto the front wheel. Detach the rear drive chain, preferably whilst the main link is on the rear wheel sprocket and then remove the chainguard. The chainguard is secured by two crosshead screws which screw into two lugs on the frame, one near the rear damper pivot bracket and the other a few inches from the rear fork pivot shaft. It is not imperative to remove the chainguard during pivot bush replacement, but removal will ensure that the guard is not damaged.

3 Remove the rear brake actuating rod at the brake plate lever by unscrewing the adjustment nut and then applying the brake. This will draw the brake rod from the lever clevis pin. Remove the adjustment spring and clevis pin to avoid loss. Detach the rear brake torque rod at the brake plate by removing the split pin, nut and washer.

4 Loosen the chain tension adjusting nuts and remove the rear wheel spindle nut from the left of the machine. The spindle may be knocked out with a rawhide mallet, which will leave the rear wheel free for removal. Note the position of the right-hand rear wheel spacing collar in relation to the brake plate and chain

tension adjuster. The chain tensioner will most probably fall free when the rear wheel is removed.

5 Remove the rear suspension units from the rear fork. They are retained by a single bolt each, running from the outside of their brackets through the damper eyes into a threaded portion on the inside bracket. There are, therefore, no nuts.

6 Remove the rear fork pivot nut from the right-hand side of the shaft and knock the shaft out to the left. The swinging arm fork is now free and may be pulled backwards away from the mounting.

7 Wear will take place mainly on the bearing surfaces of the two inner bushes and their respective outer bushes, but to a lesser degree on the pivot shaft itself. After removal and cleaning these components should be inspected and replaced where necessary. No difficulty should be encountered in pushing out the inner bushes or knocking out the outer bushes. This can be accomplished with a long screwdriver.

8 Reassemble the bushes and the swinging arm fork by reversing the procedure given for dismantling. Grease the bushes and the pivot shaft before reassembly on all machines, but particularly where no facility is given for further greasing at a later date.

9 Apart from causing MoT failure, or failure of equivalent roadworthiness tests, worn swinging arm pivot bearings will give imprecise handling, with a tendency for the rear of the machine to twitch or wander. The play can be best detected by placing the machine with the rear wheel clear of the ground and pushing and pulling the rear fork in a lateral direction, when grasped at the fork ends.

10 Rear suspension units: examination

1 Rear suspension units of hydraulically damped type are used on the Yamaha trail bikes. They can be adjusted to give five different spring loadings, without removal from the machine.

2 Each rear suspension unit has a number of peg holes immediately above the adjusting notches, to facilitate adjustment. Either a C spanner or the screwdriver supplied with the original kit can be used to turn the adjusters. If spring adjustment is regularly made, it will be possible to turn the adjuster by hand as the unit will remain loose. The higher the tension in the spring, ie the shorter the spring is made by adjustment, the harder the suspension will be.

3 The suspension units are sealed and there is no means of topping up or changing the damping fluid. If the damping fails or if the unit leaks, renewal is necessary.

4 In the interests of good roadholding it is essential that both suspension units have the same load setting. If renewal is necessary, the units must be replaced as a matched pair.

11 Prop stand: examination

1 Because of the high ground clearance necessary on any machine used for 'off the road' riding the Yamaha trail bikes are not fitted with centre stands. The prop stand therefore is the main and only stand fitted.

2 The prop stand bracket is located on the left-hand side of the machine and is welded to the lower frame tube. A bolt passing through the prop stand and the bracket acts as a pivot and is retained by a castellated nut and split pin. It is important that the split pin is replaced whenever the prop stand has been removed and replaced. Failure to do this may lead to loss of the stand during riding and the possibility of an accident. An extension spring returns the stand to the retracted position, immediately the weight is taken from it. Check that the extension spring is not over stretched or worn at the end-hooks, as an accident is almost inevitable if the stand falls down whilst the machine is on the move.

12 Foot rests: examination and removal

1 On early models, the footrest assembly comprises a cross-tube to which are bolted the two footrests and the prop stand. The cross-tube is located onto the two frame tubes running below the engine by two lugs to the rear of the tube and by two bolts forward of the tube. On removal of the two bolts the footrest assembly may be pulled forwards and off the lugs as a complete unit. Each footrest is retained on the cross-tube by a single bolt which acts as a pivot. In this way the footrests will not become damaged in the event of the machine being dropped. The footrests are prevented from jumping upwards by a spring housed on the footrest pivot pin, and within the box section of the footrest. Broken springs should be renewed as a loose footrest may cause an accident.

2 The rubber foot grips are easily removable for replacement when they become worn.

3 Later models have footrests which are adjustable in a vertical plane, these are fitted onto splined lugs welded to the frame tubes. Removal of the pinch bolt to the rear of the footrest allows the unit to be pulled from position and relocated in a different position.

13 Rear brake pedal: examination and renovation

1 The rear brake pedal pivots on a shaft which passes through a bracket on the right-hand side of the machine. The pedal is retained on the shaft by splines and a pinch bolt, therefore being adjustable over a limited distance in a vertical plane. The brake operating arm is connected to pedal assembly by means of a clevis pin, washer and split pin.

2 If the brake pedal is bent or twisted in an accident, it should be removed from the shaft, having been disconnected from the stop lamp switch operating rod and returned to its original shape. The pedal may be locked in a vice and straightened using a blowlamp flame to apply heat at the area where the bend occurs.

14 Kickstart lever: examination and renovation

1 The kickstart lever is splined and is secured to its shaft by a pinch bolt. On early models the kickstart crank swivels so that it can be tucked out of the way when the engine has been started, and is retained on the kickstart lever by a spring washer, plain washer and circlip. The coiled spring-washer provides friction to the crank thereby allowing it to be moved, but retained in whatever position it is put. If the crank becomes too loose on the kickstart lever, a new coil spring washer will remedy the fault. On late models the kickstart lever together with crank swivel at a point close the splined shaft. In this case the lever is retained on the pivot by a washer and circlip, the lever being held in the operating or folded position by a detent spring and ball bearing. On both types of lever, it is advisable to remove the crank occasionally so that the swivel surfaces can be greased.

2 It is unlikely that the kickstart lever will bend in an accident unless the machine is ridden with the kickstart in the operating, not folded position. It should be removed and straightened using the same technique as that recommended for the brake lever in the previous section.

15 Dualseat: removal and replacement

1 The dualseat is attached to the right-hand frame tube by means of a pivot on which it hinges. A catch on the left-hand frame tube locks the dualseat in position, under normal riding conditions.

2 To release the dualseat from the machine, lift the catch and raise the dualseat so that the pivot on the right-hand side is

Chapter 4: Frame and forks

13.1 Brake rod held by clevis pin, washer and split pin

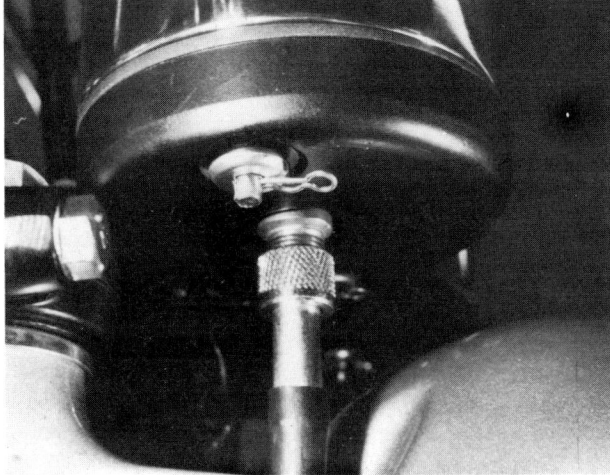

16.2 Instrument heads held by spring pins

exposed. Slide the seat prop rod along its channel and pull it out of position through the sloppy hole at the end of the channel. If the split pin through the pivot pin is removed and the pivot pin withdrawn, the dualseat can be lifted away.

3 The same operation is relevant to those machines fitted with a shorter dualseat.

4 On some later models no prop rod is fitted.

16 Speedometer and tachometer heads: removal and replacement

1 The speedometer and tachometer heads are rubber mounted on a common mounting plate, which is mounted on the top fork yoke and retained by two rubber sleeved bolts. The mounting plate complete with the two meter heads may be removed when the two mounting bolts are withdrawn, the drive cables are disconnected and the warning and lighting bulbs have been removed by pulling the holders from their seats.

2 The rubber mountings are retained to each instrument case by two split pins which pass through two short columns attached to the base of the instrument case. Do not misplace the rubber cushion interposed between the mounting bracket and the instrument case to damp out the undesirable effects of vibration.

3 Apart from defects in either the drive or the drive cable, a speedometer or tachometer that malfunctions is difficult to repair. Fit a new one, or alternatively, entrust the repair to an instrument repair specialist.

4 Remember that a speedometer in correct working order is a statutory requirement in the UK. Apart from this legal requirement, reference to the odometer reading is the best means of keeping in pace with the maintenance schedule.

17 Speedometer and tachometer drive cables: examination and maintenance

1 It is advisable to detach both cables from time to time in order to check whether they are lubricated adequately, and whether the outer coverings are compressed or damaged at any point along their run. Jerky or sluggish movements can often be attributed to a cable fault.

2 For greasing, withdraw the inner cable. After wiping off the old grease, clean with a petrol-soaked rag and examine the cable for broken stands or other damage.

3 Regrease the cable with high melting point grease, taking care not to grease the last six inches at the point where the cable enters the instrument head. If this precaution is not observed,

grease will work into the head and immobilise the movement.

4 If either instrument ceases to function, suspect a broken cable. Inspection will show whether the inner cable has broken; if so, the inner cable alone can be renewed and re-inserted in the outer casing, after greasing. Never fit a new inner cable alone if the outer covering is damaged or compressed at any point.

18 Speedometer and tachometer drive: location and examination

1 The speedometer drive gearbox is an integral part of the front wheel brake plate and is driven internally from the wheel hub. The gearbox rarely gives trouble if it is lubricated whenever the front wheel and brake plate are removed; there is no external grease nipple. If wear in the drive mechanism occurs, the worm complete with shaft can be withdrawn from the brake plate housing by unscrewing a pegged bush. The drive pinion is retained to the inside of the brake plate by a circlip, in front of the shaped driving plate that takes up the drive from the wheel hub.

2 The tachometer drive is taken from the primary drive gear through a worm gear and worm shaft to the tachometer drive cable. It is unlikely that the drive will give trouble during the normal service life of the machine. If faults occur, follow the operational sequence described in Chapter 1, Section 15, for dismantling, examination and assembly.

19 Cleaning the machine

1 After removing all surface dirt with a rag or sponge washed frequently in clean water, the machine should be allowed to dry thoroughly. Application of car polish or wax to the cycle parts will give a good finish, particularly if the machine has been neglected for a long period.

2 The plated parts of the machine should require only a wipe with a damp rag. If the plated parts are badly corroded, as may occur during the winter when the roads are salted, it is preferable to use one of the proprietary chrome cleaners. These often have an oily base which will help to prevent the corrosion from recurring.

3 If the engine parts are particularly oily, use a cleaning compound such as Gunk or Jizer. Apply the compound whilst the parts are dry and work it in with a brush so that it has the opportunity to penetrate the film of grease and oil. Finish off by washing down liberally with plenty of water, taking care that it does not enter the carburettor or the electrics. If desired, the

now clean aluminium alloy parts can be enhanced further by using a special polish such as Solvol Autosol which will fully restore their brilliance.

4 Whenever possible, the machine should be wiped down after it has been used in the wet, so that it is not garaged under damp conditions which will promote rusting. Make sure to wipe the chain and re-oil it, to prevent water from entering the rollers and causing harshness with an accompanying high rate of wear. Remember there is little chance of water entering the control cables and causing stiffness of operation if they are lubricated regularly as recommended in the Routine Maintenance Section.

20 Fault diagnosis - frame and forks

Symptom	Cause	Remedy
Machine veers either to the left or the right with hands off handlebars	Bent frame Twisted forks Wheels out of alignment	Check and replace Check and replace Check and re-align
Machine rolls at low speeds	Overtight steering head bearings	Slacken until adjustment is correct
Machine judders when front brake is applied	Slack steering head bearings Worn fork slider bushes	Tighten until adjustment is correct Dismantle forks and renew bushes
Machine pitches on uneven surfaces	Ineffective fork dampers Ineffective rear suspension units Suspension too soft	Check oil content Check whether units still have damping action Raise suspension adjustment one or two notches
Fork action stiff	Fork legs out of alignment (twisted in yokes)	Slacken yoke clamps and fork top bolts, pump fork several times then retighten from the bottom upwards
Machine wanders, steering imprecise,	Worn swinging arm pivot	Dismantle and renew bushes and pivot ot shaft

Chapter 5 Wheels, brakes and tyres

Contents

General description ... 1	Adjusting the front brake ... 8
Front wheel: examination and renovation ... 2	Adjusting the rear brake ... 9
Front brake assembly: examination and renovation ... 3	Cush drive assembly: examination and replacement ... 10
Wheel bearings: examination and replacement ... 4	Rear wheel sprocket: removal, examination and replacement 11
Front wheel: reassembly and replacement ... 5	Final drive chain: examination and lubrication ... 12
Rear wheel: examination, removal and renovation ... 6	Tyres: removal and replacement ... 13
Rear brake assembly: examination, renovation and reassembly ... 7	Security bolt ... 14
	Fault diagnosis: wheels, brakes and tyres ... 15

Specifications

	DT1	DT1-B	DT1-C	DT1-E
Tyres				
Front		3.25 x 19 inch		
Rear		4.00 x 18 inch		

	DT2	RT1-B	RT2
Tyres			
Front		3.25 x 19 inch	
Rear		4.00 x 18 inch	

	DT1	DT1-B	DT1-C	DT1-E
Tyre pressure				
Front	13 lb/inch^2	14 lb/inch^2	14 lb/inch^2	13 lb/inch^2
Rear	16 lb/inch^2	17 lb/inch^2	17 lb/inch^2	16 lb/inch^2

	DT2	RT1-B	RT2
Tyre pressure			
Front	13 lb/inch^2	13 lb/inch^2	13 lb/inch^2
Rear	16 lb/inch^2	16 lb/inch^2	16 lb/inch^2

Brakes
Type ... Internal expansion, single leading shoe
Front ... 5.8 inch (150 mm)
Rear ... 5.8 inch (150 mm)

	DT3	RT3	DT250B	DT400B
Tyres				
Front		3.00 x 21 inch		
Rear		4.00 x 18 inch		
Tyre pressure				
Front	13 lb/inch^2	13 lb/inch^2	23 lb/inch^2	23 lb/inch^2
Rear	16 lb/inch^2	16 lb/inch^2	25 lb/inch^2	25 lb/inch^2

Brakes
Type ... Internal expansion, single leading shoe
Front ... 6.3 inch (160 mm)
Rear ... 5.8 inch (150 mm)

Chapter 5: Wheels, brakes and tyres

1 General description

1 All models have 18 inch rear wheels and 19 inch front wheels, with the exception of the DT3 and RT3 and the late models which have 21 inch front wheels. Original fitted tyres are the block tread 'trials universal' type for additional grip over uneven ground. On all models steel rims are laced to cast aluminium hubs which run on journal ball bearings.

2 Front wheel: examination and renovation

1 Place the machine on blocks so that the front wheel is raised clear of the ground. Spin the wheel and check the rim alignment. Small irregularities can be corrected by tightening the spokes in the affected area, although a certain amount of practice is necessary to prevent over-correction. Any flats in the wheel rim should be evident at the same time. These are more difficult to remove and in most cases it will be necessary to have the wheel rebuilt on a new rim. Apart from the effect on stability, a flat will expose the tyre bead and walls to greater risk of damage.
2 Check for loose or broken spokes. Tapping the spokes is the best guide to tension. A loose spoke will produce a quite different sound and should be tightened by turning the nipple in an anti-clockwise direction. Always recheck for run-out by spinning the wheel again. If the spokes have to be tightened an excessive amount, it is advisable to remove the tyre and tube by the procedure detailed in Section 13 of this Chapter; this is so that the protruding ends of the spokes can be ground off to avoid punctures to the inner tube.

3 Front brake assembly: examination, renovation and reassembly

1 The front brake assembly complete with brake plate can be withdrawn from the front wheel hub after the wheel spindle has been pulled out and the wheel removed from the forks. Refer to Chapter 4, Section 2, paragraphs 7 and 8.
2 Examine the condition of the brake linings. If they are wearing thin or unevenly, the brake shoes should be renewed. The linings are bonded to the brake shoes and cannot be supplied separately.
3 To remove the brake shoes, turn the brake operating lever so that the brake is in the full-on position. Pull the brake shoes apart to free them from their operating cam and from the pivot on which the fixed ends bear. Then pull them upward in a V formation so that they can be lifted away together with the return springs. When they are well clear of the brake plate, the return springs can be detached.
4 Check the inner surface of the brake drum, on which the brake shoes bear. The surface should be free from score marks or indentations, otherwise reduced braking efficiency will be inevitable. Remove all traces of brake lining dust and wipe with a rag soaked in petrol, to remove all traces of grease and oil.
5 Before replacing the brake shoes, check that the brake operating cam is working smoothly and not binding at its pivot. The cam can be removed for greasing by detaching the operating arm from the splined shaft end. The operating arm has splines which engage with similar splines on the cam shaft end; mark the operating arm and the splined shaft to aid correct relocation.
6 To reassemble the brake shoes on the brake plate, fit the return springs and pull the shoes apart whilst holding them in the form of a V, facing upwards. If they are now located with the brake operating cam and fixed pivot, they can be pushed back into position by pressing downward. Do not use force, or there is risk of distorting the shoes.

4 Wheel bearings: examination and replacement

1 Access is available to the wheel bearings when the brake plate

3.1 Complete brake assembly will pull out

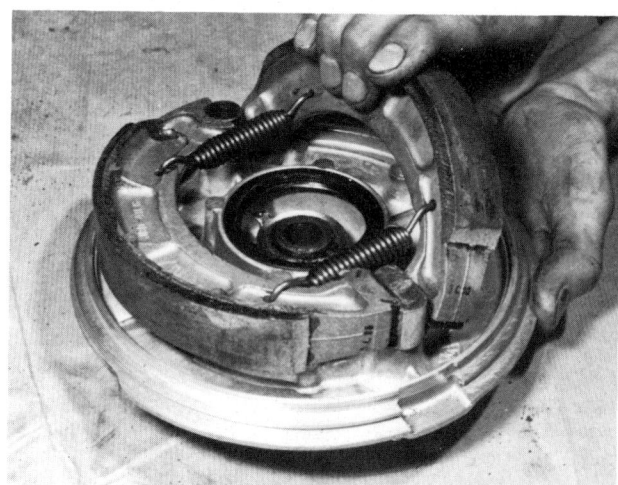

3.3 Prise brake shoes off back plate

4.2a Prise out dust cap followed by ...

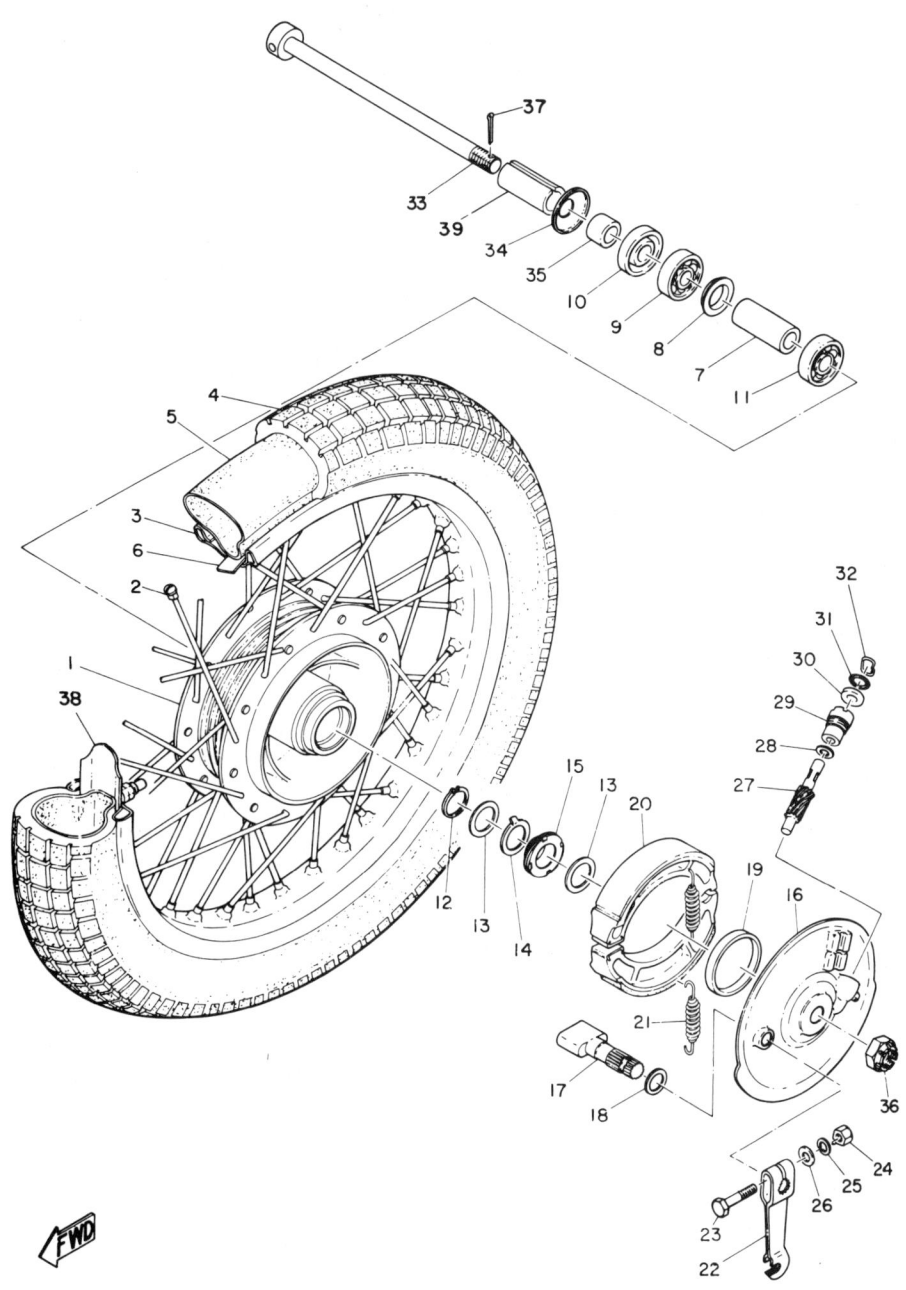

Fig. 5.1 Front wheel

1 Hub
2 Spoke set
3 Rim
4 Tyre
5 Tube
6 Rim tape
7 Bearing spacer
8 Spacer flange
9 Bearing
10 Oil seal
11 Bearing
12 Circlip
13 Thrust washer - 2 off
14 Speedometer dog
15 Speedometer drive gear
16 Brake plate
17 Brake cam
18 Shim
19 Oil seal
20 Brake shoe - 2 off
21 Return spring - 2 off
22 Operating arm
23 Pinch bolt
24 Nut
25 Spring washer
26 Plain washer
27 Worm shaft
28 Thrust washer
29 Bush
30 Oil seal
31 'O' ring
32 Clip
33 Spindle
34 Dust cover
35 Spacer
36 Nut
37 Spring washer
38 Split pin
39 Bead spacer
40 Grease nipple

has been removed. The left-hand bearing is exposed when the brake plate is lifted after the oil seal, located in front, has been prised out of position.

2   Lay the wheel on the ground with the brake drum facing upward and with a special tool, in the form of a rod with a curved end, insert the curved end into the hole in the centre of the spacer separating the two wheel bearings. If the other end of the special tool is hit with a hammer, the right-hand bearing, bearing flange washer, and bearing spacer will be expelled from the hub.

3   Invert the wheel and drive out the left-hand bearing by inserting a drift of the appropriate size, through the hub. During the removal of either bearing it may be necessary to support the wheel across an open-ended box so that there is sufficient clearance for the bearing to be displaced completely from the hub.

4   Remove all the old grease from the hub and bearings, giving the latter a final wash in petrol. Check the bearings for signs of play or roughness when they are turned. If there is any doubt about the condition of a bearing, it should be renewed.

5   Before replacing the bearings, first pack the hub with new grease. Then drive the bearings back into position, not forgetting the distance piece that separates them. Fit replacement oil seals and any dust covers or spacers that were also displaced during the original dismantling operation.

5   Front wheel: reassembly and replacement

1   Place the front brake plate and brake assembly in the brake drum and align the wheel in the forks so that the cast-in slot engages with the abutment on the left-hand fork leg. This acts as the anchorage for the front brake and must be positioned correctly.

2   Align the wheel so that the spindle can be inserted from the right. Place the spindle sleeve between the fork leg bottom and the clamp so that the slit in the sleeve is adjacent to one of the clamp edges. Push the spindle home through the wheel until the spindle head is flush with the right-hand fork leg. Replace the washer and nut and tighten the nut up. Retighten the two nuts which hold the spindle clamp.

3   Spin the wheel to ensure that it moves freely, then attach the front brake cable and the speedometer drive cable, the latter being retained by a wire clip. Make sure that both cables pass through the cable retaining loop of the mudguard to ensure that they can not come into contact with either the tyre or wheel. Check that the brake functions correctly, especially if the brake operating arm has been removed and replaced. If necessary, re-adjust the brake by following the procedure described in Section 8 of this Chapter, then spin the wheel again as a final check.

6   Rear wheel: examination, removal and renovation

1   Place the machine on blocks, so that the weight falls onto the front wheel and leaves the rear wheel clear of the ground. Check for rim alignment, damage to the rim and for broken or loose spokes, as described in Section 2 of this Chapter.

2   To remove the rear wheel, use the procedure recommended in paragraphs 2 - 4 of Section 9, Chapter 4. Remember to replace the chain master link on one end of the free chain to avoid its loss whilst the chain is disconnected.

3   The rear brake plate and brake assembly can be withdrawn from the right-hand side of the wheel hub.

4   The rear wheel bearings are a drive fit in the hub, separated by a spacer, using a general arrangement similar to that of the front wheel. Use a similar technique for removing, greasing and replacing the bearings, and for the replacement of both oil seals.

7   Rear brake assembly: examination, renovation and reassembly

1   The rear brake plate complete with the brake assembly can be withdrawn from the rear wheel after the wheel spindle has been pulled out, the distance piece removed and the wheel pulled clear of the forks.

2   If it is necessary to dismantle the brake assembly, follow the procedure described in Section 3 of this Chapter, and use the same methods for checking the different components. The brake shoes are aluminium alloy with bonded linings. To check for lining wear, with the brake plate removed but the shoes still in situ, measure the diameter across the two shoes whilst they are in their retracted position. The dimensions as originally fitted are as stated in the Specifications at the beginning of this Chapter. If the linings are worn by more than 0.157 in (4 mm) they will not function efficiently and are in need of renewal.

8   Adjusting the front brake

The front brake cable has a screw adjuster at both ends of the outer cable, the adjusters being on the handlebar lever and the outer cable stop lug on the front plate. Use the lower of the two adjusters for rough adjustment and the handlebar adjuster for day-to-day and fine adjustment. The lower adjuster has a locking nut which must be loosened before the adjuster screw can be rotated. The handlebar adjuster is fitted with a large knurled ring adjuster lock for ease of adjustment without a spanner. With the front brake adjusted correctly the play (gap) at the handlebar lever should be 3/16 - 5/16 inch (5 - 8 mm) measured between the inside edges of the fixed and moving parts of the lever assembly. With the front brake applied fully it should not be possible for the handlebar lever to touch the handlebar grip.

9   Adjusting the rear brake

1   With the rear brake correctly adjusted, the up and down movement of the brake pedal between the fully off and fully on position should be approximately 0.8 - 1.2 inch (20 - 30 mm) measured at the brake pedal foot grip. Before the amount of travel is adjusted the brake pedal should be positioned for quick operation. Because the rider's requirements may vary, the brake operating lever is retained to the camshaft by splines, giving many variations of operating angle. A simple pinch bolt arrangement holds the operating lever in place once the correct operating angle has been chosen. When selecting the operating arm angle make certain that the angle between the brake operating rod and the brake operating lever is less than 90°. If the angle is more than 90° the effective operating pressures will be reduced.

2   The length of travel is controlled by the adjuster at the end of the brake operating rod, close to the brake operating arm. If the nut is turned clockwise, the amount of travel is reduced and vice versa. Always check that the brake is not binding after adjustments have been made.

3   Note that it may be necessary to re-adjust the height of the stop lamp switch if the pedal height has been changed to any marked extent. The switch located immediately below the right-hand side cover that carries the capacity symbol of the model. The body of the switch is threaded, so that it can be raised or lowered, after the locknuts have been slackened. If the stop lamp lights too soon, the switch should be lowered and vice versa.

10   Cush drive assembly: examination and replacement

1   The cush drive assembly is contained within the left-hand side of the rear wheel hub. It comprises a set of synthetic rubber buffers, housed within a series of vanes cast in the hub shell. The drive to the rear wheel is transmitted via these rubbers, which

4.2b ... the oil seal

4.2c Knock out wheel bearing

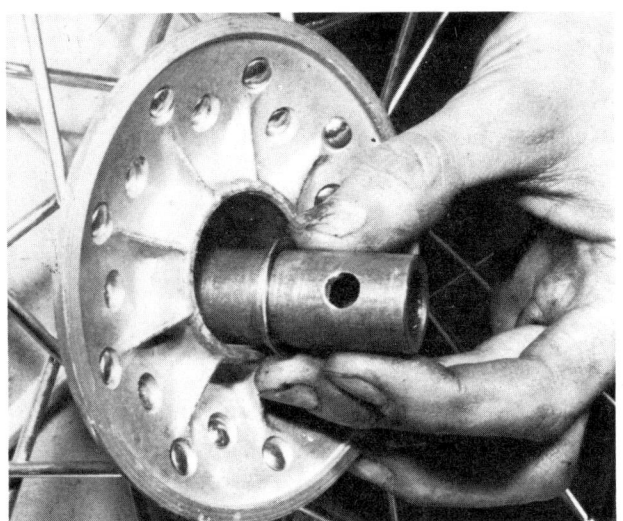
4.3 Wheel bearing spacer

4.4 Speedometer gear is held by circlip

5.1 Brake plate must engage with fork leg

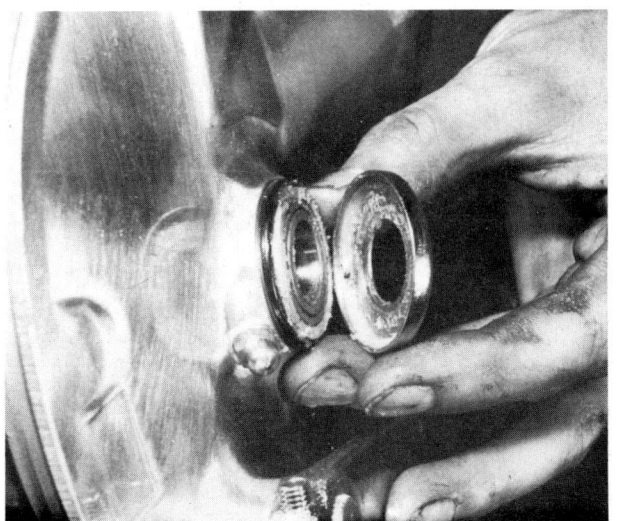
7.2a Note 'O' ring on dust cap

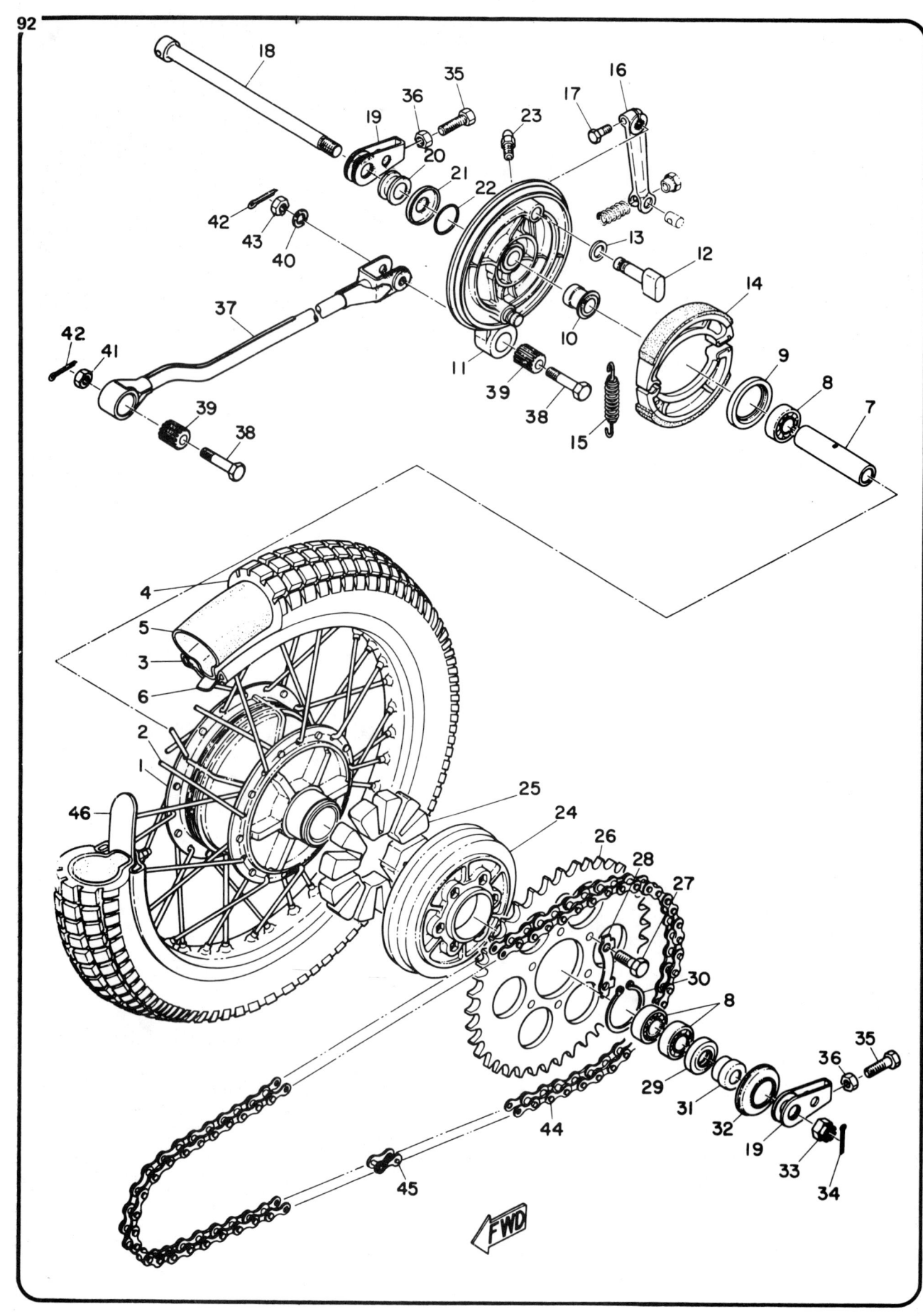

Fig. 5.2 Rear wheel

1 Hub
2 Spoke set
3 Rim
4 Tyre
5 Tube
6 Rim tape
7 Bearing spacer
8 Bearing
9 Oil seal
10 Flanged spacer
11 Brake plate
12 Brake cam
13 Washer
14 Brake shoe - 2 off
15 Return spring - 2 off
16 Operating arm
17 Bolt
18 Spindle
19 Chain adjuster - 2 off
20 Collar
21 Dust cover
22 'O' ring
23 Grease nipple
24 Sprocket carrier
25 Cush drive rubbers - 6 off
26 Sprocket
27 Bolt - 6 off
28 Tab washer - 3 off
29 Oil seal
30 Circlip
31 Spacer
32 Dust cover
33 Castellated nut
34 Split pin
35 Adjuster ball - 2 off
36 Locknut - 2 off
37 Torque arm
38 Torque arm bolt
39 Bush
40 Spring washer
41 Nut
42 Split pin - 2 off
43 Nut
44 Chain
45 Spring link
46 Security bolt

7.2b Brake plate spacer

7.2c Dust cap covers oil seal

9.1 Wheel alignment markings

10.1 Cush drive rubbers

11.1 Sprocket held by bolts and tab washers

12.7 Spring link must be refitted correctly

cushion any surges or roughness in the drive which would otherwise convey the impression of harshness.

2 Examine the rubber periodically for signs of damage or general deterioration. Renew and fit the rubbers as a set if there is any doubt about their condition; there is no difficulty in removing or replacing them as they are not under compression when the drive plate is detached.

3 To remove the cush drive assembly it will be necessary first to remove the rear wheel sprocket which is held by four or six bolts to the cush drive casing. Each set of two bolts is retained by a common tab washer, the edges of which must be knocked down with a screwdriver or blunt chisel before the bolts can be loosened. The cush drive assembly is retained in the hub by a single large circlip which locates in a groove on the outside of the left-hand bearing housing; with the circlip released the cush drive can be withdrawn.

11 Rear wheel sprocket: removal, examination and replacement

1 The rear wheel sprocket may be removed as described in the previous Section. Note the positioning of the sprocket as it is reversible, but must be replaced in its original position.

2 Check the condition of the sprocket teeth. If they are hooked, chipped or badly worn, the sprocket must be renewed. It is considered bad practice to renew one sprocket on its own. The final drive sprockets should always be renewed as a pair and a new chain fitted, otherwise rapid wear will necessitate even earlier renewal on the next occasion.

12 Final drive chain: examination and lubrication

1 The final drive chain is fully exposed, with only a light chainguard over the top run. Periodically the tension will need to be adjusted, to compensate for wear. This is accomplished by blocking up the machine and slackening the two wheel nuts on the left-hand side of the rear wheel so that the wheel can be drawn backward by means of the drawbolt adjusters in the fork ends. The rear brake torque arm bolt must also be slackened during this operation.

2 The chain is in correct tension if there is approximately 20 mm (¾ inch) slack in the middle of the lower run. Always check when the chain is at its tightest point as a chain rarely wears evenly during service.

3 Always adjust the drawbolts an equal amount in order to preserve wheel alignment. The fork ends are clearly marked with a series of horizontal lines above the adjusters, to provide a

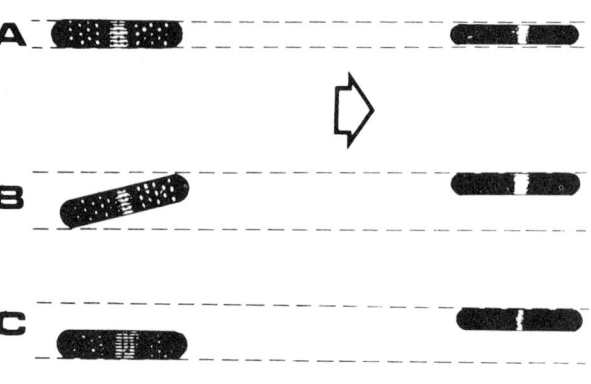

Fig. 5.3 Method of checking wheel alignment

A = Correct
B = Incorrect
C = Incorrect

Tyre removal: Deflate inner tube and insert lever in close proximity to tyre valve

Use two levers to work bead over the edge of rim

When first bead is clear, remove tyre as shown

Tyre fitting: Inflate inner tube and insert in tyre

Lay tyre on rim and feed valve through hole in rim

Work first bead over rim, using lever in final section

Use similar technique for second bead, finish at tyre valve position

Push valve and tube up into tyre when fitting final section, to avoid trapping

simple visual check. If desired, wheel alignment can be checked by running a plank of wood parallel to the machine, so that it touches the side of the rear tyre. If wheel alignment is correct, the plank will be equidistant from each side of the front wheel tyre, when tested on both sides of the rear wheel. It will not touch the front wheel tyre because this tyre is of smaller cross section. See the accompanying diagram.

4 Do not run the chain overtight to compensate for uneven wear. A tight chain will place undue stress on the gearbox and rear wheel bearings, leading to their early failure. It will also absorb a surprising amount of power.

5 After a period of running, the chain will require lubrication. Lack of oil will greatly accelerate the rate of wear of both the chain and the sprockets and will lead to harsh transmission. The application of engine oil will act as a temporary expedient, but it is preferable to remove the chain and clean it in a paraffin bath before it is immersed in a molten lubricant such as Linklyfe or Chainguard. These lubricants achieve better penetration of the chain links and rollers and are less likely to be thrown off when the chain is in motion. Aerosol type chain lubricants are also available, which will prove equally effective and obviate the need to remove the chain prior to application.

6 To check whether the chain is due for replacement, lay it lengthwise in a straight line and compress it endwise so that all the play is taken up. Anchor one end and measure the length. Now pull the chain with one end and anchored firmly, so that the chain is fully extened by the amount of play in the opposite direction. If there is a difference of more than ¼ inch per foot in the two measurements, the chain should be renewed in conjunction with the sprockets. Note that this check should be made AFTER the chain has been washed out, but BEFORE any lubricant is applied, otherwise the lubricant may take up some of the play.

7 When replacing the chain, make sure that the spring link is seated correctly, with the closed end facing the direction of travel.

13 Tyres: removal and replacement

1 At some time or other the need will arise to remove and replace the tyres, either as the result of a puncture or because a renewal is required to offset wear. To the inexperienced, tyre changing represents a formidable task yet if a few simple rules are observed and the technique learned, the whole operation is surprisingly simple.

2 To remove the tyre from the wheel, first detach the wheel from the machine by following the procedure in Chapter 4, Sections 2.6 and 2.7 or paragraphs 2.4 of Section 9, Chapter 4 depending on whether the front or the rear wheel is involved. Deflate the tyre by removing the valve insert and when it is fully deflated, push the bead of the tyre away from the wheel rim on both sides so that the bead enters the centre well of the rim. Remove the locking cap and push the tyre valve into the tyre itself.

3 Insert a tyre lever close to the valve and lever the edge of the tyre over the outside of the wheel rim. Very little force should be necessary; if resistance is encountered it is probably due to the fact that the tyre beads have not entered the well of the wheel rim all the way round the tyre.

4 Once the tyre has been edged over the wheel rim, it is easy to work around the wheel rim so that the tyre is completely free on one side. At this stage, the inner tube can be removed.

5 Working from the other side of the wheel ease the other edge of the tyre over the outside of the wheel rim furthest away. Continue to work around the rim until the tyre is free from the rim.

6 If a puncture has necessitated the removal of the tyre, re-inflate the inner tube and immerse it in a bowl of water to trace the source of the leak. Mark its position and deflate the tube. Dry the tube and clean the area around the puncture with a petrol-soaked rag. When the surface has dried, apply rubber solution and allow this to dry before removing the backing from the patch and applying the patch to the surface.

7 It is best to use a patch of the self-vulcanising type, which will form a very permanent repair. Note that it may be necessary to remove a protective covering from the top surface of the patch, after it has sealed in position. Inner tubes made from synthetic rubber may require a special type of patch and adhesive, if a satisfactory bond is to be achieved.

8 Before replacing the tyre, check the inside to make sure the agent that caused the puncture is not trapped. Check also the outside of the tyre, particularly the tread area, to make sure nothing is trapped that may cause a further puncture.

9 If the inner tube has been patched on a number of past occasions, or if there is a tear or large hole, it is preferable to discard it and fit a new one. Sudden deflation may cause an accident, particularly if it occurs with the front wheel.

10 To remove the tyre, inflate the inner tube sufficiently for it to assume a circular shape but only just. Then push it into the tyre so that it is enclosed completely. Lay the tyre on the wheel at an angle and insert the valve through the rim tape and the hole in the wheel rim. Attach the locking cap on the first few threads, sufficient to hold the valve captive in its correct location.

11 Starting at the point furthest from the valve, push the tyre bead over the edge of the wheel rim until it is located in the central well. Continue to work around the tyre in this fashion until the whole of one side of the tyre is on the rim. It may be necessary to use a tyre lever during the final stages.

12 Make sure there is no pull on the tyre valve and again commencing with the area furthest from the valve, ease the other bead of the tyre over the edge of the rim. Finish with the area close to the valve, pushing the valve up into the tyre until the locking cap touches the rim. This will ensure the inner tube is not trapped when the last section of the bead is edged over the rim with a tyre lever.

13 Check that the inner tube is not trapped at any point. Re-inflate the inner tube, and check that the tyre is seating correctly around the wheel rim. There should be a thin rib moulded around the wall of the tyre on both sides, which should be equidistant from the wheel rim at all points. If the tyre is unevenly located on the rim, try bouncing the wheel when the tyre is at the recommended pressure. It is probable that one of the beads has not pulled clear of the centre well.

14 Always run the tyres at the recommended pressures and never under or over inflate. The correct pressures for solo use are given in the Specifications Section of this Chapter.

15 Tyre replacement is aided by dusting the side walls, particurlarly in the vicinity of the beads, with a liberal coating of French chalk. Washing up liquid can also be used to good effect, but this has the disadvantage of causing the inner surfaces of the wheel rim to rust.

16 Never replace the inner tube and tyre without the rim tape in position. If this precaution if overlooked there is a good chance of the ends of the spoke nipples chafing the inner tube and causing a crop of punctures.

17 Never fit a tyre that has a damaged tread or side walls. Apart from the legal aspects, there is a very great risk of a blow-out, which can have serious consequences on any two-wheel vehicle.

18 Tyre valves rarely give trouble, but it is always advisable to check whether the valve itself is leaking before removing the tyre. Do not forget to fit the dust cap, which forms an effective second seal.

14 Security bolt

1 It is often considered necessary to fit a security bolt to the rear wheel of an off-road model because of the initial take up of drive may cause the tyre to creep around the wheel rim and tear the valve from the inner tube. The security bolt retains the bead of the tyre to the wheel rim and prevents this occurrence.

Chapter 5: Wheels, brakes and tyres

14 Fault diagnosis - wheels, brakes and tyres

Symptom	Cause	Remedy
Handlebars oscillate at low speeds	Buckled front wheel Incorrectly fitted front tyre	Remove wheel for specialist attention. Check whether line around bead is equidistant from rim.
Forks 'hammer' at high speeds	Front wheel out of balance	Add weights until wheel will stop in any position.
Brakes grab, locking wheel	Ends of brake shoes not chamfered	Remove brake shoes and chamfer ends.
Brakes feel spongy	Stretched brake operating cables, weak pull-off springs	Replace cables and/or springs, after inspection.
Tyres wear more rapidly in middle of tread	Over inflation	Check pressures and run at recommended settings.
Tyres wear rapidly at outer edges of tread	Under inflation	Ditto.

Chapter 6 Electrical system

Contents

General description ... 1	Stop and tail lamp: replacing bulb ... 9
Flywheel magneto: checking output ... 2	Flashing indicators ... 10
Battery: examination and maintenance ... 3	Flasher unit: location and replacement ... 11
Battery: charging procedure ... 4	Warning lamps: replacement of bulbs ... 12
Rectifier: general description ... 5	Horn: location and examination ... 13
Fuse: location and replacement ... 6	Wiring: layout and examination ... 14
Headlamp: replacing bulbs and adjusting beam height ... 7	Ignition and lighting switch ... 15
Handlebar switch assembly: examination ... 8	Fault diagnosis: electrical system ... 16

Specifications

Model	DT1 and DT1-C	DT2, DT3, RT2 and RT3
Battery		
Type	MV1-6D	6N4-2A-6D
Make	Nippon	Nippon
Voltage	6v	6v
Capacity	2AH	4AH
Magneto		
Make	Mitsubishi	Mitsubishi
Model	FZA-1BL	FZA-1BL
Rectifier		
Make	Mitsubishi	Mitsubishi
Model	DS10HJ-1	DS10HJ-8
***Bulbs**		
Main headlamp	35w/35w	35w/35w
Tail lamp	5.3w/17w	5.3w/17w
Instrument lamp	3w x 2	3w x 2
Main beam indicator	1.5w	1.5w
Flasher indicator	3w	3w
Flashing lamps	17w	17w

Model	DT1-B, DT1-E, RT1 and RT1-B
Battery	
Type	MV1-6D
Make	Nippon
Voltage	6v
Capacity	2AH
Magneto	
Make	Mitsubishi
Model	FZC-1AIL
Rectifier	
Make	Mitsubishi
Model	DS10HJ-1

Chapter 6: Electrical system

*Bulbs

Main headlamp	35w/35w
Tail lamp	5.3w/17w
Instrument lamp	3w x 2
Main beam indicator	1.5w
Flasher indicator	3w
Flashing lamps	17w

*All bulbs rated 6 volt.

1 General description

The Yamaha trail bikes are fitted as standard with a 6 volt electrical systems utilising a two or three coil flywheel magneto (depending on the model) which supplies the ignition, lighting and charging power.

Although the ignition source coils are contained within the same component as the lighting coils, they are completely separate from the charging coils and circuit, being interconnected at no point. Because the output from the charging and lighting coils is AC (alternating current) a rectifier is included in the circuit to convert the current to DC (direct current) in order to maintain the battery charge.

All those electrical components related to the ignition and starting operations have their functions described in Chapter 3.

2 Flywheel magneto: checking output

As previously mentioned in Chapter 3, Section 2, there is no satisfactory method of checking the output from the flywheel magneto without test equipment of the multi-meter type. If the performance of the unit is suspect, it should be checked by either a Yamaha service agent or an auto-electrical technician.

3 Battery: examination and maintenance

1 The type of battery fitted to each model is described in the Specifications Section at the beginning of this Chapter. Maintenance methods as set out below are common to all batteries fitted as standard to the Yamaha trail bike range.

2 The transparent plastic case of the battery permits the upper and lower levels of the electrolyte to be observed when the battery is lifted from its housing below the dualseat. Maintenance is normally limited to keeping the electrolyte level between the prescribed upper and lower limits and by making sure the vent pipe is not blocked. The lead plates and their separators can be seen through the transparent case, a further guide to the general condition of the battery.

3 Unless acid is spilt, as may occur if the machine falls over, the electrolyte should always be topped up with distilled water, to restore the correct level. If acid is spilt on any of the machine, it should be neutralised with an alkali such as washing soda and washed away with plenty of water, otherwise serious corrosion will occur. Top up with sulphuric acid of the correct specific gravity (1.260 - 1.280) only when spillage has occurred. Check that the vent pipe is well clear of the frame tubes or any of the other cycle parts, for obvious reasons.

4 Battery: charging procedure

1 Refer to the written instructions on the side of the battery for information regarding the correct charging rates. Over-high charge rates should be avoided since they will shorten the battery life.

2 Make sure that the battery charger connections are correct; red to positive and black to negative. It is preferable to remove the battery from the machine whilst it is being charged and to remove the vent plugs from each cell. When the battery is reconnected to the machine, the black lead must be connected to the negative terminal and the red lead to the positive terminal. This is most important as the machine has a negative earth. If the terminals are inadvertently reversed, the electrical system will be damaged permanently. The rectifier will be destroyed by a reversal of the current flow.

5 Rectifier: general description

1 The conversion of alternating current to direct current, on all models with flywheel magnetos, is made by the use of a rectifier, an electrical component which allows a one-way movement of current only. The rectifier is of the single phase half-wave silicon type, and converts the current before it is used to charge the battery.

2 In the event of failure of the battery to maintain a fully charged condition, it is possible that the rectifier is malfunctioning. Unfortunately, there is no easy way of checking without the appropriate test equipment. Provided that the electrical connections have not been inadvertently transposed at the battery, a check by substitution of the correct replacement is the only practicable method of verification.

6 Fuse: location and replacement

1 A fuse is incorporated in the electrical system to give protection from sudden overload, which may occur during a short circuit. The fuse is contained within a plastic fuse holder that forms part of the electrical wiring. It is located close to the positive terminal of the battery, under the dualseat. The fuse is rated at 10 amps. A spare fuse is supplied as standard; it should be renewed every time it has to be utilised.

2 Before renewing a fuse that has blown, check that no obvious short circuit has occurred, otherwise the replacement fuse will blow immediately it is inserted. It is always wise to check the electrical circuit thoroughly, to trace the fault and eliminate it.

3 When a fuse blows while the machine is running and no spare is available, a 'get you home' remedy is to remove the blown fuse and wrap it in silver paper before replacing it in the fuse holder. The silver paper will restore the electrical continuity by bridging the broken fuse wire. This expedient should NEVER be used if there is evidence of a short circuit or other major electrical fault, otherwise more serious damage will be caused. Replace the 'doctored' fuse at the earliest possible opportunity, to restore full circuit protection.

7 Headlamp: replacing bulbs and adjusting beam height

1 To remove the headlamp rim, detach the small screw in the right-hand underside of the headlamp shell. The rim can then be prised off, from the bottom edge of the shell, complete with the reflector unit.

2 On most early models the bulb is a twin-filament sealed beam unit. If a failure occurs the complete lens assembly must be removed and a new one fitted. The lens assembly is retained in the rim by two screws through tabs in the rim and lens assembly.

Later models have a conventional twin-filament bulb which is retained in the rear of the reflector by a rubber boot which

Chapter 6: Electrical system

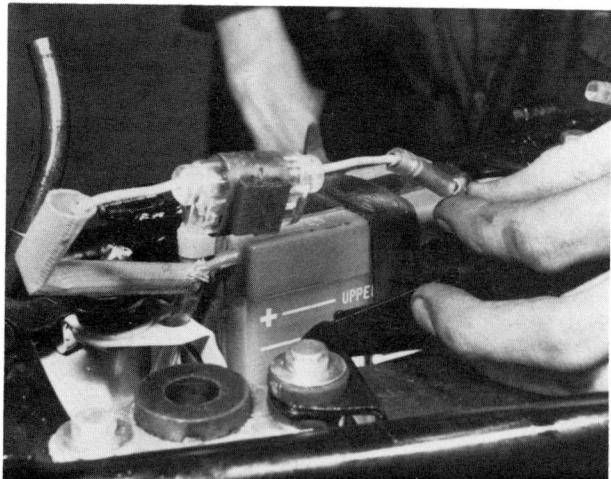
6.1 Spare fuse is contained in fuse pod

7.1 Rim held by countersunk screw

7.2a Main bulb holder retained by rubber boot

7.2b Bulb spring located on three pins

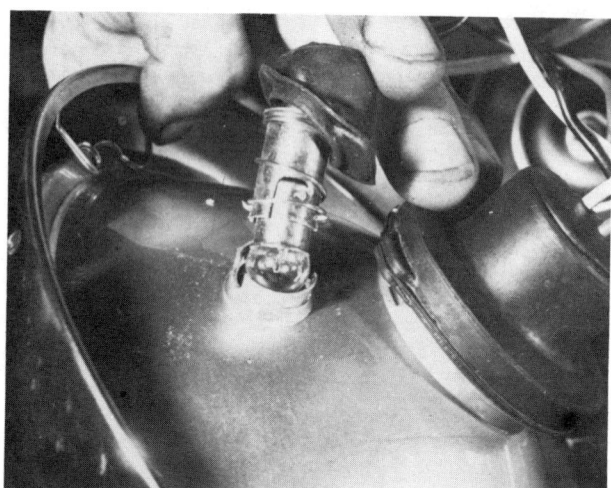
7.3 Pilot bulb bayonet fixed in housing

covers the bulb holder. The bulb is fixed to the holder by a spring loaded three prong arrangement.

3 The pilot bulb (where fitted) is housed in a metal holder which is located on the pilot bulb window in the reflector by a rubber sleeve. The bulb may be removed by pulling the holder from the window. The bulb is of the opposite pin bayonet fixing type. Pilot bulbs are only fitted to machines originally delivered to countries or states where the law requires their fitting. The bulb rating is 6v 3W, but variations in the wattage may occur according to the state or country for which the machine is supplied.

4 Beam alignment on early models is effected by means of a small screw through the left-hand side of the headlamp rim. The screw passes through a plate attached to the reflector shell, into a threaded nylon insert. By turning the screw, the headlamp beam can be ranged either left or right, in a horizontal plane.

5 The headlamp fitted to late models is adjustable for beam alignment by virtue of the detachable headlamp shell brackets. The bracket is retained on the headlamp shell by two bolts running through 'sloppy' holes and into 'capped' nuts in the headlamp. With the headlamp in situ on the machine the two bracket bolts can be slackened, and the headlamp shell moved to left or right.

6 Beam height is adjusted by slackening the two bolts that

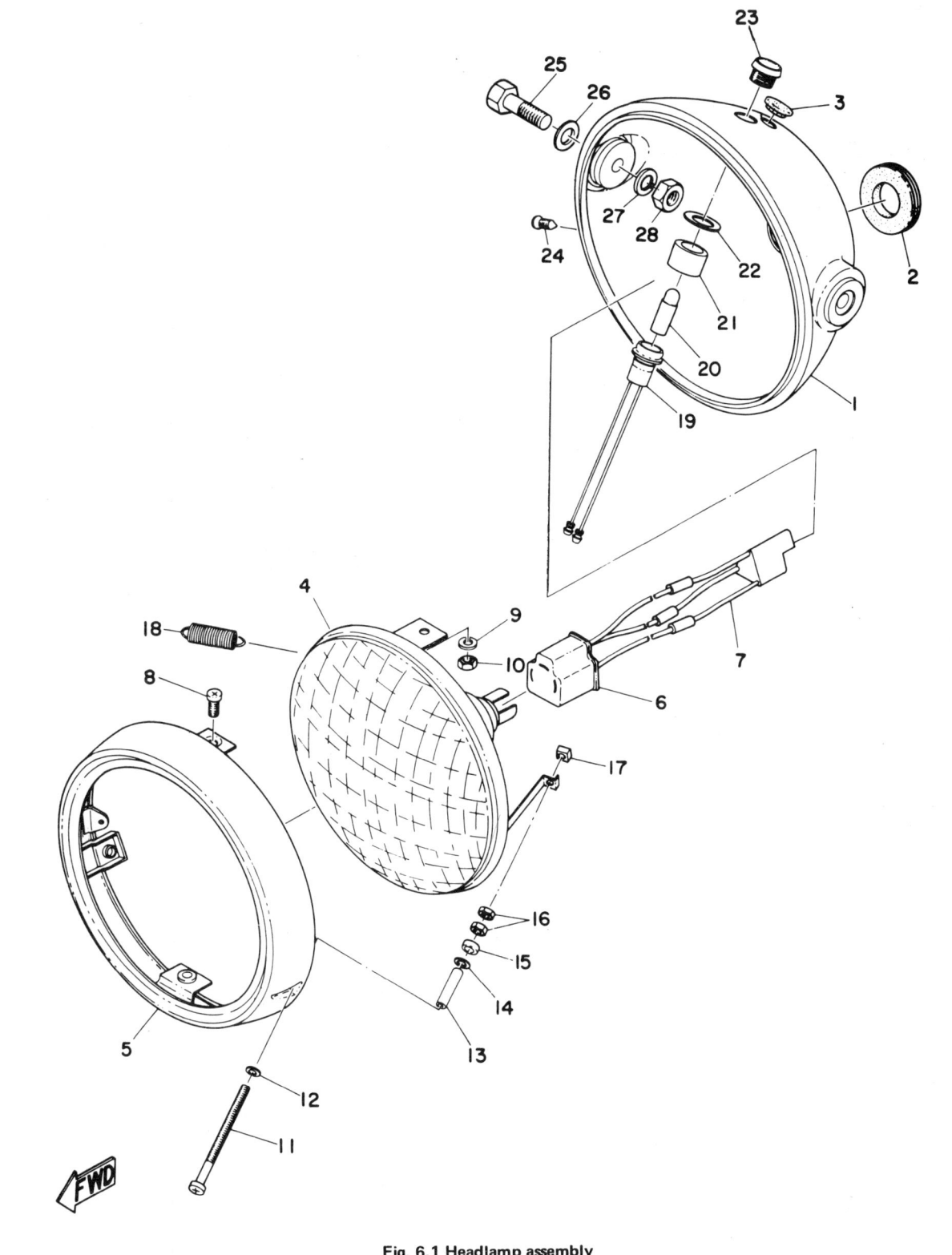

Fig. 6.1 Headlamp assembly

1 Headlamp shell
2 Grommet
3 Grommet
4 Sealed beam unit
5 Rim
6 Lead socket
7 Harness
8 Screw - 2 off
9 Spring washer - 2 off
10 Nut - 2 off
11 Lens adjusting screw
12 Plain washer
13 Spacer
14 Plain washer
15 Spacer
16 Nut
17 Adjuster block
18 Tension spring
19 Warning light leads
20 Bulb
21 Bulb holder nut
22 Washer
23 Warning lamp body
24 Screw
25 Bolt - 2 off
26 Plain washer - 2 off
27 Spring washer - 2 off
28 Nut - 2 off

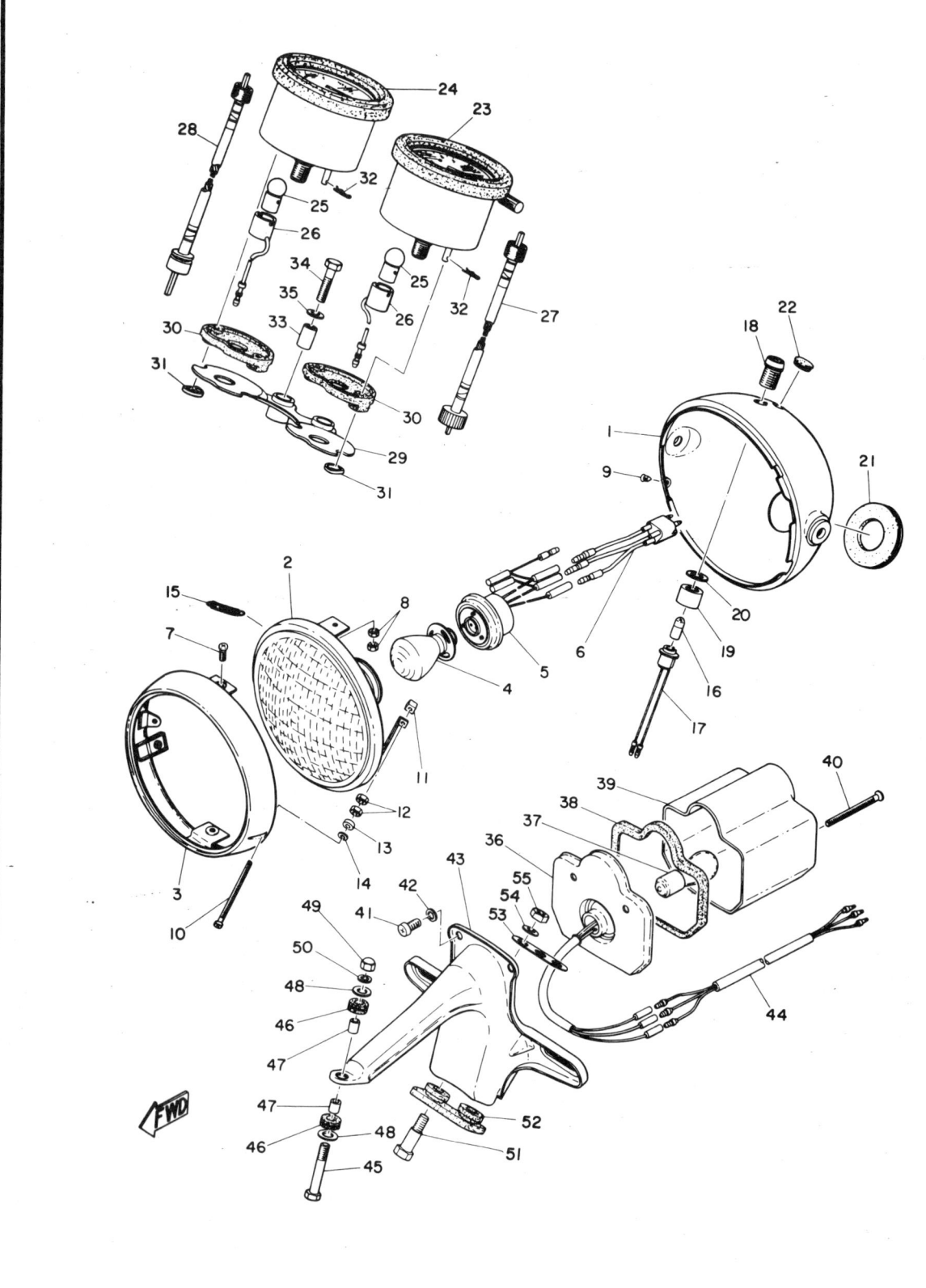

Fig. 6.2 Headlamp, tail lamp and instrument leads

1 Headlamp shell
2 Reflector unit
3 Headlamp rim
4 Bulb
5 Bulb holder
6 Harness
7 Screw - 2 off
8 Nut - 4 off
9 Rim retaining screw
10 Rim adjuster screw
11 Adjuster block
12 Nut - 2 off
13 Spacer
14 Washer
15 Tension spring
16 Warning bulb
17 Warning lamp leads
18 Lamp body
19 Nut
20 Washer
21 Grommet
22 Grommet
23 Speedometer head
24 Tachometer head
25 Bulb - 2 off
26 Bulb holder - 2 off
27 Speedometer cable complete
28 Tachometer cable complete
29 Instrument bracket
30 Rubber seating
31 Special washer
32 Spring clip - 4 off
33 Rubber bush - 2 off
34 Bolt - 2 off
35 Plain washer - 2 off
36 Tail lamp base
37 Tail lamp bulb
38 Gasket
39 Lens
40 Screw - 2 off
41 Spring washer - 2 off
42 Screw - 2 off
43 Tail lamp bracket
44 Lead
45 Bolt
46 Damper
47 Spacer - 2 off
48 Washer - 2 off
49 Nut
50 Spring washer
51 Bolt - 2 off
52 Damper
53 Special washer
54 Nut - 2 off
55 Plain washer - 2 off

retain the headlamp shell in position (through the lugs from the telescopic forks) and tilting the shell either upwards or downwards before retightening.

7 To check the headlamp alignment, place the machine on level ground facing a wall 25 yards distant, with the rider seated normally. The height of the centre of the headlamp from the ground, when the dip switch is in the 'full on' position. The concentrated area of light should be centrally disposed. Adjustments in either direction are made as detailed in the preceding paragraphs. Note that a different setting for the beam height will be required when a pillion passenger is carried.

8 The above instructions for beam setting relate to the requirements of the UK lighting regulations. Other settings may be required in countries other than the UK.

8 Handle bar switch assembly: examination

1 The switch assembly which forms part of the left-hand dummy twist grip combines the dipswitch, indicator switch and the horn button. In the event of failure, the switch assembly complete must be renewed, it is not practicable to effect a permanent repair. On late models an engine stop button is incorporated in the throttle twist grip.

9 Stop and tail lamp: replacing bulb

1 To gain access to the bulb, remove the two screws that retain the moulded plastic lens cover to the tail lamp assembly, and remove the cover complete with gasket. The bulbs fitted to all models are of the 'double filament' type, which combine the filaments for the stop lamp and the tail lamp in one bulb. The bulb has a staggered pin bayonet fixing, which prevents the bulb contacts from being reversed.

2 If the tail lamp bulb keeps blowing, suspect either vibration in the rear mudguard assembly, or more probably, a poor earth connection.

3 The stop lamp is operated by a stop lamp switch on the right-hand side of the machine, immediately above the brake pedal. It is connected to the pedal by an extension spring, which acts as an operating link. The body of the switch is threaded, so that a limited range of adjustment is available, to determine when the lamp will operate.

10 Flashing indicators

1 The forward flashing indicator lamps are connected to 'stalks' that are threaded into the fork shroud 'ears' which serve as headlamp mounting brackets. A locknut ensures that the 'stalks' are retained so that the indicator lamps are in the horizontal plane. The rear indicators are also mounted on stalks which thread into lugs at the rear of the dualseat carrying frame.

2 In each case, access to the bulb is gained by removing the moulded plastic lens cover, which is retained by two crosshead screws. The bulbs are retained by bayonet fixings.

11 Flasher unit: location and replacement

1 The flasher unit is bolted to the frame below the dualseat and behind the battery, or below the frame top tube next to the ignition coil.

2 A series of audible clicks will be heard if the flasher unit is functioning correctly. If the unit malfunctions, the usual symptom is one initial flash before the unit goes dead. It will be necessary to replace the flasher unit complete if the fault cannot be attributed to either a burnt-out flasher bulb or a blown fuse. Take great care when handling the unit because it is easily damaged if dropped.

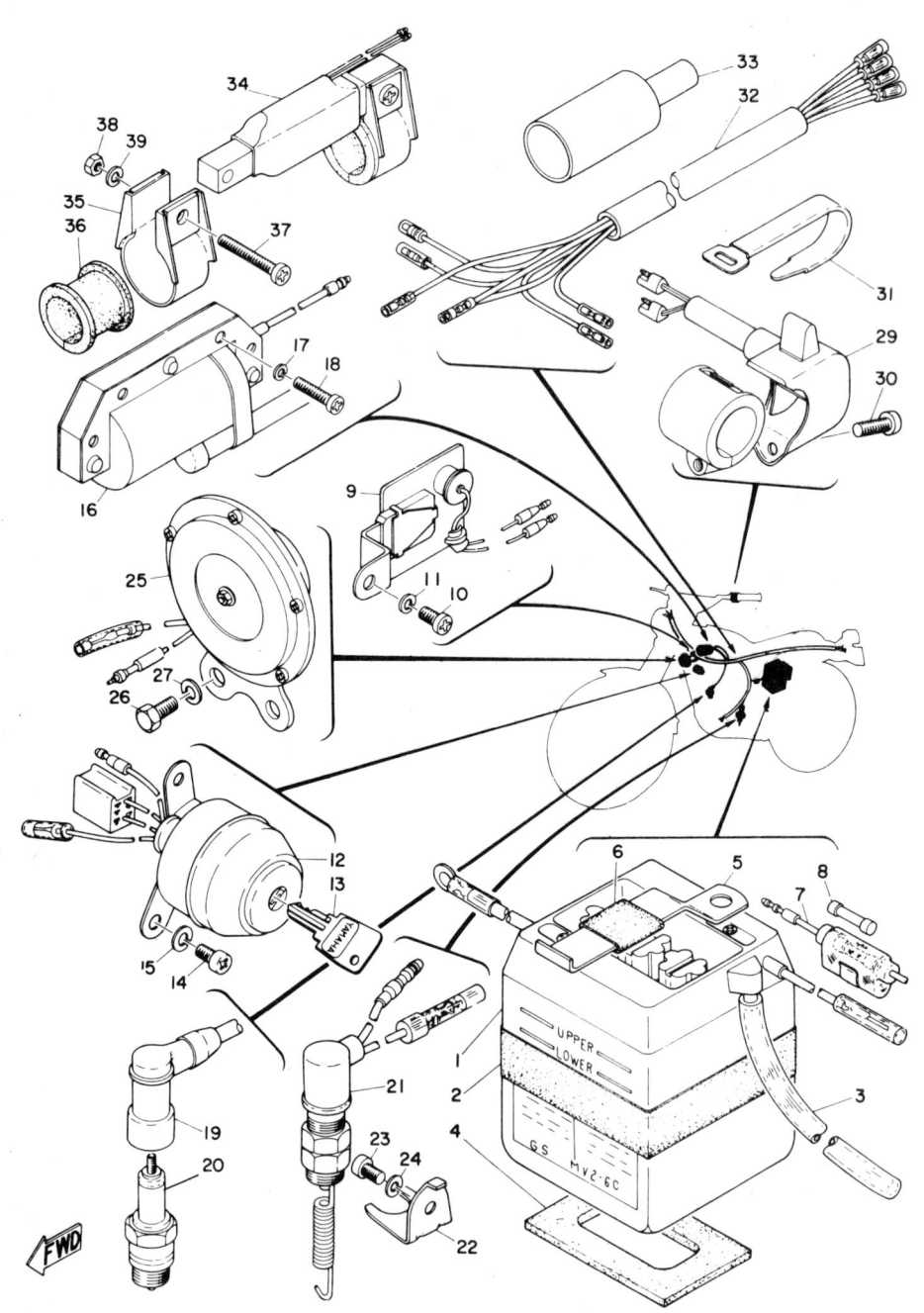

Fig. 6.3 Electrical fittings

1. Battery
2. Damper strap
3. Breather pipe
4. Battery seat
5. Battery strap
6. Pad
7. Fuse holder
8. Fuse - 2 off
9. Rectifier
10. Screw
11. Spring washer
12. Main switch
13. Key - 4 off
14. Screw - 2 off
15. Spring washer - 2 off
16. Ignition coil
17. Pan head screw - 2 off
18. Spring washer - 2 off
19. Plug cap
20. Spark plug
21. Stop lamp switch
22. Stop lamp bracket
23. Screw
24. Spring washer
25. Horn
26. Bolt - 2 off
27. Spring washer - 2 off
28. Handlebar switch holder
29. Handlebar switch
30. Screw
31. Lead strap
32. Wiring harness
33. Wiring cover
34. Choke coil
35. Choke coil braket strap - 2 off
36. Rubber damper
37. Screw - 2 off
38. Nut - 2 off
39. Washer - 2 off

8.1a Left-hand handlebar switch

8.1b Engine stop on throttle twist grip

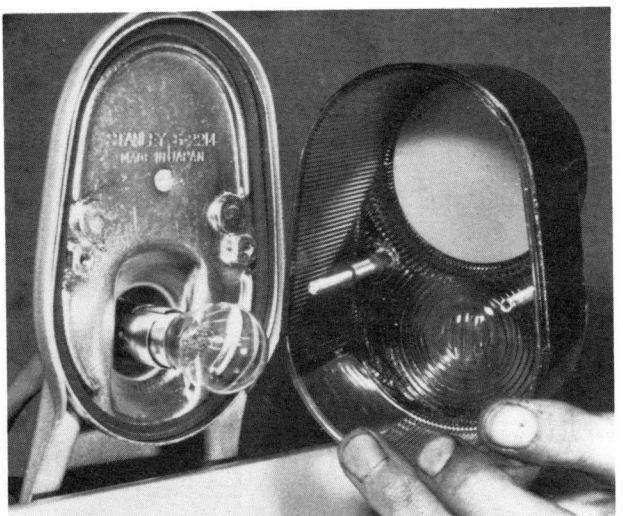

9.1 Stop lamp lens held by two screws

10.1 Indicator lens held by two screws

11.1 Flasher unit next to coil (late models)

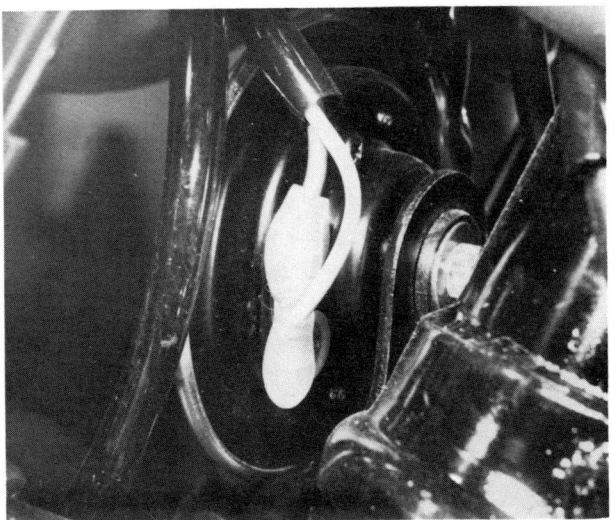

13.1 Horn located under headlamp

12 Warning lamps: replacement of bulbs

1 With the exception of the headlamp main beam warning light, the warning lamps are fitted in the instrument heads together with the dial illuminating lamps, all of which are a push fit in their holders which in turn are a push fit in the underside of the instruments.

Access to the bulbs can be made after the instruments have been lifted from their common mounting bracket. Each instrument is retained by spring pins which fit through pegs which are fixed in the base of each instrument and pass through the bracket.

2 All bulbs are rated at 3W with the exception of the high beam lamp, which is mounted in a holder in the headlamp shell and is rated at 1.5 watts.

13 Horn: location and examination

1 The horn is fixed via a flexible steel strip to the frame tube below the fuel tank. The flexible steel strip isolates the horn from the undesirable effects of high frequency vibration.

2 The horn has no external means of adjustment. If it malfunctions it must be renewed; it is statutory requirement in most countries that the machine must be fitted with a horn in working order.

14 Wiring: layout and examination

1 The wiring harness is colour coded and will correspond with the accompanying wiring diagram. Where socket connectors are used, they are designed so that reconnection can be made in the correct position only.

2 Visual inspection will show whether there are any breaks or frayed outer coverings which will give rise to short circuits. Another source of trouble may be the snap connectors and sockets, where the connector has not been pushed fully home in the outer housing.

3 Intermittent short circuits can often be traced to a chafed wire that passes through or is close to a metal component such as a frame member. Avoid tight bends in the lead or situations where a lead can become trapped between castings.

15 Ignition and lighting switch

1 The ignition and lighting switch is combined in one unit and housed either between and behind the speedometer and tachometer heads on the top fork yoke or mounted on the left-hand side of the machine to the rear of the steering head and below the fuel tank. The switch is operated by a key which cannot be removed when the ignition is turned on.

2 The number stamped on the ignition key will match that of the steering head lock. A replacement key can be obtained if the number is quoted; if either the ignition switch or steering head lock is renewed, additional keys will be required.

3 It is not practicable to repair the ignition switch if it malfunctions. It should be renewed with a new switch and key to match.

16 Fault diagnosis - electrical system

Symptom	Cause	Remedy
Complete electrical failure	Blown fuse	Check wiring and electrical components for short circuit before fitting new 15 amp fuse. Check battery connections, also whether connections shown signs of corrosion.
Dim lights, horn inoperative	Discharged battery	Recharge battery with battery charger and check whether alternator is giving correct output (electrical specialist).
Constantly 'blowing' bulbs	Vibration, poor earth connection	Check whether bulb holders are secured correctly. Check earth return or connections to frame.

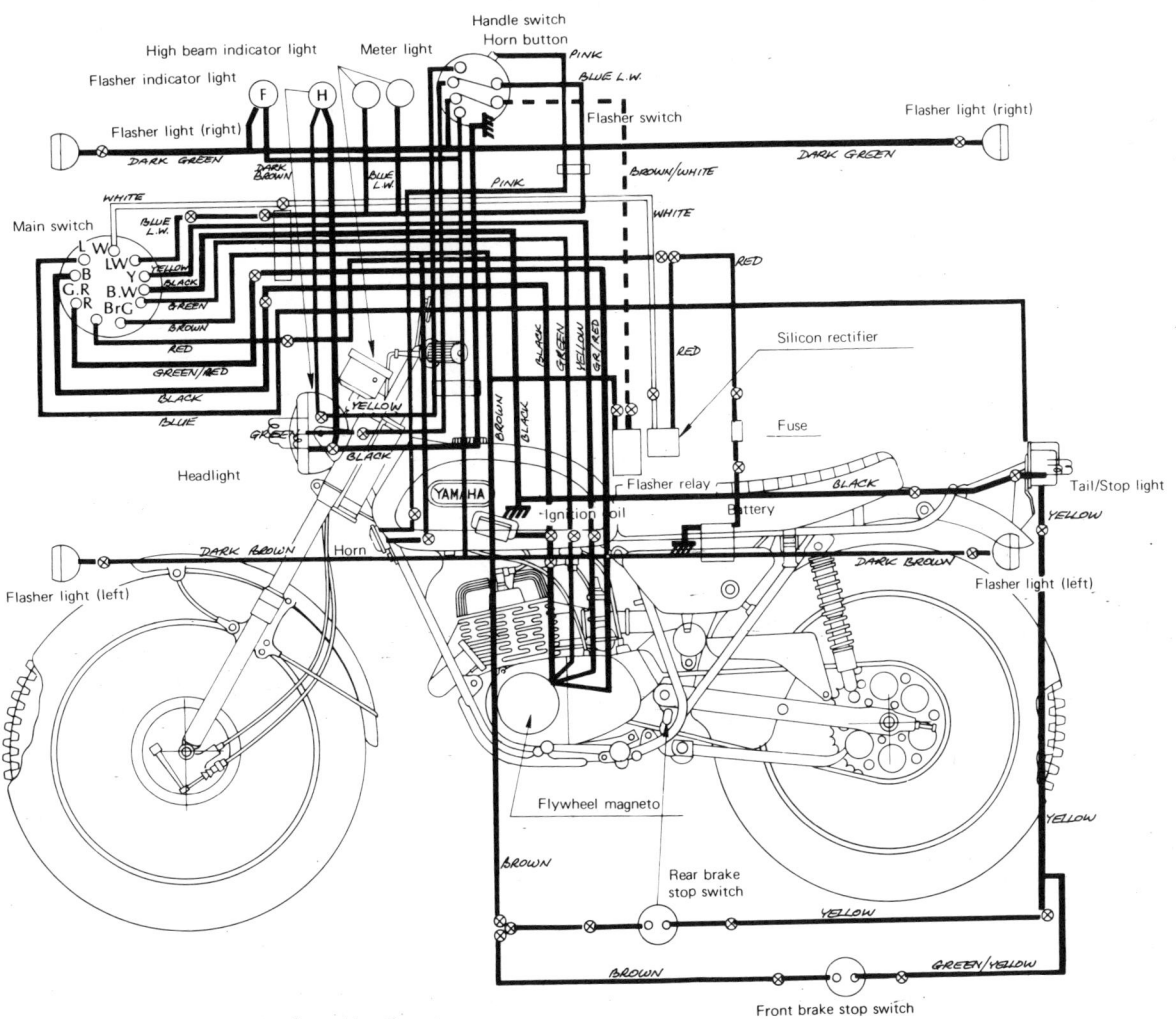

Fig. 6.4 Wiring diagram DT/RT models

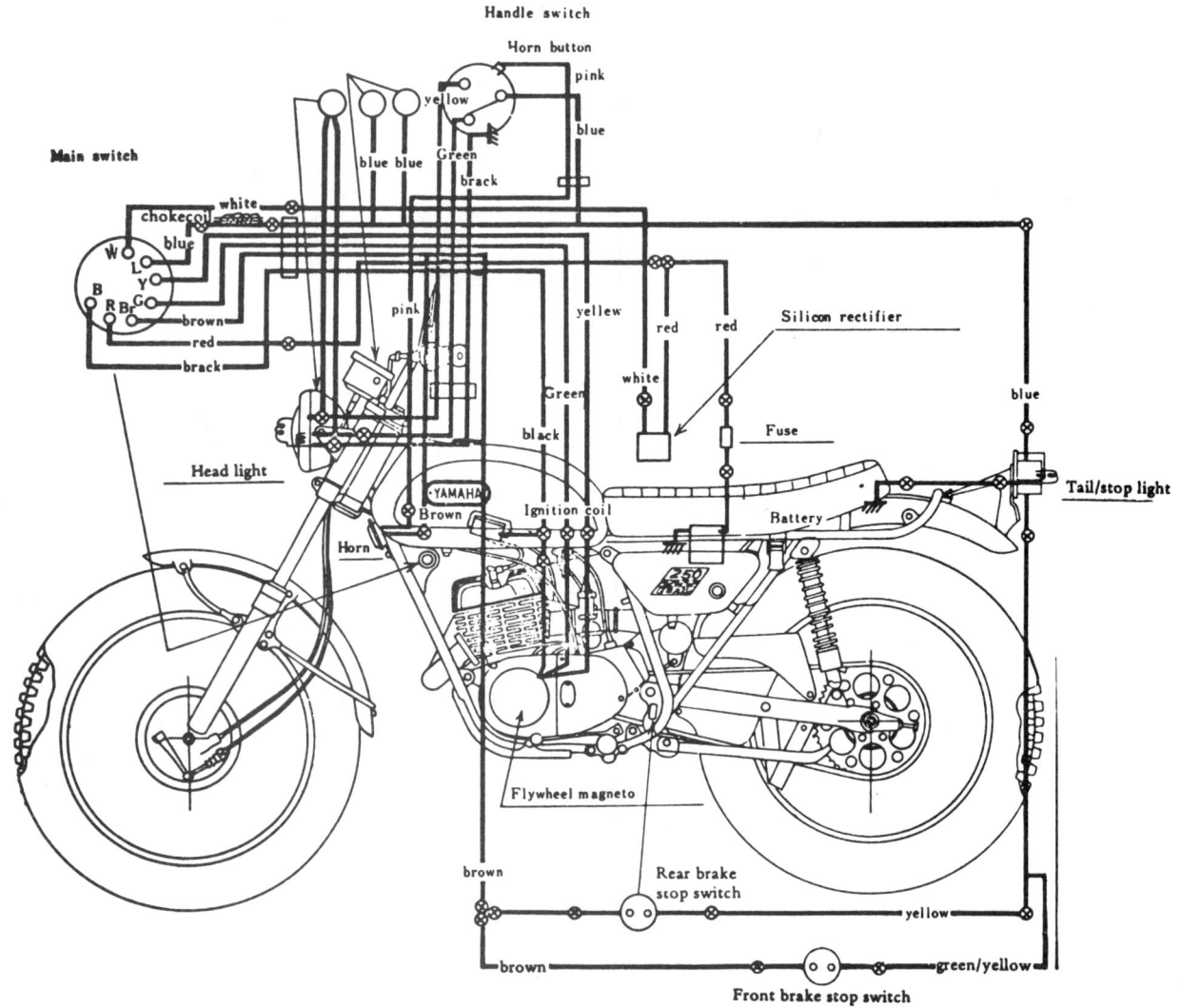

Fig. 6.5 Wiring diagram DT1A/DT1B/DT1C V11 models

Right-hand view of 1979 DT 250 monoshock model

Chapter 7 The Yamaha 250 and 400 D and E monoshock models

Contents

General description ... 1	Throttle cable free play adjustment ... 6
Oil pump: bleeding the main feed pipe ... 2	Adjustment and removal of the rear suspension shock absorber ... 7
Oil pump: bleeding the oil pump and distribution pipe ... 3	Rear sub-frame: examination, renovation and replacement ... 8
Oil pump: checking and adjusting the maximum pump stroke ... 4	Other modifications ... 9
Carburettor: idle mixture and idle speed adjustment ... 5	

Specifications

Model	DT250D and E	DT400D and E
Dimensions:		
Overall length	2,185 mm (86.0 in)	2,185 mm (86.0 in)
Overall width	870 mm (34.3 in)	870 mm (34.3 in)
Overall height	1,165 mm (45.9 in)	1,165 mm (45.9 in)
Seat height	855 mm (33.7 in)	855 mm (33.7 in)
Wheelbase	1,420 mm (55.9 in)	1,415 mm (55.7 in)
Minimum ground clearance	255 mm (10.0 in)	255 mm (10.0 in)
Weight:	129 kg (284 lbs)	133 kg (293 lbs)
Engine		
Type	two-stroke	two-stroke
Bore	70 mm (2.76 in)	85 mm (3.35 in)
Stroke	64 mm (2.52 in)	70 mm (2.76 in)
Cylinders	One	One
Displacement	246 cc	397 cc
Compression ratio	6.7 : 1	6.4 : 1
Piston and rings		
Piston clearance	0.035–0.040 mm (0.0014–0.0016 in)	0.040–0.045 mm (0.0016–0.0018 in)
Ring end gap (installed):		
Top	0.2–0.4 mm (0.0079–0.0157 in)	0.3–0.5 mm (0.012–0.020 in)
2nd	0.2–0.4 mm (0.0079–0.0157 in)	0.3–0.5 mm (0.012–0.020 in)
Piston ring side clearance	0.03–0.05 mm (0.0012–0.0020 in)	0.03–0.05 mm (0.0012–0.0020 in)
Maximum	0.08 mm (0.0031 in)	0.08 mm (0.0031 in)
Cylinder barrel		
Standard bore size	70.00–70.02 mm (2.756–2.757 in)	85.00–85.02 mm (3.347–3.349 in)
Maximum	70.1 mm (2.760 in)	85.1 mm (3.350 in)
Cylinder taper limit	0.08 mm (0.0031 in)	0.08 mm (0.0031 in)
Cylinder wear limit	0.05 mm (0.0020 in)	0.05 mm (0.0020 in)
Crankshaft		
Deflection tolerance	0.03 mm (0.0012 in)	0.03 mm (0.0012 in)
Connecting rod side clearance	0.25–0.75 mm (0.0098–0.030 in)	0.25–0.75 mm (0.0098–0.030 in)
Maximum	1.00 mm (0.040 in)	1.00 mm (0.040 in)
Connecting rod axial clearance	0.4–1.0 mm (0.016–0.039 in)	0.4–1.0 mm (0.016–0.039 in)
Maximum	2.0 mm (0.079 in)	2.0 mm (0.079 in)

Chapter 7: Yamaha 250 and 400 D and E monoshock models

Gearbox		
Type	5-speed, constant mesh, drum change	5-speed, constant mesh, drum change
Bottom	33/13 2.538 7.172	38/14 2.714 7.669
2nd	34/19 1.789 5.056	34/19 1.789 5.056
3rd	26/20 1.300 3.674	26/20 1.300 3.674
4th	23/23 1.000 2.826	23/23 1.000 2.826
Top	20/26 0.769 2.173	20/26 0.769 2.173
Final drive:		
Type	Roller chain, 104 link (inc. joining link)	Roller chain, 102 link (inc. joining link)
Size/make	DK520DS, Daido	DK520DS, Daido
Reduction ratio	47/14 3.357	45/16 2.687
Primary drive:		
Type	Helical gear	Helical gear
Teeth ratio	65/23 2.826 : 1	65/23 2.826 : 1
Clutch		
Type	Wet, multi-plate	Wet, multi-plate
Friction plate thickness	3.0 mm (0.12 in)	3.0 mm (0.12 in)
Minimum	2.7 mm (0.11 in)	2.7 mm (0.11 in)
Clutch plate warp limit	0.05 mm (0.002 in)	0.05 mm (0.002 in)
Clutch spring length standard	34.9 mm (1.374 in) 6 pcs	34.9 mm (1.374 in) 6 pcs
Minimum	33.9 mm (1.335 in)	33.9 mm (1.335 in)
Clutch pushrod run out max	0.2 mm (0.008 in)	0.2 mm (0.008 in)
Lubrication system	Yamaha Autolube (separate system)	
Oil pump	Plunger type	
Colour code	Red	Yellow
Minimum stroke	0.25–0.30 mm (0.0098–0.012 in)	0.25–0.30 mm (0.0098–0.012 in)
Maximum stroke	1.85–2.05 mm (0.0073–0.081 in)	1.85–2.05 mm (0.0073–0.081 in)
Total reduction ratio	18/23 x 55/1 = 43.0	18/23 x 32/1 = 25.0
Oil discharge:		
Minimum stroke	0.50–0.63 cc (0.017–0.021 fl ozs)	0.50–0.63 cc (0.017–0.021 fl ozs)
Maximum stroke	4.65–5.15 cc (0.157–0.174 fl ozs)	4.65–5.15 cc (0.157–0.174 fl ozs)
Pump adjustment	at full throttle	at full throttle
Carburettor		
Make	Mikuni	Mikuni
Type	VM28SC,1M100	VM34SC,1M200
Main jet	150	190
Needle jet	N–8	O–2
Pilot jet	50	80
Starter jet	60	60
Jet needle	5DP33–3	6F9–3
Float level	15.8 mm	22.9 mm
Pilot screw (turns out)	1–¾	1–½
Air jet	2.5 mm (diameter)	2.5 mm (diameter)
Engine idle speed	1,300–1,400	1,400–1,500
Air filter	Oiled foam rubber	Oil foam rubber
Ignition system		
Type	Flywheel magneto ignition	CDI ignition system
Spark plug	NGK B–8ES or Champion N–2	NGK B–8ES or Champion N–2
Ignition timing	3.2 ± 0.15 mm (0.126 ± 0.006 in) BTDC	2.9 ± 0.15 mm (0.114 ± 0.006 in) BTDC
Condenser		
Condenser capacity	0.25 microfarad	0.25 microfarad
Insulation resistance	50 M ohms or more	50 M ohms or more
Ignition coil		
Type	Mitsubishi F6T412	Mitsubushi F6T411
Primary resistance	N/A	1.0 ohms ± 10% (20°C/68°F)
Secondary resistance	5.9 K ohms ± 20% (20°C/68°F)	5.9 K ohms ± 20% (20°C/68°F)

Chapter 7: Yamaha 250 and 400 D and E monoshock models

CDI unit		
Type	N/A	Mitsubishi 8T00371
Frame	Tubular, double cradle	Tubular, double cradle
Suspension		
Front (type/travel)	Telescopic fork/197 mm (7.6 in)	Telescopic fork/197 mm (7.6 in)
Rear (type/travel)	Swinging arm (monoshock) 140 mm (5.5 in) 82 mm (shock absorber travel) (3.23 in)	Swinging arm (monoshock) 140 mm (5.5 in) 82 mm (shock absorber travel) (3.23 in)
Front forks		
Spring free length	399 mm (15.7 in)	399 mm (15.7 in)
Preload length	385 mm (15.2 in)	385 mm (15.2 in)
Fork oil capacity	190.5 cc (6.4 fl ozs) per leg	190.5 cc (6.4 fl ozs) per leg
Rear shock absorber		
Gas pressure	213 lbs/in^2 (15 kg/cm^2)	213 lbs/in^2 (15 kg/cm^2)
Absorber travel	82 mm (15 kg/cm^2)	82 mm (15 kg/cm^2)
Spring free length	265 mm (10.43 in)	265 mm (10.43 in)
Preload length	257 mm (10.12 in)	257 mm (10.12 in)
Wheels		
Rim horizontal run out:		
Front	0.5 mm (0.020 in)	0.5 mm (0.020 in)
Rear	0.5 mm (0.020 in)	0.5 mm (0.020 in)
Tyre pressure front:		
Normal solo riding	18.5 lbs/in^2 (1.3 kg/cm^2)	18.5 lbs/in^2 (1.3 kg/cm^2)
High speed/two up riding	21.3 lbs/in^2 (1.5 kg/cm^2)	21.3 lbs/in^2 (1.5 kg/cm^2)
Tyre pressure rear:		
Normal solo riding	21.3 lbs/in^2 (1.5 kg/cm^2)	21.3 lbs/in^2 (1.5 kg/cm^2)
High speed/two up riding	25.6 lbs/in^2 (1.8 kg/cm^2)	25.6 lbs/in^2 (1.8 kg/cm^2)
Brakes		
Front drum diameter	160 mm (63.0 in)	160 mm (63.0 in)
Minimum diameter	156 mm (61.4 in)	156 mm (61.4 in)
Rear drum diameter	150 mm (59.1 in)	150 mm (59.1 in)
Minimum diameter	146 mm (57.5 in)	146 mm (57.5 in)
Tyres		
Front	3.00–21 4PR, Dunlop	3.00–21 4PR, Dunlop
Rear	4.00–18 4PR, Dunlop	4.00–18 4PR, Dunlop
Electrical system		
Flywheel magneto		
Type	Mitsubishi FIT350	F3T350
Output	2,500 rpm/0.9 $\pm$ 0.3A 7,000 rpm/2.3 $\pm$ 0.5A	2,500/0.9 $\pm$ 0.3A 7,000/2.3 $\pm$ 0.5A
Source coil resistance	1.65 ohms $\pm$ 10% (20°C/68°F)	1.65 ohms $\pm$ 10% (20°C/68°F)
Coil resistance	166 ohms $\pm$ 10%	166 ohms $\pm$ 10%
Regulator	Mitsubishi 071 or Stanley SRS–610	Mitsubishi 071 or Stanley SRS–610
Regulated voltage	7.0 V (Mitsubishi) 7.2 V (Stanley)	7.0 V (Mitsubishi) 7.2 V (Stanley)
Allowable amperage	8.0 A	8.0 A
Rectifier	Stanley DE41	Stanley DE41
Battery		
Capacity	6 volt 6 amps	6 volt 6 amps
Battery dimensions	56 x 110 x 98 mm (2.20 x 4.33 x 3.86 in)	56 x 110 x 98 mm (2.20 x 4.33 x 3.86 in)
Type	6N6–3B–1	6N6–3B–1
Charging rate	0.6A at 10 hrs	0.6A at 10 hrs
Flasher relay		
Type	Condenser	Condenser
Make	Nippondenso	Nippondenso
Model	061300–5010	061300–5010
Charge coil resistance	0.33 ohms $\pm$ 10% (20°C/68°F)	0.38 ohms $\pm$ 10% (20°C/68°F)

Chapter 7: Yamaha 250 and 400 D and E monoshock models

Lighting coil resistance ...	0.19 ohms ± 10% (20°C/68°F)	0.22 ohms ± 10% (20°C/68°F)

Bulbs

Headlight ...	6V 35/35w (sealed beam)	6V 35/35w (sealed beam)
Tail/stop lamp ...	6V 5.3/25w	6V 5.3/25w
Licence plate lamp ...	6V 5.3w	6V 5.3w
Indicator lamps ...	6V 17w (4 lamps)	6V 17w (4 lamps)
Instrument lamps ...	6V 3.0w (2 lamps)	6V 3.0w (2 lamps)
Full beam indicator lamp ...	6V 3.0w	6V 3.0w
Oil level warning lamp ...	6V 3.0w	6V 3.0w
Neutral indicator lamp ...	6V 3.0w	6V 3.0w

Torque wrench settings:

Engine

Cylinder head nut ...	14 ft f lb (2.0 kg f m)
bolt ...	18 ft f lb (2.5 kg f m)
Spark plug ...	14 ft f lb (2.0 kg f m)
Cylinder nut ...	29 ft f lb (4.0 kg f m)
bolt ...	33 ft f lb (4.5 kg f m)
Primary drive gear ...	54 ft f lb (7.5 kg f m)
Clutch boss ...	54 ft f lb (7.5 kg f m)
Clutch spring ...	7 ft f lb (1.0 kg f m)
Drive spring ...	54 ft f lb (7.5 kg f m)
Kick-starter ...	18 ft f lb (2.5 kg f m)
Reed valve ...	0.7 ft f lb (0.1 kg f m)
Rotor nut ...	51 ft f lb (7.0 kg f m)
Stator ...	7 ft f lb (1.0 kg f m)
Clutch pressure plate ...	18 ft f lb (2.5 kg f m)

Frame

Engine mountings front upper ...	18 ft f lb (2.5 kg f m)
front lower ...	18 ft f lb (2.5 kg f m)
rear upper ...	18 ft f lb (2.5 kg f m)
rear lower ...	36 ft f lb (5.0 kg f m)
Pivot shaft nut ...	47 ft f lb (6.5 kg f m)
Rear shock absorber front ...	36 ft f lb (5.0 kg f m)
rear ...	18 ft f lb (2.5 kg f m)
Handlebar clamp bolts ...	40 ft f lb (5.5 kg f m)
Handlebar upper bracket ...	11 ft f lb (1.5 kg f m)
lower pinch bolt ...	11 ft f lb (1.5 kg f m)
Front spindle bracket ...	7 ft f lb (1.0 kg f m)
Front spindle nut ...	61 ft f lb (8.5 kg f m)
Rear spindle nut ...	80 ft f lb (11.0 kg f m)
Driven sprocket nut ...	29 ft f lb (4.0 kg f m)
Footrest nut ...	43 ft f lb (6.0 kg f m)

1 General description

1 The Yamaha DT400B model was first imported into the UK during February 1976. Its importation was discontinued during December 1977, shortly after the introduction of the Monoshock version. The only remaining Yamaha trail bike now available from the 250, 360, and 400 range in the UK is the DT250E model.

2 None of the models have altered to any great extent from those described in the earlier sections of this manual, apart from the use of a Monoshock rear suspension system in 1977. Where changes in specification have been made that necessitate different procedures from those detailed earlier, they are described in this Chapter.

3 The oil pump is one such item and the procedure for bleeding it is different as it no longer has a nylon pinion.

4 A different type of carburettor is used on both the 250 and 400 models.

5 The modified exhaust system incorporates a spark arrester.

6 The most fundamental change occurred during the 1977 season, when the rear suspension system was changed to one of the Monoshock type. Only one suspension unit is used, the cantilever construction of the rear sub-frame having a greatly extended range of travel.

1.5 DT250E modified exhaust system

2 Oil pump: bleeding the main feed pipe

1 This must be carried out whenever the oil tank has run dry, or whenever any part of the Autolube system has been disconnected. If the system is not bled or is incompletely bled of air, seizure of the engine may result.
2 To bleed the pump and/or oil pipe it is first necessary to remove the pump cover and then the bleed screw. It is advisable to have some kind of clean container at hand, to collect the oil which flows out.
3 Allow the oil to run from the bleed screw opening until all the air bubbles have disappeared. Reinstall the bleed screw (check the bleed screw gasket and if it is in any way damaged, replace it) and tighten it. Then replace the pump cover.

3 Oil pump: bleeding the oil pump and distribution pipe

1 The procedure here is the same as the procedure described in Chapter 2, except (due to there being no plastic pinion) the engine must be started and kept running at around 2000 rpm instead of rotating the plastic pinion.

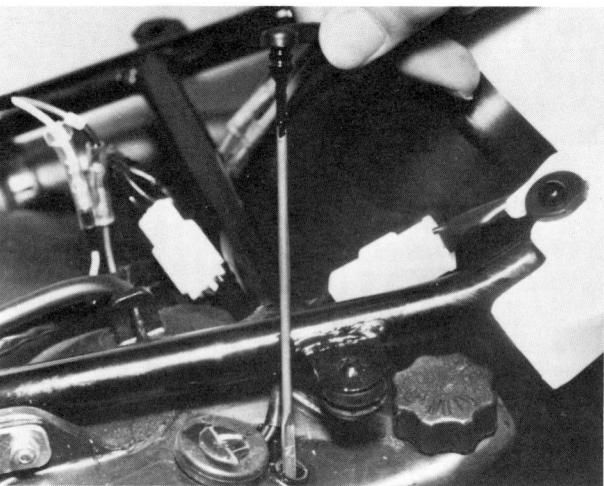

2.1 Checking the oil level

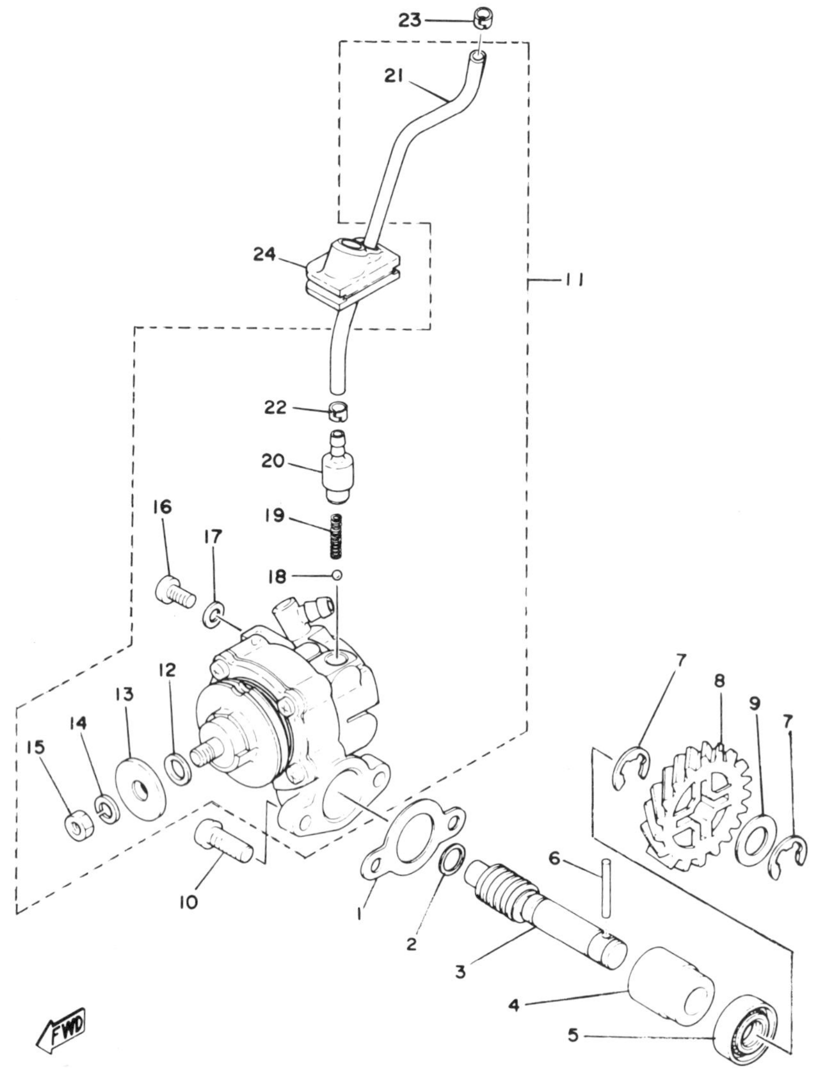

Fig. 7.1 Oil pump assembly

1 Gasket
2 Washer
3 Worm shaft
4 Worm shaft sleeve
5 Oil seal
6 Dowel pin
7 'E' clip - 2 off
8 Drive gear
9 Washer
10 Screw
11 Oil pump assembly
12 Shim
13 Adjusting plate
14 Spring washer
15 Nut
16 Screw
17 Gasket
18 Ball bearing
19 Spring
20 Nozzle
21 Hose
22 Hose clip
23 Hose clip
24 Oil pump seating

Chapter 7: Yamaha 250 and 400 D and E monoshock models

4 Oil pump: bleeding and adjusting the maximum pump stroke

1 This is not usually necessary. However, should the need arise (for example, if the engine overheats due to lack of lubrication, or conversely is using an excessive amount of engine oil) the procedure is as follows:
2 Remove the pump cover and start the engine.
3 Whilst the engine is running at its idling speed, watch the pump adjustment plate carefully. As soon as the adjustment plate has moved to its outermost limit, stop the engine immediately.
4 Using a feeler gauge, measure the gap between the raised boss on the pump adjustment pulley and the adjustment plate. Do not force the feeler gauge into the gap as this will result in a false measurement being obtained.
5 Repeat 3 and 4 several times so that an average measurement can be obtained. The pump is set at its minimum pump stroke when the gap is at its largest.

Pump stroke settings
  Minimum pump stroke   0.25—0.30 mm (0.010—0.012 in)
  Maximum pump stroke   1.85—2.05 mm (0.073—0.081 in)

6 If the measurement obtained is incorrect, remove the adjustment plate locknut, and adjustment plate.
7 Remove or add an adjustment shim as required.
8 Replace the adjustment plate locknut and tighten it securely.
9 Remeasure the gap by repeating 3 and 4.
10 Continue to adjust until the correct measurement is obtained.

5 Carburettor: idle mixture and idle speed adjustment

1 Run the engine for several minutes until it is fully warmed up. Then turn the pilot air screw in until it is lightly seated.
2 Turn the pilot air screw back out to:
  DT250   2.0 turns out
  DT400   1.5 turns out
Then adjust to the desired idle speed from this point, noting that it should not be necessary to change the setting much beyond that recommended.

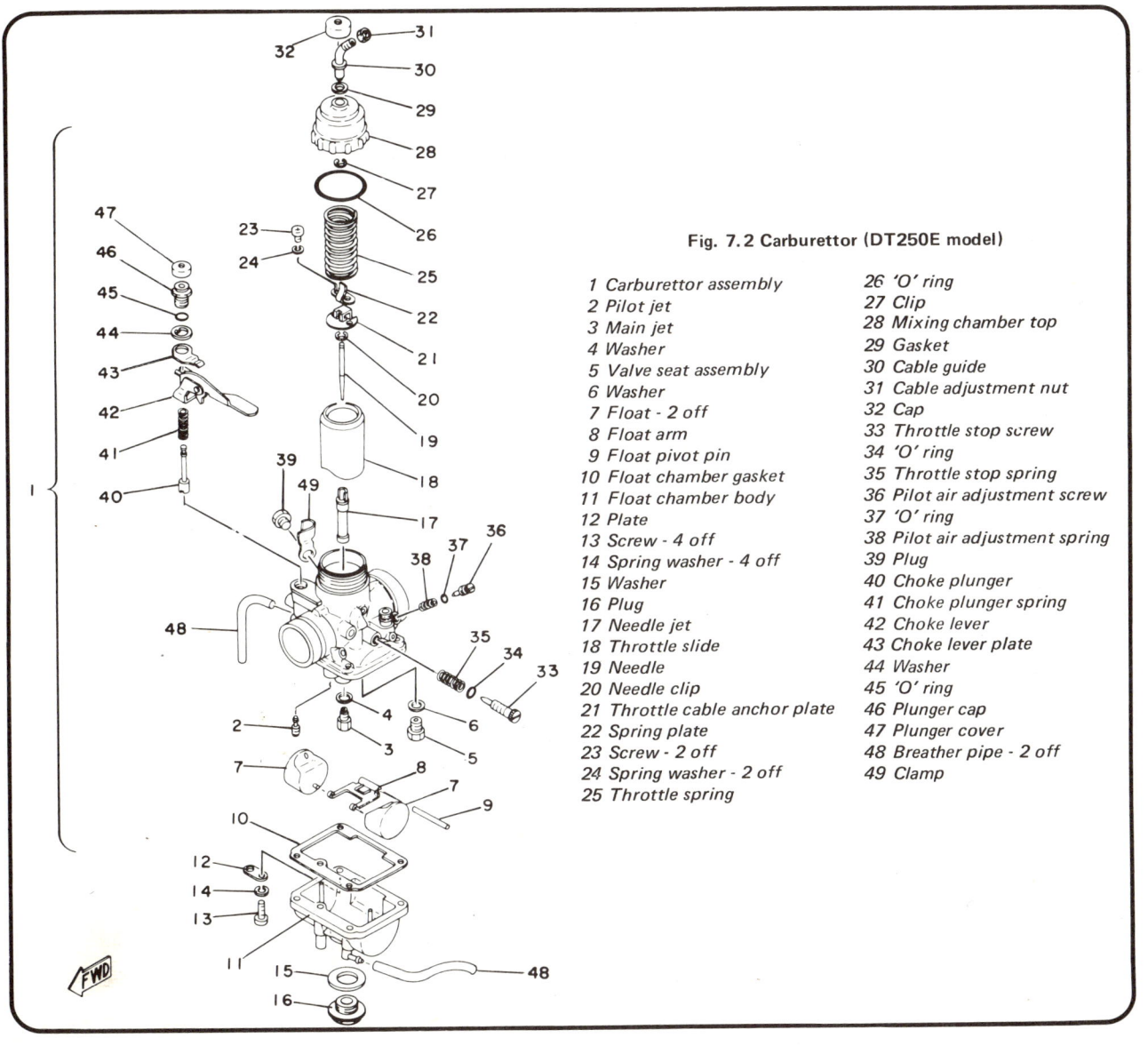

Fig. 7.2 Carburettor (DT250E model)

1 Carburettor assembly
2 Pilot jet
3 Main jet
4 Washer
5 Valve seat assembly
6 Washer
7 Float - 2 off
8 Float arm
9 Float pivot pin
10 Float chamber gasket
11 Float chamber body
12 Plate
13 Screw - 4 off
14 Spring washer - 4 off
15 Washer
16 Plug
17 Needle jet
18 Throttle slide
19 Needle
20 Needle clip
21 Throttle cable anchor plate
22 Spring plate
23 Screw - 2 off
24 Spring washer - 2 off
25 Throttle spring
26 'O' ring
27 Clip
28 Mixing chamber top
29 Gasket
30 Cable guide
31 Cable adjustment nut
32 Cap
33 Throttle stop screw
34 'O' ring
35 Throttle stop spring
36 Pilot air adjustment screw
37 'O' ring
38 Pilot air adjustment spring
39 Plug
40 Choke plunger
41 Choke plunger spring
42 Choke lever
43 Choke lever plate
44 Washer
45 'O' ring
46 Plunger cap
47 Plunger cover
48 Breather pipe - 2 off
49 Clamp

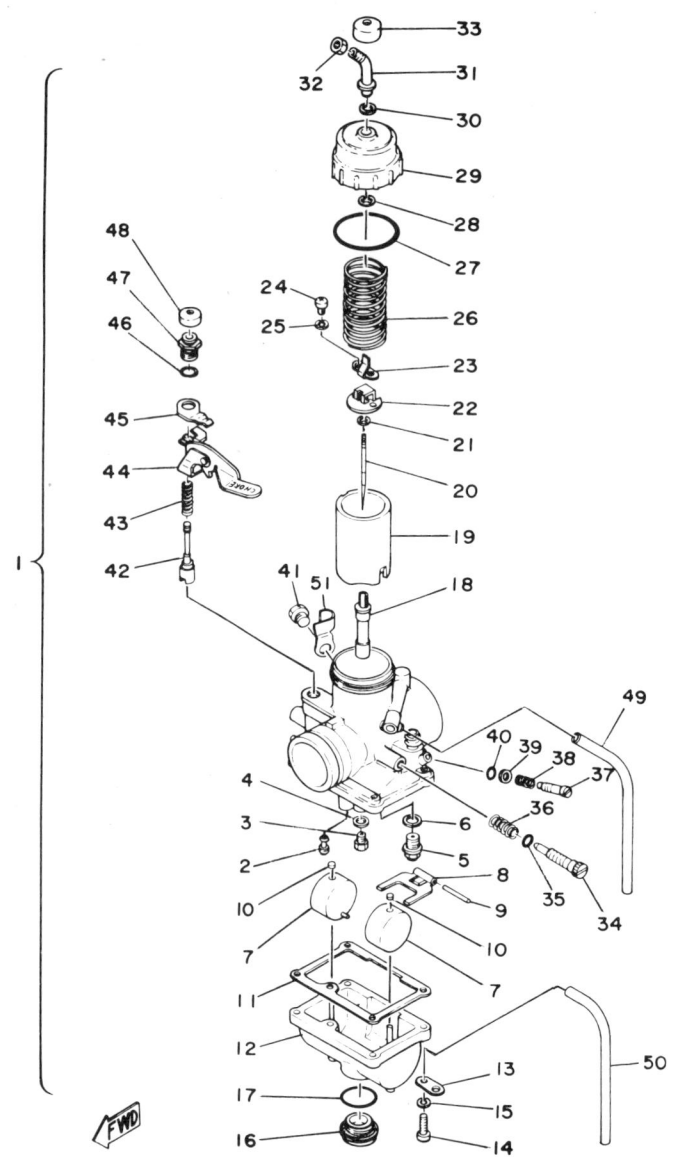

Fig. 7.3 Carburettor (DT400E model)

1 Carburettor assembly
2 Pilot jet
3 Main jet
4 Washer
5 Valve seat assembly
6 Washer
7 Float
8 Float arm
9 Float pivot pin
10 Float cap
11 Float chamber gasket
12 Float chamber body
13 Plate
14 Screw
15 Spring washer
16 Plug
17 'O' ring
18 Needle jet
19 Throttle valve
20 Needle
21 Needle clip
22 Throttle cable anchor plate
23 Spring plate
24 Screw - 2 off
25 Spring washer - 2 off
26 Throttle valve spring
27 'O' ring
28 Clip
29 Mixing chamber top
30 Gasket
31 Cable guide
32 Cable adjustment nut
33 Cap
34 Throttle stop screw
35 'O' ring
36 Throttle stop spring
37 Pilot air adjustment screw
38 Pilot air adjustment spring
39 Washer
40 'O' ring
41 Plug
42 Choke plunger
43 Choke plunger spring
44 Choke lever
45 Choke lever plate
46 'O' ring
47 Plunger cap
48 Plunger cap cover
49 Breather pipe
50 Overflow pipe
51 Clamp

6 Throttle cable: free play adjustment

1 There should be 5–8 mm (0.20–0.31 in) free play at the throttle grip flange. Having adjusted the throttle cable be sure to securely fasten the locknut.

7 Adjustment and removal of the rear suspension shock absorber

1 Adjustment can be carried out with the rear suspension shock absorber unit in place in the frame. To adjust, unscrew the retaining screw (7.1a) and using a 'C' spanner, turn the sleeve around to adjust the suspension as required. Turning the sleeve clockwise (towards the arrow marked 'S') will give softer suspension, turning the sleeve anti-clockwise (towards the arrow marked 'H') will give harder suspension. Replace the retaining screw and tighten it. Replace the plastic cover and seat.

2 The rear shock absorber on these models contains highly compressed nitrogen gas. The manufacturer advises that you should not tamper with or attempt to open the cylinder assembly, nor subject the cylinder to extreme heat or open flame.

3 When removing the shock absorber from the machine it is first necessary to detach the following items: seat, fuel tank, side-cover, air filler cap, oil tank, and mudguard grommets. Having done this, remove the upper pivot shaft that passes through the lower end of the suspension unit, swinging arm pivot shaft. Next remove the upper suspension unit bolt and pull out the shock absorber carefully, to avoid bending it. Do not lose the two washers as these must be replaced on re-assembly. If a new spring is to be fitted the shock absorber may be dismantled as shown in the accompanying photographs.

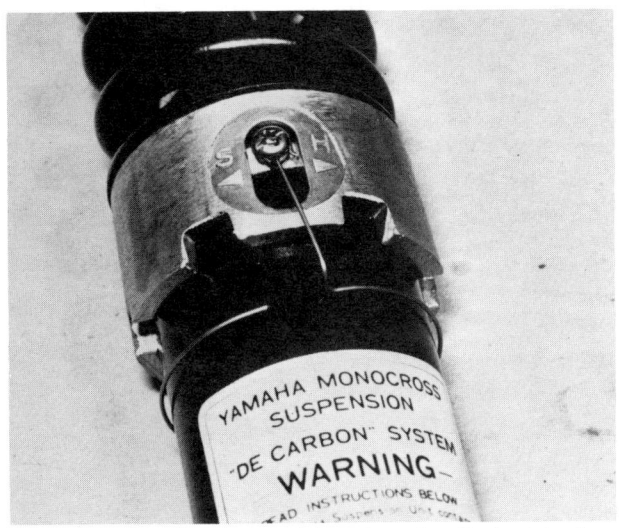
7.1a Release locating screw and turn sleeve to adjust pre-load

7.1b Adjustment can be carried out with suspension unit in position

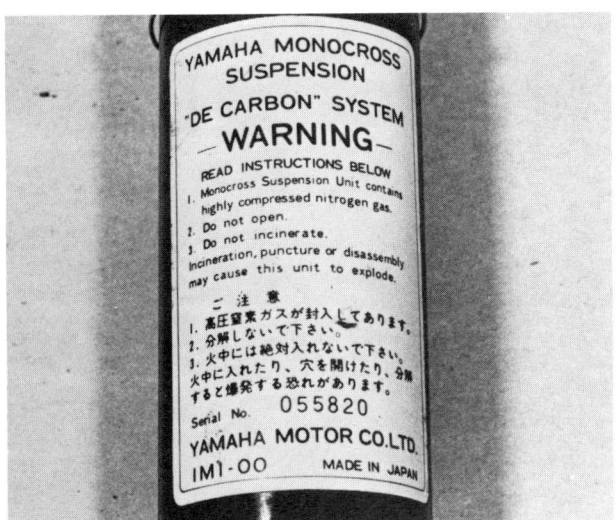
7.2 Shock absorber warning

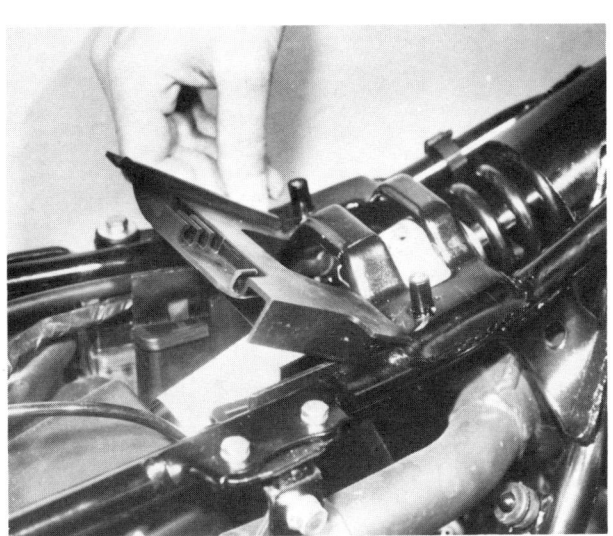
7.3a Cover incorporates spare fuse holder

7.3b Rear sub-frame is suspended by a single, central unit

7.3c Remove split pin from trunnion . . .

7.3d . . . and unscrew from shock absorber end

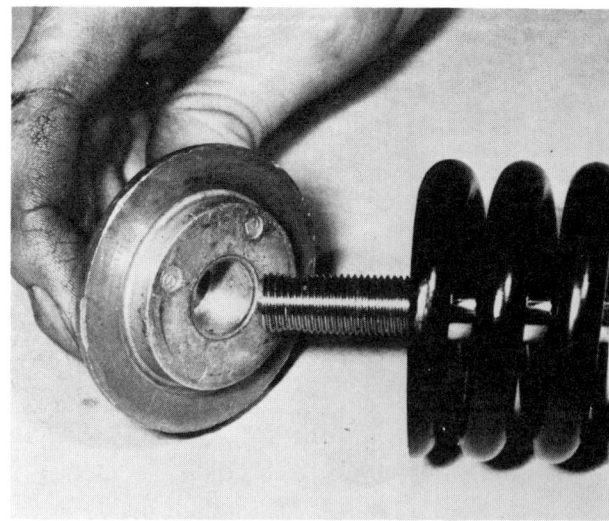
7.3e Remove upper spring seating

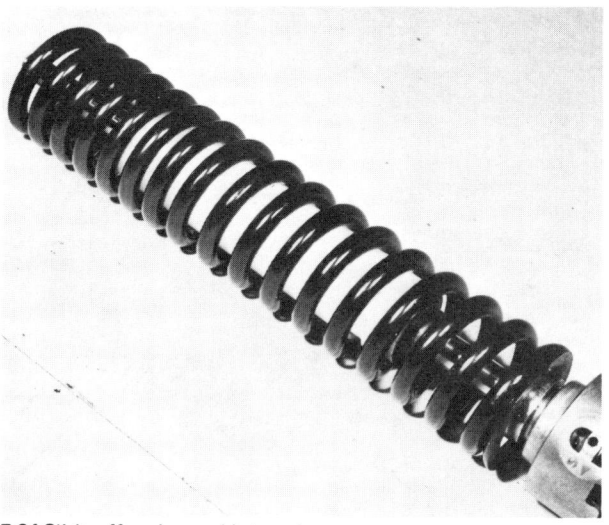
7.3f Slide off spring and internal spacer

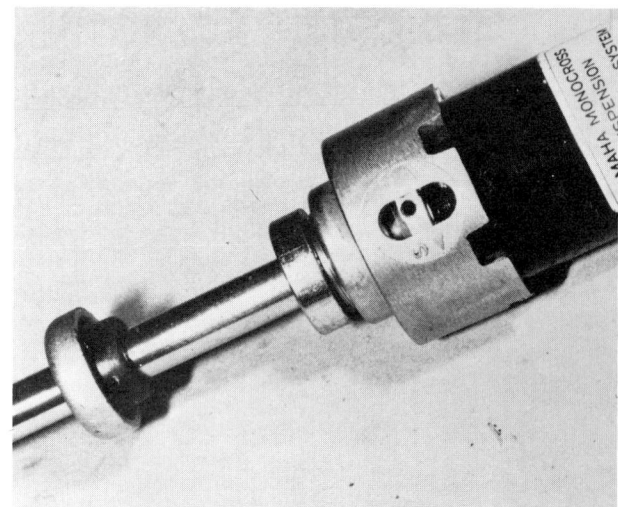
7.3g Note bump stop fitted against suspension unit

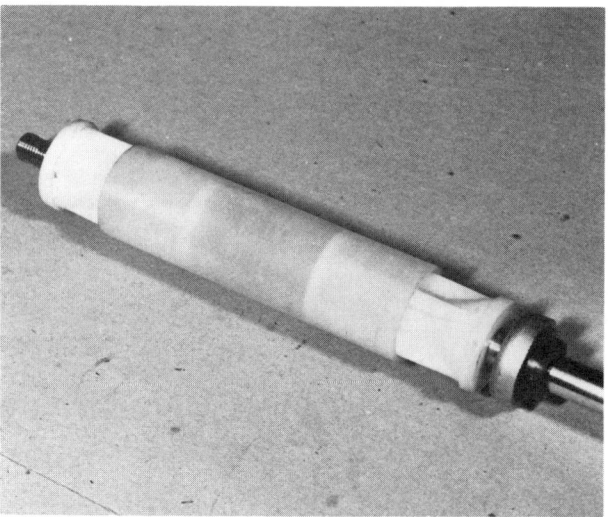
7.3h Internal spacer and bump stop fitted as shown

Chapter 7: Yamaha 250 and 400 D and E monoshock models

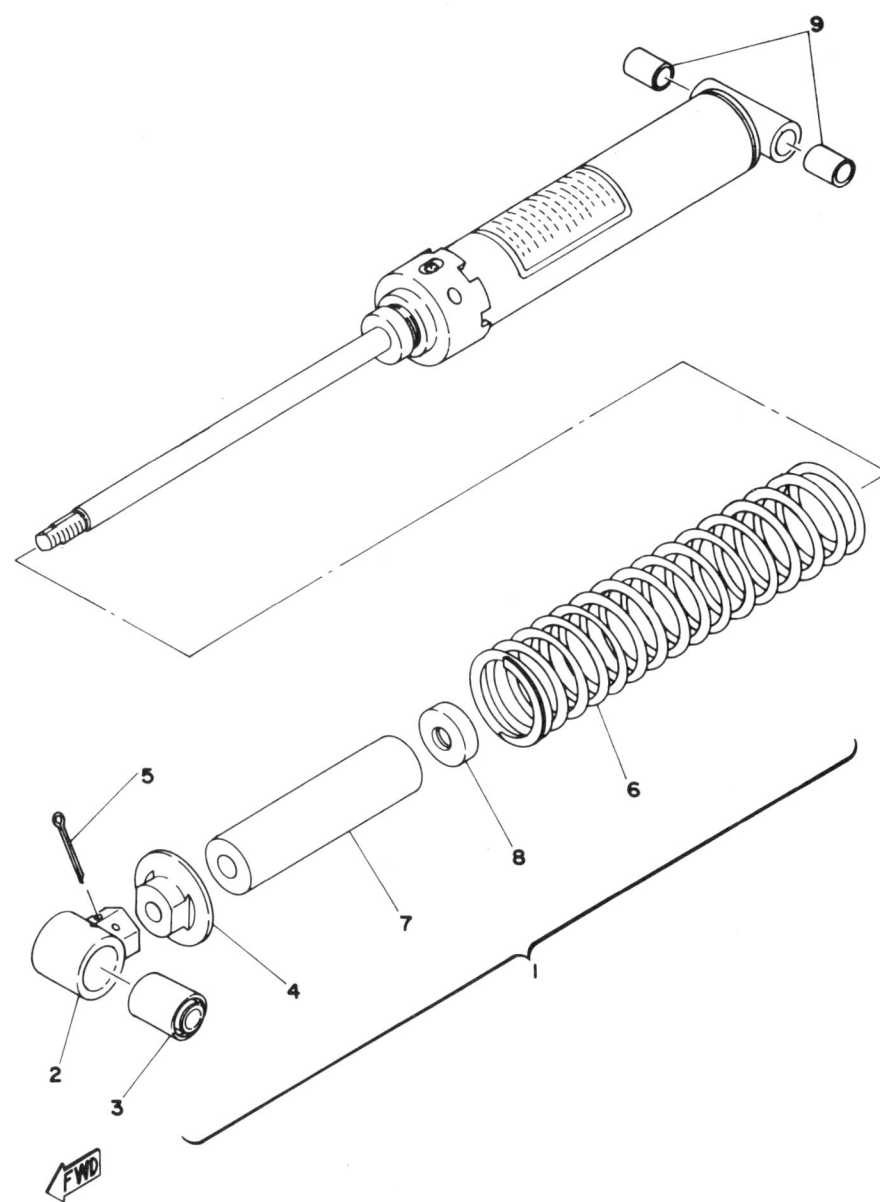

Fig. 7.4 Rear suspension unit

1. Rear suspension unit
2. Upper bracket
3. Bush
4. Upper spring seating
5. Split pin
6. Compression spring
7. Sleeve
8. Damper
9. Bush - 2 off

8 Rear sub-frame: examination, removal and replacement

1 To inspect the rear sub-frame it is first necessary to remove the rear wheel and then the shock absorber, as described in Section 7.3. Having done this, take hold of the ends of the rear sub-frame and move them from side-to-side. There should not be any readily perceptible free play, although the manufacturers advise that up to 1 mm is permissible. If there is more than this amount the rear sub-frame will have to be removed and the swinging arm bushes replaced.

2 To remove the rear sub-frame, firstly remove the nut from the swinging arm pivot bolt, and tap out the shaft. It is important to note the location of both the spacing washers and shims so that they can be replaced in their correct positions. Tap out the old bushes. The new bushes may be driven in using a hammer, but make sure that the rear sub-frame itself is well supported so that it is not damaged. Coating the bushes with grease or a little oil may prove beneficial when trying to insert new ones, and these along with the pivot shaft should be well greased before replacing the rear sub-frame. The pivot bolt torque setting is 5.6–8.0 kgf m (35–58 lbf ft).

9 Other minor modifications

1 The engine no longer has fluted anti-vibration blocks. Instead, solid blocks are used.
2 The new DT models have an extra bolt on the crankcase. There are now 6 instead of 5.
3 An extra washer is used in the selector fork mechanism.
4 A different type of stand is used on new models.
5 The headlamp is now of the sealed beam type and the tail/stop lamp has been altered slightly from the original.
6 The oil tank on the new DT250E and DT400E has a low oil level warning switch which activates a warning light on the instrument panel. You should always check the oil level of the machine at regular intervals (see Routine maintenance) and do not rely upon this device to tell you when to top up the tank.

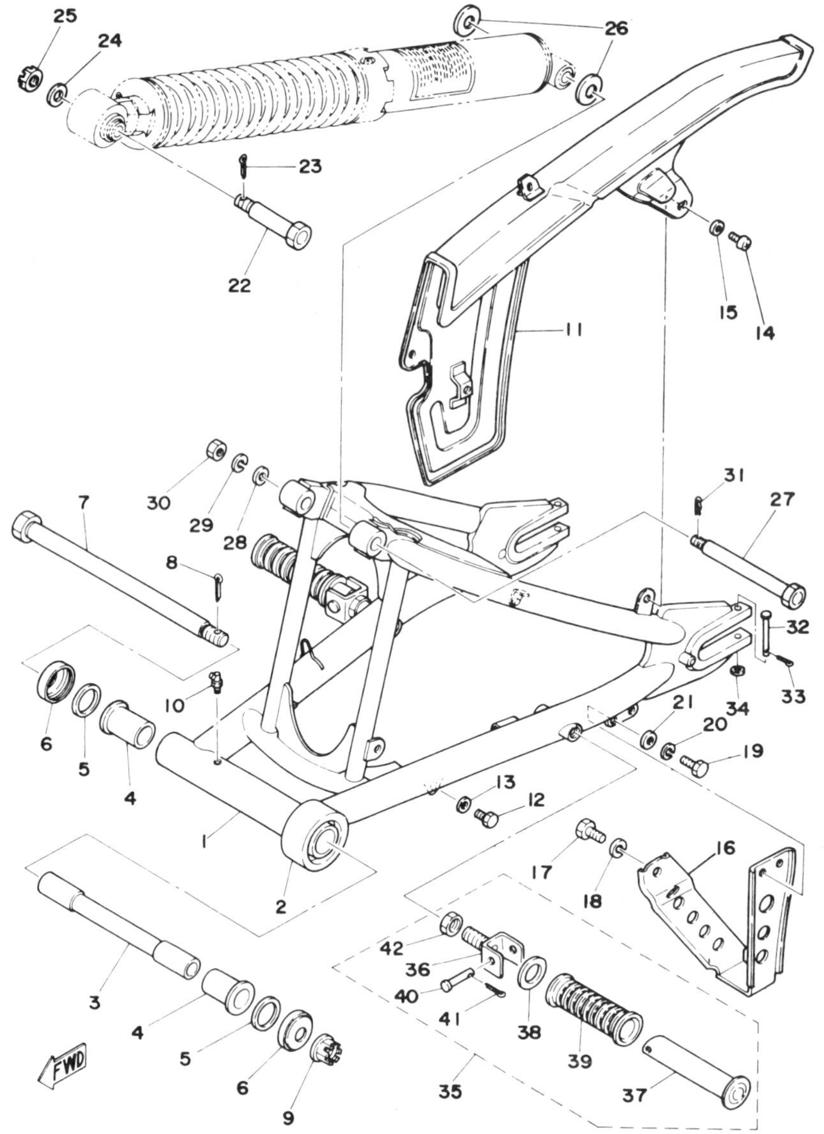

Fig. 7.5 Rear cantilever frame and chainguard

1 Rear sub-frame complete
2 Chainguard seal
3 Collar
4 Bush - 2 off
5 Shim
6 Dust cover - 2 off
7 Pivot shaft
8 Split pin
9 Nut
10 Grease nipple
11 Chaincase
12 Bolt
13 Washer
14 Screw - 3 off
15 Washer - 3 off
16 Chainguard
17 Bolt
18 Spring washer
19 Bolt - 2 off
20 Spring washer - 2 off
21 Washer - 2 off
22 Bolt
23 Split pin
24 Washer
25 Nut
26 Damper
27 Bolt
28 Washer
29 Spring
30 Nut
31 'R' pin
32 Clevis pin - 2 off
33 Split pin - 2 off
34 Washer - 2 off
35 Pillion footrest assembly - 2 off
36 Pillion footrest bracket - 2 off
37 Pillion footrest - 2 off
38 Washer - 2 off
39 Pillion footrest cover - 2 off
40 Clevis pin - 2 off
41 Split pin - 2 off
42 Nut - 2 off

8.2a Rear sub-frame can be removed for attention to the bushes

8.2b Headed bushes can be tapped out from the opposite side

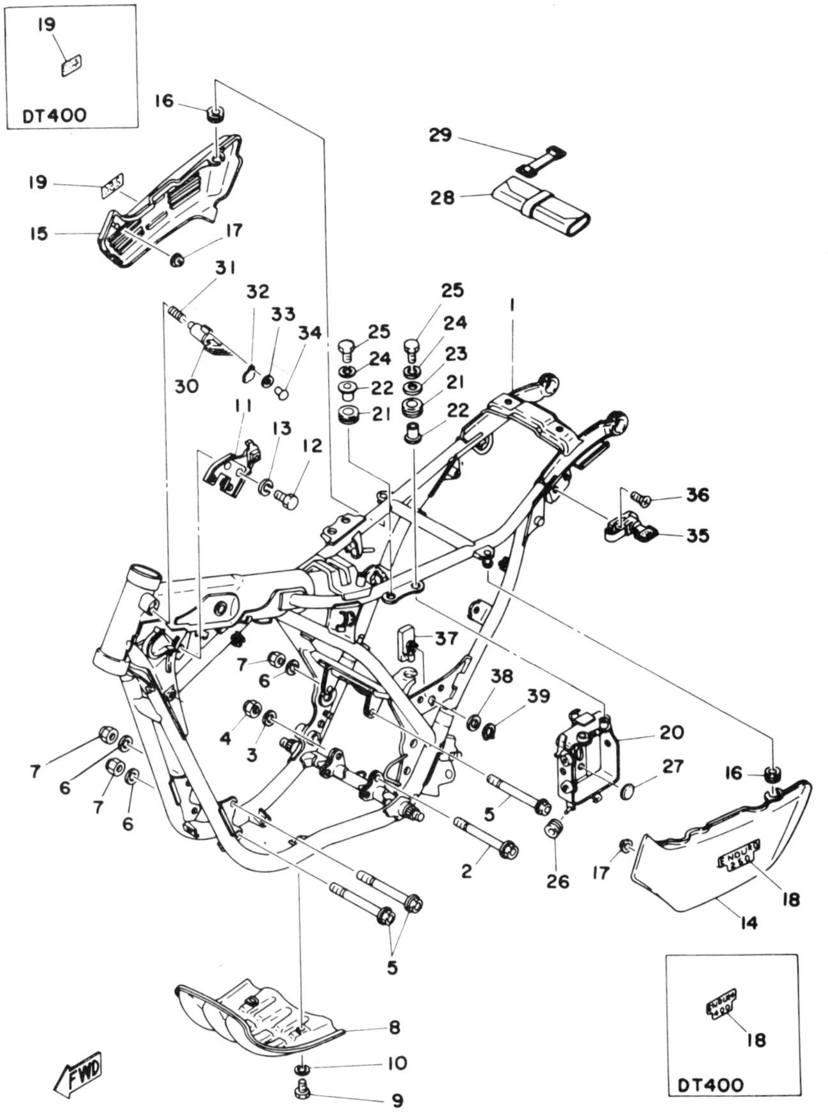

Fig. 7.6 Frame and side covers

1 Frame
2 Bolt
3 Washer
4 Nut
5 Bolt
6 Washer
7 Nut
8 Crankcase shield
9 Bolt
10 Spring washer
11 Spring seating
12 Bolt
13 Spring washer
14 Side cover assembly, left-hand
15 Side cover assembly, right-hand
16 Grommet - 4 off
17 Grommet - 2 off
18 Emblem - left-hand side cover
19 Emblem - right-hand side cover
20 Battery seating
21 Grommet - 2 off
22 Collar - 2 off
23 Washer
24 Spring washer - 2 off
25 Bolt - 2 off
26 Grommet
27 Battery pad
28 Tool kit
29 Tool kit retaining band
30 Steering lock
31 Spring
32 Cap
33 Wave washer
34 Rivet
35 Helmet lock assembly
36 Screw
37 Chain protector
38 Wave washer
39 Circlip

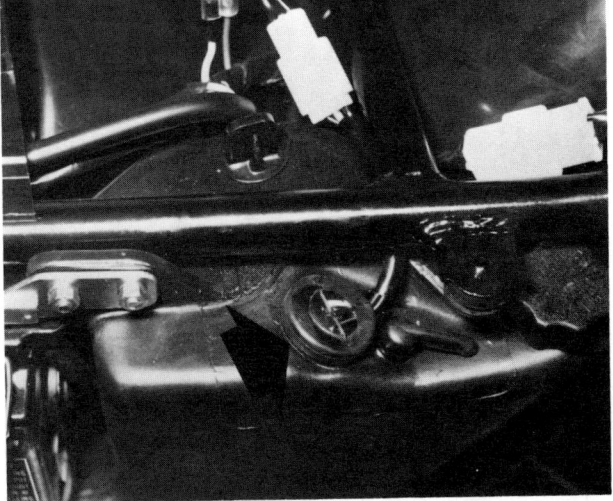

9.6 Oil tank incorporates low oil level warning switch

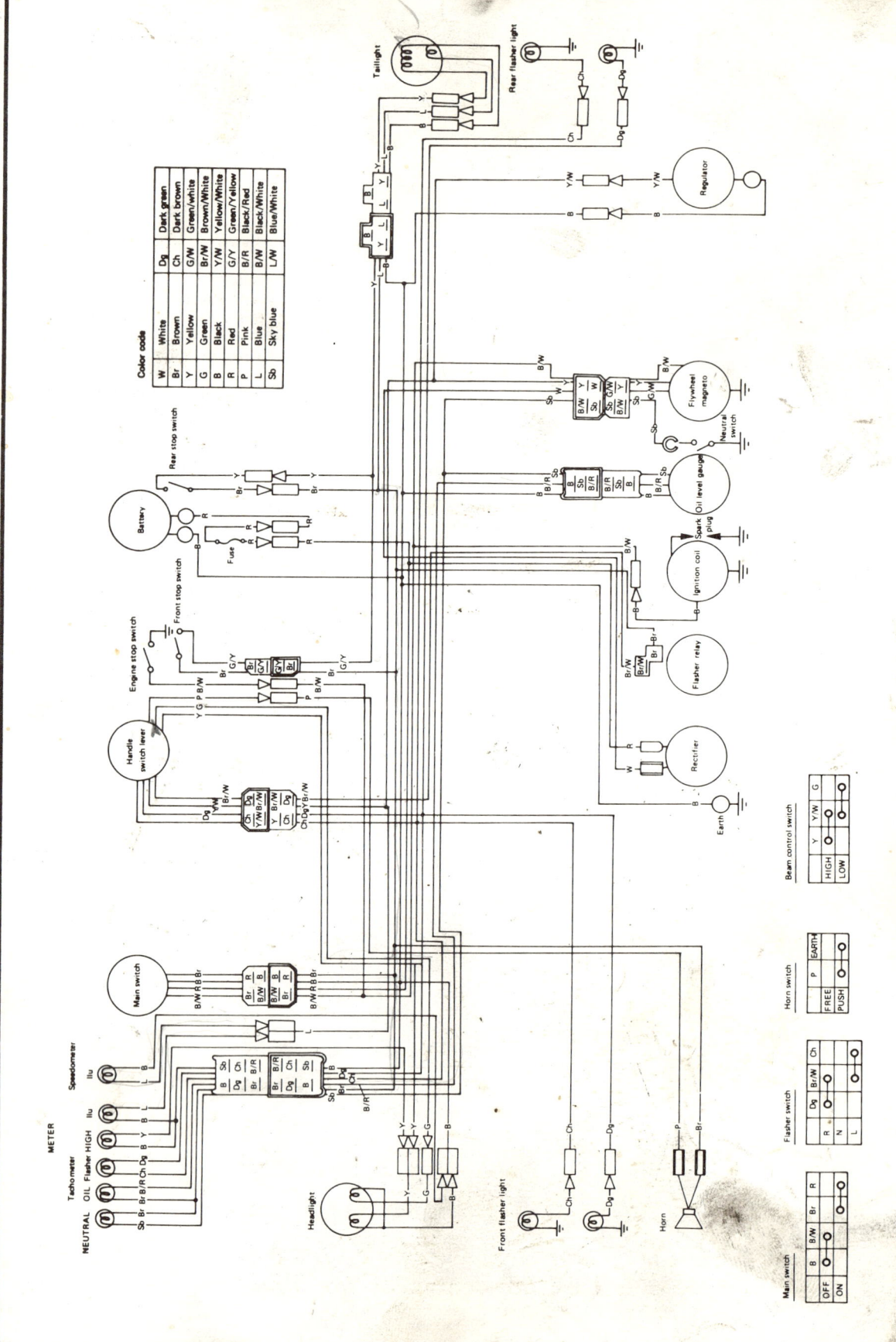

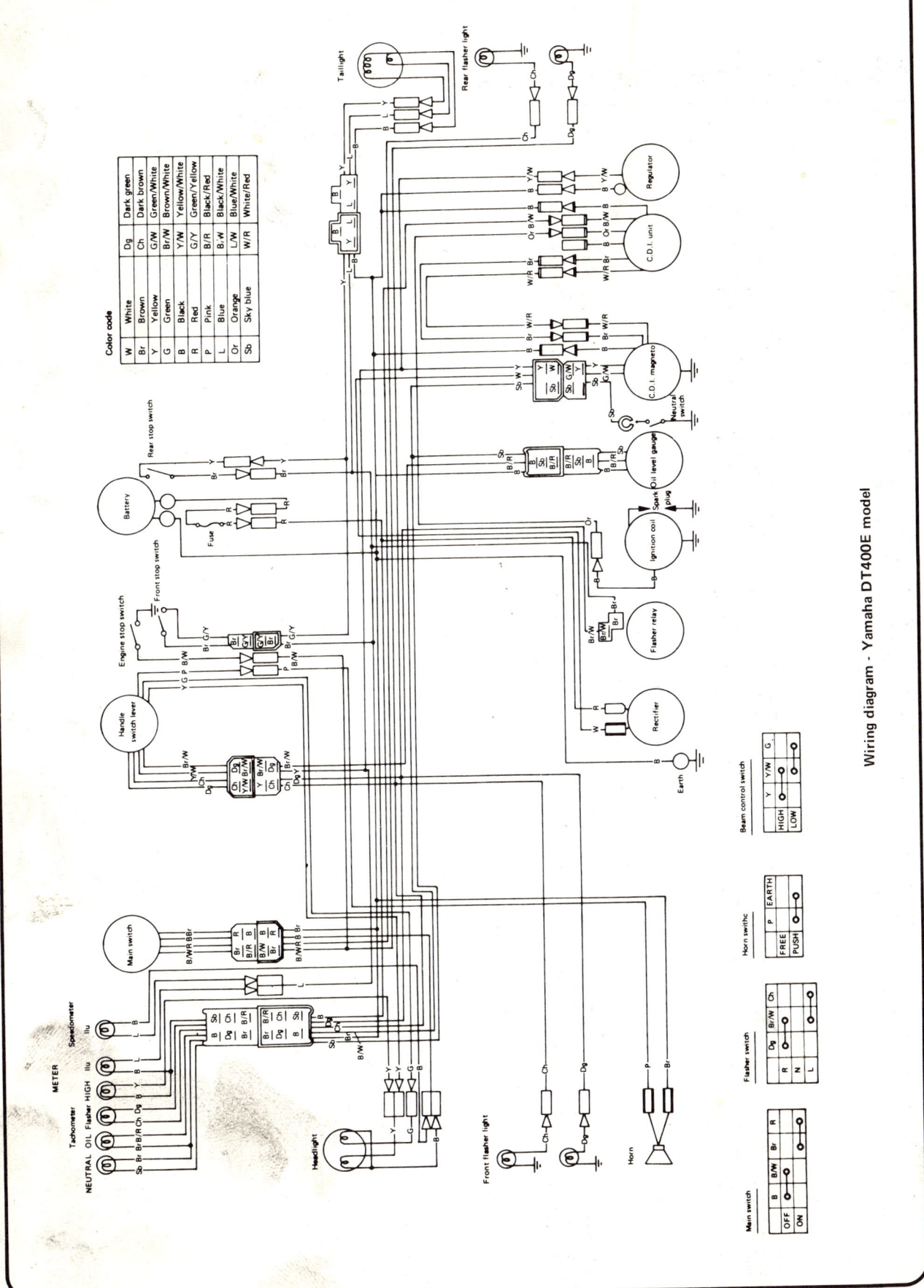

Metric conversion tables

Inches	Decimals	Millimetres	Millimetres to Inches		Inches to Millimetres	
			mm	Inches	Inches	mm
1/64	0.015625	0.3969	0.01	0.00039	0.001	0.0254
1/32	0.03125	0.7937	0.02	0.00079	0.002	0.0508
3/64	0.046875	1.1906	0.03	0.00118	0.003	0.0762
1/16	0.0625	1.5875	0.04	0.00157	0.004	0.1016
5/64	0.078125	1.9844	0.05	0.00197	0.005	0.1270
3/32	0.09375	2.3812	0.06	0.00236	0.006	0.1524
7/64	0.109375	2.7781	0.07	0.00276	0.007	0.1778
1/8	0.125	3.1750	0.08	0.00315	0.008	0.2032
9/64	0.140625	3.5719	0.09	0.00354	0.009	0.2286
5/32	0.15625	3.9687	0.1	0.00394	0.01	0.254
11/64	0.171875	4.3656	0.2	0.00787	0.02	0.508
3/16	0.1875	4.7625	0.3	0.01181	0.03	0.762
13/64	0.203125	5.1594	0.4	0.01575	0.04	1.016
7/32	0.21875	5.5562	0.5	0.01969	0.05	1.270
15/64	0.234375	5.9531	0.6	0.02362	0.06	1.524
1/4	0.25	6.3500	0.7	0.02756	0.07	1.778
17/64	0.265625	6.7469	0.8	0.03150	0.08	2.032
9/32	0.28125	7.1437	0.9	0.03543	0.09	2.286
19/64	0.296875	7.5406	1	0.03937	0.1	2.54
5/16	0.3125	7.9375	2	0.07874	0.2	5.08
21/64	0.328125	8.3344	3	0.11811	0.3	7.62
11/32	0.34375	8.7312	4	0.15748	0.4	10.16
23/64	0.359375	9.1281	5	0.19685	0.5	12.70
3/8	0.375	9.5250	6	0.23622	0.6	15.24
25/64	0.390625	9.9219	7	0.27559	0.7	17.78
13/32	0.40625	10.3187	8	0.31496	0.8	20.32
27/64	0.421875	10.7156	9	0.35433	0.9	22.86
7/16	0.4375	11.1125	10	0.39370	1	25.4
29/64	0.453125	11.5094	11	0.43307	2	50.8
15/32	0.46875	11.9062	12	0.47244	3	76.2
31/64	0.48375	12.3031	13	0.51181	4	101.6
1/2	0.5	12.7000	14	0.55118	5	127.0
33/64	0.515625	13.0969	15	0.59055	6	152.4
17/32	0.53125	13.4937	16	0.62992	7	177.8
35/64	0.546875	13.8906	17	0.66929	8	203.2
9/16	0.5625	14.2875	18	0.70866	9	228.6
37/64	0.578125	14.6844	19	0.74803	10	254.0
19/32	0.59375	15.0812	20	0.78740	11	279.4
39/64	0.609375	15.4781	21	0.82677	12	304.8
5/8	0.625	15.8750	22	0.86614	13	330.2
41/64	0.640625	16.2719	23	0.90551	14	355.6
21/32	0.65625	16.6687	24	0.94488	15	381.0
43/64	0.671875	17.0656	25	0.98425	16	406.4
11/16	0.6875	17.4625	26	1.02362	17	431.8
45/64	0.703125	17.8594	27	1.06299	18	457.2
23/32	0.71875	18.2562	28.	1.10236	19	482.6
47/64	0.734375	18.6531	29	1.14173	20	508.0
3/4	0.75	19.0500	30	1.18110	21	533.4
49/64	0.765625	19.4469	31	1.22047	22	558.8
25/32	0.78125	19.8437	32	1.25984	23	584.2
51/64	0.796875	20.2406	33	1.29921	24	609.6
13/16	0.8125	20.6375	34	1.33858	25	635.0
53/64	0.828125	21.0344	35	1.37795	26	660.4
27/32	0.84375	21.4312	36	1.41732	27	685.8
55/64	0.859375	21.8281	37	1.4567	28	711.2
7/8	0.875	22.2250	38	1.4961	29	736.6
57/64	0.890625	22.6219	39	1.5354	30	762.0
29/32	0.90625	23.0187	40	1.5748	31	787.4
59/64	0.921875	23.4156	41	1.6142	32	812.8
15/16	0.9375	23.8125	42	1.6535	33	838.2
61/64	0.953125	24.2094	43	1.6929	34	863.6
31/32	0.96875	24.6062	44	1.7323	35	889.0
63/64	0.984375	25.0031	45	1.7717	36	914.4

Metric conversion tables

1 Imperial gallon = 8 Imp pints = 1.20 US gallons = 277.42 cu in = 4.54 litres

1 US gallon = 4 US quarts = 0.83 Imp gallon = 231 cu in = 3.78 litres

1 Litre = 0.21 Imp gallon = 0.26 US gallon = 61.02 cu in = 1000 cc

Miles to Kilometres		Kilometres to Miles	
1	1.61	1	0.62
2	3.22	2	1.24
3	4.83	3	1.86
4	6.44	4	2.49
5	8.05	5	3.11
6	9.66	6	3.73
7	11.27	7	4.35
8	12.88	8	4.97
9	14.48	9	5.59
10	16.09	10	6.21
20	32.19	20	12.43
30	48.28	30	18.64
40	64.37	40	24.85
50	80.47	50	31.07
60	96.56	60	37.28
70	112.65	70	43.50
80	128.75	80	49.71
90	144.84	90	55.92
100	160.93	100	62.14

lbf ft to kgf m		kgf m to lbf ft		lbf/in^2 to kgf/cm^2		kgf/cm^2 to lbf/in^2	
1	0.138	1	7.233	1	0.07	1	14.22
2	0.276	2	14.466	2	0.14	2	28.50
3	0.414	3	21.699	3	0.21	3	42.67
4	0.553	4	28.932	4	0.28	4	56.89
5	0.691	5	36.165	5	0.35	5	71.12
6	0.829	6	43.398	6	0.42	6	85.34
7	0.967	7	50.631	7	0.49	7	99.56
8	1.106	8	57.864	8	0.56	8	113.79
9	1.244	9	65.097	9	0.63	9	128.00
10	1.382	10	72.330	10	0.70	10	142.23
20	2.765	20	144.660	20	1.41	20	284.47
30	4.147	30	216.990	30	2.11	30	426.70

Index

A

Air cleaner - 58

B

Battery - 99
Bleeding, oil pump - 114
Brake pedal, rear - 84
Brakes:
    adjustment - 90
    fault diagnosis - 97
    front - examination, dismantling, reassembly - 88
    rear - examination, dismantling, reassembly - 90
    specifications - 87
Bulbs, renewal - 99, 103, 106

C

Carburettor:
    adjusting - 58, 115
    dismantling, inspection & reassembly - 56
    fault diagnosis - 56
    removal - 54
    specifications - 53
CDI unit - 69
Clutch:
    inspection - 28
    fault diagnosis - 52
    reassembly and replacement - 43
    removal and dismantling - 18
    specifications - 9
Condenser - 65, 69
Contact breaker - 64, 65
Crankcase covers - 28, 49
Crankcases:
    jointing - 31
    separating - 23
Crankshaft:
    inspection - 26
    removal - 23
    replacement - 31
Cush drive - 90
Cylinder barrel:
    inspection - 27
    replacement - 47
    removal - 15
Cylinder head:
    decarbonising - 27
    inspection - 27
    removal - 15
    replacement - 47

D

Decompressor unit - 48
Dual seat - 84

E

Electrical system - fault diagnosis - 106
Electrical system, specifications - 98
Engine:
    components, examination - 25
    dismantling - 13
    fault diagnosis - 51
    reassembly - 28
    specifications - 8
Engine/gearbox unit:
    removal - 11
    replacement - 48
Exhaust system - 44, 58

F

Final drive chain - 94
Final drive sprocket - 94
Flasher unit - 103
Flashing indicators - 103
Footrests - 84
Forks, front:
    dismantling - 73
    fault diagnosis - 86
    inspection - 78
    removal - 71
    replacement - 78
Fork, rear - 79, 86
Frame:
    examination and renovation - 79
    fault diagnosis - 86
Fuel feed pipe - 54
Fuel system:
    fault diagnosis - 62
    specifications - 53
Fuel tank - 54
Fuel tap - 54
Fuse - 99

G

Gearbox:
    components - examination - 27
    dismantling - 13
    fault diagnosis - 51
    reassembly - 31
    specifications - 9

Index

Gearbox/engine unit:
    removal - 11
    replacement - 48
Gearchange assembly - 21, 34

H

Headlamp - 99
Horn - 106

I

Ignition coil - 69
Ignition source coil - 64
Ignition system:
    fault diagnosis - 70
    specifications - 63
Ignition switch - 69
Ignition timing - 69

K

Kickstarter - 21, 38, 84

L

Lubricants, recommended - 7
Lubrication system - 59, 62

M

Magneto - 18, 44, 99
Maintenance, routine - 6
Metric conversion tables - 124, 125

O

Oil pipes - 48
Oil pump - 25, 45, 48, 61, 114, 115
Oil seals - 27
Oil tank - 62, 119
Ordering spare parts - 5

P

Petrol feed pipe - 54
Petrol tank - 54
Petrol tap - 54
Pistons:
    inspection - 26
    removal - 15
    replacement - 47
Piston rings - 26, 47
Primary drive gear - 18, 23, 43
Prop stand - 84

R

Recommended lubricants - 7
Rear sub-frame, removal and replacement - 124
Rectifier - 99
Reed valve - 58
Routine maintenance - 6
Running-in - 49

S

Shock absorber, removal and adjustment - 116
Small-end bearing - 26
Spare parts, ordering - 5
Spark plug - 69
Spark plug chart (colour) - 67
Speedometer - 85
Sprockets:
    final drive - 44
    rear wheel - 94
Starting and running rebuilt engine - 49
Steering damper - 78
Steering head races - 78
Stop lamp - 103
Suspension, fault diagnosis - 86
Suspension units, rear - 84
Swinging arm - 79, 86
Switches:
    handlebar assembly - 103
    ignition - 69, 106
    lighting - 106

T

Tachometer - 25, 45, 85
Tail lamp - 103
Throttle cable, adjustment - 116
Tyres:
    pressures - 87
    removal and replacement - 96
    security bolt - 96
    specifications - 87
Tyre changing sequence (colour) - 95
    fault diagnosis - 97

W

Warning lamps - 106
Wheel bearings - 188
Wheel, front - 88, 90
Wheel, rear - 90
Wiring diagrams - 107, 108, 122, 123
Wiring layout and examination - 106

Printed by
Haynes Publishing Group
Sparkford Yeovil Somerset
England